A Labour of Love

THE EXPERIENCE
OF PARENTHOOD
IN BRITAIN 1900–1950

STEVE HUMPHRIES

AND

PAMELA GORDON

SIDGWICK & JACKSON
LONDON

First published 1993 by Sidgwick & Jackson Limited

This trade paperback published 1993 by Sidgwick & Jackson Limited
a division of Pan Macmillan Publishers Limited
Cavaye Place London SW10 9PG
and Basingstoke

Associated Companies throughout the world

ISBN 0 283 06195 2

1 3 5 7 9 8 6 4 2

A CIP catalogue record for this book is available from
the British Library

Phototypeset by Intype, London
Printed by Mackays of Chatham Plc

To the memory of my beautiful mother.
Marjorie Humphries (1924–1992)

Steve Humphries

To mum and dad.
With love from Smuts and Ela J.

Pamela Gordon

CONTENTS

ACKNOWLEDGEMENTS

We would like to thank all those who have helped us in writing this book. We are indebted to Peter Salmon and Sam Organ of BBC Bristol for their advice and support for the television series which this book accompanies. Special thanks also to Paul Thompson and Dr Irvine Loudon for their advice and perceptive comments on reading the draft of the book. Thanks also to Helen Gummer at Sidgwick and Jackson.

We would also like to thank Rob Blann. Fred Brewster. Chailey Heritage. The Children's Society. Bernicia Evison. Valerie Fildes. Sally Humphries. Dolly Lander. Jane Lewis. Joanna Mack. Lara Marks. Elsie and John McCabe. Mary Parsons. Rob Perks. Hazel Prince. Carey Smith. Carys Thomas and Justin Toper.

Thanks to Maggi Cook. Felicity Goodall. Lola Hardingham. Steve Haskett. Mike Humphries. Sally Jenkinson. John Quinn. Ashley Ramage. Madge Reed. John Shan. Liz White. Jules Williamson and especially to Daniel De Waal. Fred Hart and Sharon Tanton for their own contributions towards the book and the series.

Finally we are indebted to all the people who have shared their memories with us over the course of this project. We could not have written this book without them.

INTRODUCTION

We know surprisingly little about the experience of parent-hood in Britain during the first half of the century. It is not difficult to map out the broad contours of family life and its changes over the decades: there was a gradual decrease in family size; most parents enjoyed more leisure time and had more money to spend on their children than in the past; and many family homes became more spacious and comfortable with the massive inter-war expansion into the suburbs. But when it comes down to the everyday detail and drama of what went on behind closed doors in the nation's living rooms, parlours and bedrooms, the picture is much more blurred. We have little idea what it was like to give birth at home in the days when most families could not afford a doctor and when the death rate of mothers and babies was appallingly high. We know little about how it felt to be a poor mother struggling to feed a family of ten in the city slums. We know even less about how middle-class suburban mothers coped in their new servantless homes. Women's magazines trumpeted the virtues of the 'new mother', equipped with all the latest domestic gadgetry, but the voices of the mothers who read these magazines have never been heard. One of the biggest silences, though, comes from the fathers. Most male autobiographies focus on work and public achievements and tell us little about life as a father. Certainly the home was seen − as frequently it is today − as the mother's natural domain. In the child-care literature of the period the father was a distant figure who came home from work to his pipe and slippers, and who was expected to play only the most minor role in looking after the children and the home. It is intriguing to explore to what extent fathers conformed to this stereotype. What is missing most of all from our knowledge of

1

family life in the recent past is any real sense of the relationships that were formed between mothers and fathers and their children.

The aim of this book – and the television series it accompanies – is to begin to fill this important gap in our social history by providing detailed accounts of the experiences of 'ordinary' parents. The only way to document this experience is through personal reminiscence. In writing the book we have collected stories from more than two thousand people born between the 1890s and the 1930s. Most wrote to us in answer to our call for memories published in local newspapers all over Britain. We followed up the letters with hundreds of interviews. By drawing on this material we have tried to provide a new view of parenthood in the past. The book portrays the lives of mothers and fathers through their own eyes and in their own words. We have also complemented this 'adult' view with that of children of the time, describing family life from their own perspective. The relationships formed between parents and children are, of course, highly personal and unique to each family: we have tried to capture the individuality of different parents' experiences by quoting their stories at some length. But we have also tried, in the introduction to each chapter, to set the context for these experiences and to unravel some broad patterns in parenting and show how it changed over time and varied between different social classes.

The voices heard in the book are those of around fifty people who contacted us and whom we interviewed in depth. Most of these interviews were filmed for the television series. We chose them because they reflected a broad spectrum of experience of parenting and family life in the first half of the century. By documenting their memories we are able to hear for the first time the authentic voice of parents of the period from the top to the bottom of the social scale.

CHAPTER ONE
Childbirth

At the beginning of the century childbirth dominated many women's lives. In the 1900s working-class women who married in their teens or early twenties experienced an average of ten pregnancies. Of these around three would end in miscarriage, two in death during birth or infancy and only five would survive. They could expect, in all, to spend around fifteen years either pregnant or nursing babies. Middle-class women generally had fewer children – on average about three in the 1900s – but because they often married later childbirth also dominated their married life. They, too, lost many babies in pregnancy, childbirth or in infant deaths.

Victorian taboos on sex meant that there was widespread ignorance among men and women about their bodies and contraception, which was greatest among the poorer sections of society. Many of the pregnancies of working-class women at this time were unplanned or unwanted. No birth-control clinics were provided: the official view was that advice of this kind was immoral, threatening the mother's 'natural' reproductive role. Contraception was often left to the man but most husbands could not afford condoms, or were too embarrassed to buy or use them. It has been estimated that only about 1 per cent of working-class husbands used condoms in the 1900s. Instead they used the unreliable method of withdrawal. Middle-class couples were more successful in reducing their family size. They had begun to do this in mid Victorian times, driven by a desire to improve their standard of living. Although more professional couples could afford to buy condoms the most common methods of contraception among the middle classes were probably also withdrawal and abstention.

Many women did what they could to reduce the burdens of

birth and childcare. Some working-class women resorted to abortion – which was then illegal – to terminate unwanted pregnancies. Either they took abortifacient pills made of a variety of substances such as rye, lead, and gunpowder coated in margarine, which rarely worked, or turned in desperation to back-street abortionists. In the 1920s the BMA estimated that as many as 16 to 20 per cent of all pregnancies ended in abortion. This was probably a slightly exaggerated figure, however, for the majority of women – encouraged by Church and state – looked upon childbirth with attitudes of resignation and fatalism.

Ignorance about contraception was matched by a lack of knowledge among young mothers-to-be about childbirth itself. In the first decades of the century many women having their first baby had little or no idea what to expect. Ante-natal classes or instruction from midwives and doctors was rare; family and friends were often loath to talk about childbirth. Pregnancy and childbirth were almost as taboo as the sex act itself as subjects for information and conversation. Most attempts to explain what would happen were heavily euphemistic: many who asked where the baby would come from were told 'it comes out where it went in'. Some went into labour believing that the baby would come out of their umbilicus or even their anus.

In the 1900s the vast majority of women had their babies at home. In cities like Birmingham, Liverpool, Hull and in many parts of London, more than 95 per cent of all births were home births. In the late 1920s home births still accounted for 85 per cent of all births in Britain. The well-to-do mother would often be examined regularly by a doctor during her pregnancy and well rested prior to the birth. But the working-class mother had no time for elaborate preparations for the birth of a new baby. Childbirth had to be fitted in with the urgent day-to-day demands of earning a living and looking after a family. Pregnant women would normally have to work – either in paid employment, running a family home, or both – right up until they went into labour. This might involve cooking, washing, scrubbing, lifting heavy weights and carrying other infants around: many went into childbirth already exhausted.

Home births were often difficult and dangerous. Most women were attended by a midwife, but many midwives were unqualified or had only a basic training. Sometimes there was no midwife: the cost of employing one – in the 1900s about ten shillings (50p), almost a week's wages for the more low-paid worker – was too expensive. These families often turned to the services of a 'handy-woman', usually a neighbour experienced in childbirth, who would supervise the birth for a small consideration or sometimes for nothing. Few working-class families could afford to pay a doctor up to £2 to be present and he was usually called only in an emergency.

Poor housing conditions meant that the home was not an ideal place to deliver a baby. Even though many mothers worked tirelessly to keep their homes clean, bugs, crumbling ceilings, damp, cramped rooms, inadequate light and no running water could create major problems. The preparations for birth were basic: at the onset of labour the experienced mother would lay out brown paper or newspaper on her bed to protect the mattress while she was giving birth and which was later used to collect the afterbirth, which was normally wrapped up and burnt on the fire. Little or no pain relief was available: the expectant mother would be told to lie on her left side and a towel was knotted at the end of the bed for her to pull on during contractions. Pain was made worse by ignorance and fear: many thought they were dying.

Yet mothers often seem to have made virtually no noise during labour. Most suffered in silence. Any shouting or screaming received a stern reprimand and occasionally a slap across the face from the midwife. It was a matter of pride to give birth without 'making a fuss'. Mothers didn't want to disturb their neighbours, their children or their husband who were often close by.

Most women didn't want their husbands with them during labour or at the birth. Some wanted them out of the house alto-gether and it was common practice for them to be sent to the pub, to a football match or to stay with a relative. One reason for this was the fear that their husbands would see them naked for the first time. (Remarkably, many mothers with large families seem to have got through their entire married life without their husbands ever seeing them completely undressed.) Childbirth was seen as the preserve of women, which was why the presence of a midwife was preferred to that of a male doctor. Men seem to have shared this view. Although their babies were born in their home few had any desire to witness birth. The oral testimony we have collected suggests that they were probably even more frightened and embarrassed at the idea than their wives.

If the birth was uncomplicated, mother and baby would usually survive, despite the difficult conditions and lack of adequate medical care. If the birth was not straightforward – and many were not – then mother and baby found themselves in grave danger. In the 1900s around 3,000 mothers lost their lives giving birth every year. This appallingly high figure increased in subsequent decades so that by the 1930s around 3,500 mothers were dying each year. At a time when social and medical advances were rapidly reducing death through infectious disease, maternal mortality was virtually the only death rate that was going up. By the mid 1930s the risk of a mother dying in childbirth was as high as it had been in the mid nineteenth century. This issue became one of the big medical scandals of the inter-war years, for it was estimated at the time that almost half of these deaths could have been prevented.

What is most surprising – and most shocking to contemporary commentators – was that death in childbirth among well-to-do mothers was proportionately as high as, or sometimes even higher than among the poor, despite the social, medical and health advantages enjoyed by the better-off. In Leeds in the 1920s, for example, the maternal mortality rate was almost twice as high in middle-class compared to working-class areas. In 1931 the maternal mortality rate in middle-class Chelsea was 5.4 per thousand while in working-class Hackney it was 3.2. Private nursing homes favoured by the middle classes often had the worst mortality records of all.

It gradually emerged that general practitioners were largely responsible for this extraordinary pattern of maternal mortality. From the 1870s onwards GPs, influenced by the growth of obstetrics, began to intervene in normal labour to a disturbing degree, partly because they were paid more if they used instruments during birth. Forceps began to be used as a matter of course. At the turn of the century it was reported that they were used in 50–75 per cent of all births attended by GPs in Glasgow. A similar figure was reported in Carmarthenshire in the 1930s. By then the link between the indiscriminate and sometimes unhygienic use of instruments with mortality was becoming clear. Andrew Topping, medical officer of health in Rochdale in the 1930s, stated that the conduct of some GPs delivering babies in the town was 'little short of murder'. There were, of course, many careful and conscientious GPs – but there were many more who were not. Ironically, working-class mothers who could not afford the doctor were often spared his fatal mistakes.

Most women escaped death in childbirth but frequently suffered impaired health afterwards. In the 1920s Marie Stopes found that among her first 10,000 birth-control patients 1,321 had slit cervixes, 335 serious prolapses and 1,508 internal deformations. A leading obstetrician estimated in 1931 that 10 per cent of all mothers were disabled by the experience of childbirth.

Birth was also dangerous for new-born babies: in the 1900s around 25,000 died every year during birth or within four weeks of being born. Most deaths were due to prematurity, congenital malformations or birth injuries. Here, again, the indiscriminate use of instruments by GPs added to the high death toll.

During the early part of the century, in line with the growing concern about the high rate of mortality in birth, infant and maternal welfare became a national issue. The anxiety was closely linked to fears, expressed strongly in the Boer War and the First World War, that the mother's role was of supreme importance in rebuilding a strong and healthy nation fit to 'rule the waves'. However, most of the government's efforts were concentrated on improving the health of babies and infants (see Chapter 2). Improved maternal care for women was considered less of a priority.

The first major initiative to make childbirth safer was the Midwifery Act of 1902 which aimed to improve the quality of midwives by requiring a minimal training period. GPs untrained in obstetrics. who presented the biggest hazard to mothers' lives. were not considered to be such a problem. The legislation led to the gradual demise of the 'handywoman' but loopholes existed which meant that until the 1920s most midwives remained untrained.

The main intervention to attempt to make childbirth safer – especially from the late 1920s onwards – was hospitalization. Before then. most hospital provision was archaic: many maternity wards were attached to Poor Law infirmaries. charity hospitals or workhouses and were mostly used by poor or unmarried mothers on the verge of destitution. The death rate in hospital births was generally higher even than in home births. but in 1929 when local authorities took control of Poor Law hospitals conditions changed rapidly.

Childbirth increasingly came to be seen as a 'surgical event' which ought to take place under close medical supervision in hospital. It was now thought by most members of the medical profession that home births. like kitchen table surgery. should be relegated to the past. The surgical procedures began as soon as the mother-to-be arrived in hospital when her pubic hair was shaved and she was given an enema. These measures were designed to protect the patient from any dangerous infection. The delivery position recommended in hospitals reflected the greater emphasis on surgical techniques: medical attendants insisted that women should lie on their backs with their feet secured in stirrups. to make obstetric manoeuvres easier. and physical intervention with instruments became normal obstetric practice.

As maternity wards increased in numbers and were modernized. losing their old Poor-Law image. so more and more mothers started to have their babies in hospital. In 1927 15 per cent of births were in hospital; by 1933 this had risen to 24 per cent. Nevertheless many still preferred to have their babies at home: although standards in health care and hygiene were generally higher in the new hospitals. they were often frightening places for expectant mothers. Many experienced a loss of control over the birth of their baby with the new surgical procedures. some of which – for example. shaving and enemas – have since been rejected as unnecessary. An authoritarian and impersonal atmosphere often prevailed in maternity wards which contrasted sharply with the familiar surroundings that helped to reassure mothers when having their babies at home.

Hospitalization had little impact on maternal mortality until the mid 1930s when there was a dramatic reduction: between the mid 1930s and 1940s the maternal death rate fell 40 per cent and infant deaths during birth also steadily declined. This was largely due to a number of medical advances: the introduction of antibiotics and penicillin reduced deaths from puerperal sepsis; blood transfusions prevented deaths from haemorrhage; safe Caesarian deliveries became common practice; the rising standard of obstetric education increased the skills of doctors reducing the number of fatal accidents; and finally during this period the provision of ante-natal care in clinics and hospitals alerted doctors to births which were likely to be difficult or dangerous. The safety record of hospital deliveries reduced the apprehension that many mothers had once felt. With the introduction of the National Health Service in 1948 the number of consultant obstetricians and maternity beds was greatly increased all over Britain and by the end of that decade more than half of all births took place in hospital. Childbirth was no longer overshadowed by fear of the death of the mother and her baby.

Mothers' lives ceased to be dominated by constant pregnancy and childbirth: by the 1930s around three-quarters of all families consisted of three or less children. only 10 per cent of parents producing five or more. More and more couples practised more effective birth control: men used condoms and women were fitted with caps at the birth-control clinics pioneered by Marie Stopes in the 1920s. The clinics. though. met with considerable official opposition and even in the late 1930s still only a quarter of all local authorities provided parents with information about contraception. fearing that greater knowledge of birth control would encourage immorality. liberate women from their 'duties' as mothers and reduce the fertility rate in Britain to such an extent that there would be a population crisis. The lack of education and persistence of old attitudes of shame about contraception meant that with-drawal and abstinence remained the most commonly employed methods. However. inspired perhaps by a desire for more freedom and a better standard of living. many felt a new determination to have smaller families than in previous generations. Now that women could be and were spared the pain and drudgery of child-bearing year in year out. their health – and that of their babies – improved. Childbirth was increasingly seen as a special and momentous event in a woman's life. to be planned by the parents.

Ivy Summers

Ivy was born in Grimsby in 1901, the daughter of a 'top skipper' and one of eleven children. When she left school at fourteen she was apprenticed to a milliner for a shilling a week. Ivy met her husband when she was seventeen. He was twenty-two, had recently been demobbed from the army after the First World War and worked as a fish splitter on Grimsby Docks. They married in 1919 and went to live with Ivy's sister. Ivy supplemented their income by taking in washing. Her first child was born in 1920, thirteen months after her marriage.

I would like to have had about four and that would have been my limit, I think. Didn't plan for any of them. They just rolled up. You just had them. The first thing, there wasn't the things there is today, was there? If there had been I wouldn't have had all them bairns, but there was nothing in them days, they didn't even tell you anything. You didn't know anything. You either had them or you killed yourself trying to get rid of them, which I would never do.

I used to worry about it when I first used to fall. I used to think, 'Oh, all that to go through again', you know, and then I used to think to myself, 'Well, it's no good, it's there and there's nowt I can do about it.' And I just used to carry on, and have another one. And the first three months whenever I was having one I used to feel terrible, you know, what I was going to go through, and then I used to think, 'Well, I've got to make the best of it so let's get on with me work.' You didn't have much time to think, you were working all the time. The nurse used to come and she'd say, 'Are you having another baby?' and I'd say, 'It looks like it', and she'd say, 'Oh, I don't know, Mrs Summers.' I'd be blackleading the grate, perhaps, when she walked in and she would say, 'Well, you haven't got much but you're always lovely and clean, and your babes are always so lovely we can always pick them up 'cos they always smell so nice and clean.'

13

Everybody did the same. You had to prepare for everything. Well, I used to any road. You see, when you went to book the nurse they told you what you had to get for the first one, of course, and then after that you knew what you had to do. If you got up in the morning and you was in labour you got through your day to see that your house was all in order, you got the bairns to school and then you'd make your bed ready to be confined on. You used to fold a sheet up to about that square and then you put a sheet of brown paper on that and that's what you laid on to be confined. You had to get all the baby's clothes out and all the things that the nurse wanted, the bowl and jug, and then I used to go downstairs and tell one of the neighbours, the neighbours would be in, to go and book the nurse for me, fetch the nurse, and she used to come upstairs and we used to get it over.

I wouldn't let my husband see me having the bairns. But, anyway, the nurse would never have allowed him to be in the room, not in them days. You see, my husband, of all the years I was married, he never saw me without anything on and I never saw him without anything on. People would think it was hard to believe when you had all them bairns but it was true. I've never in me life seen him without anything on and he never seen me without anything on. I don't know if anyone else was the same as what I was but that's how I was. Perhaps it was because I'd had a sheltered upbringing or something in our family because my mother never spoke about anything and, I mean, up to me getting married I was proper ignorant about everything.

I used to send him to the match. I'd say, 'Go to the football match.' And if there was no football match I'd say, 'Go to our father's.' Send him out the road, get rid of him. When he come back it was all over and done with. I didn't want to worry him – he couldn't do no good. He'd only have been worried about me and that would have done him no good so I never bothered. I used to say, 'Go next door.' 'Cos his father lived next door to us. 'Go next door to your father's.' Well, it was a private thing. We just had one woman.

14

When I was in labour you was walking around the room with a nurse there until you were just about to have the baby. You couldn't explain what the pain was like because I don't think there is another pain on earth like it. You just feel as though it's a red hot poker going through you. They was very good to you. If you was stood at the bottom of the bed they used to stroke you, stroke your back, and help with your labour and that, and then, when the pains got real bad you knew the babe was going to be born, they used to say, 'You'd better get on the bed now because the baby will be born.' Then you had to hold on to a towel when you had your pains to bring the baby. Well, in them days you had a roller towel. We used to put it on the bed rail and you used to pull on that when the baby was being born, and then when the baby was born they used to put that around your body.

You didn't make a row 'cos the kids was in the next bedroom, weren't they? You didn't want to frighten them to death. No. I never made no noise. I just used to hold meself. Grin and bear it. I don't think with any of my children I ever made a sound. No. I'd 'a' frightened them to death if I had 'a' done. No, I never bothered about making a row. I just used to have a handkerchief in me hand and I had the towel to pull on and I just held myself like that. First thing they heard was the baby crying and that's how it was with them all.

And then when the baby was born they just took that brown paper away from under you, wrapped it up and used to burn all that on the fire downstairs. And they used to burn it on the fire, the afterbirth, and you laid in bed for nine days and on the tenth day when you got up you felt ten feet tall. And then you had to start all over again, looking after the kids and that.

And you'd got your new baby and all the other bairns to see to, so what I used to do, I used to leave the baby in bed, come down, see to the bairns, get the kids off to school, them that went to school. Then the little uns, used to sit them on the mat, give them something to play with, then I'd fetch the baby down, bath him, feed him, settle him down and start the day's work. That's what you had to do in them days. You had to do it but

15

you didn't know how you did it. Course, you think the world of your own bairns when they're born. As many as you have you still think the same about them.

Mary Siddall

Mary was born in 1899 in Wrexham, the daughter of a coal miner. When she was a child the family moved to Oldham. She began working half time in a cotton mill at the age of twelve, and full time when she left school at the age of fourteen. She met her future husband, a twenty-year-old soldier on leave during the First World War, at the cinema when she was eighteen. They began writing to each other and married three years later in 1921. Both had jobs in a local cotton mill, although he became a storeman in later years. They started a family immediately after the marriage.

Well, the pain was terrible when I were having my first baby. I were in pain from Tuesday night to the Friday morning when she was born. I worked up till the Tuesday night in the cotton mill. And when I came home during the evening I started labour pains. I could scream with it I was that much in pain. I were on me hands and knees laid on the rug for part of it. There was no gas and air in those days. I just had this bolster tied to the bed, you know, and I'd to pull that till the baby come. I bent the bed rail, pulling. It were terrible. I screamed terrible 'cause it were a big baby.

When she was born she was blue. And the nurse, she says, 'I'm sorry, but this baby's not going to live because it's been so long in birth.' But, anyway, the baby got right gradually. It took a while for her to get right but then it was such a relief.

I didn't have a doctor for none of them, I had just the midwife. I had five at home and five in hospital. I did feel safe with a woman, especially the midwives, the old-fashioned midwives that used to come in them days. She were the motherly type, you see, and she helped me a lot. She used to push up, push the baby and rub me back for me – did everything what she could to help to bring the birth on. Better than a doctor, really.

I'll tell you what my husband used to do. I were in labour pushing and crying and screaming. He'd be outside listening, and

17

when he could hear the baby's cries he'd come in then, he were all right then. That were my husband, he didn't want to be there. If he saw a baby born it'd have carried him out. I didn't want him there because I never undressed in front of him, always in the dark or else him turning the other way. Couldn't help it, that was just how I was. To say that I'd had all them children and I couldn't undress me in front of my husband!

I were twenty-one when I had me first child. I had ten children, four in four years and a month. I didn't want a lot of children at all, I just wanted the two, but they just come, you know, and I had to accept them, hadn't I, and they were all looked after. When they came they were welcome, and I were happy with them. There wasn't one too many when they were all born, I hadn't one to spare. When I got up to five somebody asked me did I want to go to the family planning. I told my husband I were fed up of having babies. 'Well,' he says. 'You've so many to have.' And that were it. He took it that way, but he didn't believe in birth control, my husband didn't, no. But I kept believing when I had another it would be the last now, but they still kept coming. If I ever wanted him to be there, he wouldn't be, he were missing.

I were nearly forty-five when I had my last baby. And I used to be ashamed of going to the hospital. I were eight month pregnant before I went to book in 'cause I were ashamed of going there. I used to ask one of my daughters, 'Will you go to the front door and see if there's anybody about.' If Mrs Suchabody was outside I used to go through the back, not because I were ashamed of having the children, I were thinking of what they thought. That were on my mind. 'She's been doing it again, she's having sex all the time.' And I wasn't.

Mary Morton Hardie

Mary was born in Lanarkshire in 1912. Her father was a civil servant. She left school at thirteen when she started work as a domestic servant. Mary met her husband, James (see also page 21), when she was sixteen, in the dairy where he was working. They were married three months later. Their first child, a son, was born in 1930. After the birth Mary decided that she didn't want any more children and, like many couples at that time, she and James decided to abstain from sex to prevent further pregnancies. Mary's second child was born in 1938, followed by three daughters in 1942, 1946 and 1948, another son in 1952, and finally a daughter in 1954. They now have eleven grandchildren and six great-grandchildren.

I didn't associate the fun that I'd had with my husband with childbirth at all. I didn't know it would ever lead to pain like this. So there and then after my first baby was born I made up my mind there would never be another baby. When I got home I told my husband I was having no more babies. 'Well,' he said, 'I can't blame you, you seem to have had a bad time.' I just wasn't going to have any more babies, it wasn't worth it. I had my baby now and I loved the baby.

My husband was really very nice about it all and I slept in a different bed with the baby. Instead of putting him in a cot I took him in bed with me. I wasn't frightened, I was terrified. I wouldn't have gone through that again for a man. I refused to sleep with him in the bed – not that he demanded it. He realized that I was terrified of having more children and he was very good, though we did have one or two sessions. But we were so careful and he always stopped before he completed. I managed seven and a half years when I didn't sleep with him to avoid being tempted.

Eventually I went down to the clinic, the doctor's surgery, and there were other young women there. I asked around to see what they did to avoid having children. So they giggled among themselves and said, 'Tell your man to get a French letter.' They call them condoms now, but I didn't know that. I'd never heard of such things. And I said to him, 'Now, look, I've been asking around at the clinic and they say you should get a French letter.' Well, my husband was so quiet and withdrawn about this. He says, 'Oh.' And he didn't say 'Yes' or 'No' and he didn't, so we didn't. As simple as that. He was really as much embarrassed as I was. Even more so.

By then my little boy was getting too big. He was about six and going to school. And so I decided I would go back and sleep with my husband because the boy needed a bed to himself. And a year later I had another baby. I didn't want to but I accepted them gratefully. I really just thought that these belong to me – I had all these children and as each one came I was so happy to have them. These were mine.

James Hardie

James was born in Motherwell in 1910. His father was an esti-
mations clerk in the steelworks in Motherwell. When James left
school at the age of fourteen he couldn't find a job so he worked
in a garage for a year without pay. He then found a job as a butter
scalper making butter pats in the Maple Dairy where he later
became the manager. It was there that he met Mary in 1928.
After the birth of their first child in 1931 James considered using
condoms as a form of contraception but like many men at that
time, however, found them expensive and was sometimes too
embarrassed to buy them at all. He and Mary turned to the most
common methods of the time, withdrawal and abstention.

We just had our family. There wasn't the same precautions
or the same things as there are today and it was a case of,
well, I suppose there was some kind of luck attached to it. We
had to be careful, that was all. Hope for the best. I used to buy
condoms if I was working away from home. When I came home
I used to bring a packet of condoms with me, of course, and that
was the best way. But they were difficult to get in those days.
There used to be certain shops where you knew they sold them
and you used to go by as if you were asking for something that
you shouldn't ask for, you know, that kind of thing. It was
looked down on a wee bit, when they saw you walking in with
a kind of sheepish look on your face you see, knowing, 'Ah ha,
here's another one.' Yes, mmm. If you went in and there was a
girl behind the counter you were a bit embarrassed, you used to
try and get the owner of the shop, in those days it was usually a
man who prescribed the medicines, and if you could get hold of
him he would slip you a packet. You just said what you wanted
to him and the girl would turn her head the other way.

But it worked all right, yes. Trouble was they were quite
expensive, you see. Just, I never got used to them and it didn't
seem the same, it wasn't a natural thing to do, put it that way.

21

As you know, a condom's not the same at all as the natural thing so I felt that way about it. I suppose the main way of doing it, of course, was withdrawal, yes. If you didn't have a condom that was the next best thing.

So we decided we'd be strong-willed and sleep in separate beds. Yes, we did that for a while. Well, it was just a case of either that or more kiddies, you know. It was quite difficult but we stuck it out and we did quite well. We actually had eight years between the first and second babies. But we used to cheat on it occasionally if you understand. But you just get kind of blasé about it and start off sleeping with each other again.

Nine times out of ten we were lucky – we've got a big family. That's what happens, you see, and then the odd accident happens sometimes. You're happy about it, it doesn't really matter, you're quite happy to have your family, yes. Other times it came at a time when you would not want another baby. I suppose we could have had a wee bit of an argument about it. Not terribly long, but we just accepted it. It was an expensive business – another mouth to feed. But the kiddies grew up to be healthy and we enjoyed them very much because of that. So we've got no regrets at all about the family.

Betty Jones

Betty was born in 1920, near Woking. Her father worked for the council and her mother looked after Betty and her five brothers and sisters. At the age of fourteen Betty was put into service in Woking. She met her first boyfriend cycling in the countryside on her half-day off. Betty became pregnant in 1937. Like many young women she was completely ignorant of the facts of life and did not guess that she was pregnant until she went into labour. Her boyfriend died after an accident before the baby was born. So after the birth, dismissed from her job, Betty took her baby to her parents' home where she stayed until she married in 1938. She had four other children: a boy in 1941, a girl in 1942, and two more boys in 1944 and 1945. She now has seventeen grand-children and eighteen great-grandchildren.

In my home sex was never ever mentioned. Babies were never mentioned, as I can remember. When my brother was born I was eleven. I came home from school and the lady next door told me that I had a little brother and asked me if I wanted to see him. And I thought I suppose I better had. So I went to see my little brother and my mum. Of course, naturally enough they were in bed. And still I never thought, 'What's my mother doing in bed?' I did not know a thing.

I met my first boyfriend when I was sixteen or round about sixteen. We used to go for bike rides out into the country, into the fields, really. We used to stick the bikes down and cuddle down on the grass, have sex. But I didn't know what was going to be at the end of it, though. I didn't know I was going to have a baby. I just thought it was the in thing. So I had no idea that I was pregnant. In those days people used to say if you had a bad cold, your periods would stop or if you did extra exercise – 'Oh, don't be surprised if your periods stop.' Well, my periods stopped and, of course, I thought that was just it. Something had hap-pened. But I didn't think I was pregnant. 'It must be because I'm

23

biking, cycling too much.' Because we did do a lot of cycling when we used to go out into the country. I was very well built and it didn't show. And I didn't feel anything.

One day I got up with such a stomach ache. I couldn't remember if I'd eaten anything or not. I tried to carry on working, setting the table for the mistress's breakfast but then the pain was getting much worse and I thought, 'Well, I can't stick this here I'm going back to bed.' So back to bed I went. This stomach ache was killing me. And then I had this terrific pain – and what happened? I looked down and I thought, 'Where the Dickens has that come from?' There was my baby. I couldn't understand where it had come from. And she was tied to me somewhere. Of course the cord was still there. I remember putting my hands down and thinking that I'd have to walk about like that all my life. I didn't shout for anybody but then one of the maids came to see if I felt better and she just screamed, 'Oh, my God!' And she went flying down to get the mistress. Well, she ranted and raved. 'Oh, my God, girl! Look what you've done. Look at the mess.' I didn't answer. I was too petrified. 'Look what you've got there,' she said. 'Didn't you know? Look at the mess you've made. You've ruined my bed. Don't be surprised if I charge you for a new bed. You can get out and stop out! You will not get your wages.' I was stunned.

In the finish they sent for the ambulance. They had to come for me right up to this attic where I had me bedroom. And one of the men must have cut the cord. Then I got that stomach ache again and I thought it was all going to happen again. But that was the afterbirth. So then off I went with this baby to the maternity home. And I honestly did not know how it had all happened till one of the nurses said to me, 'You've been a silly girl, haven't you? Why ever did you have this little baby?' 'Well,' I said, 'I didn't know I was going to have her.' And so she explained to me how I must have got pregnant.

Jane Williams

Jane was born in Stratford. London. in 1902. worked as a shop assistant and barmaid from the age of fourteen and married in 1921. The couple lived in the East End of London where her husband found it difficult to find work. He was unemployed for much of the 1920s and 1930s. Despite constant abortions Jane had five children.

I had two children, one was ten, one was seven. I was living with Alec and of course we were in poverty. And I had to get a job because he was out of work. Anyway, I found myself pregnant, and I knew I just couldn't have a child; the job was the most important thing of all, it was your bread and butter. In fact, I used to bring food home from the job. If I couldn't go into work my money was stopped, I had no money coming in. And the dear landlady would put the bailiffs in if we owed a week and a half's rent.

Thousands of women were in the same boat as me. There were lots of things you heard, if you didn't want the baby, how to get rid of it. It wasn't that you didn't want your baby, you just couldn't afford to have any more.

Nothing was known about contraception. I'd heard the word 'French letter' when I was quite a grown woman, but I thought it was something you read. And the ordinary common man would never think of buying those things. Not to my knowledge, not the part of life I lived in. Sex wasn't mentioned like it is today. I expect people grew up secretly, they made love secretly, whatever they done, but it was quite kept under cover.

So I had to get rid of it, the baby. I'd been told what to do, and I had done it. I brought this pregnancy on myself. I'd done something before I went to work in the morning. I got in the train at the Oval to go to work, and I think it was Leicester Square where I had to change to get to Hammersmith. And, this miscarriage come on, I could feel it happening. I got as far as the platform, and then I had to kneel down by the wall, because I was in trouble. Two ladies come along, and I can remember very plainly, one had an ear trumpet. She said, 'She's haemorrhaging.' They went and got the porter, and he put a sacking screen around me, and I put my handkerchief over my face, in case anybody knew me. And, from there I had to wait for an ambulance to take me to hospital, Charing Cross. I was near death. The ambulance driver said, 'I can't take her, she hasn't got a pulse.' Funny thing about it, they thought I was unconscious but I could hear everything. Then I was sinking down a big black hole, it felt like to me. I thought I was dying but I was evidently going unconscious.

They didn't like abortions in those days. The doctors asked who done it, or where you had it done. You said, 'It just happened.' Naturally you wouldn't say. But they cleaned me up though they weren't very nice to me because abortions were frowned on very badly. The very word abortion was strong. If it had all come away I'd have had no more trouble. But I came out of hospital after a few days and went back to work. And it all started again, the bleeding. I had to get back to bed and it was tipped up at one end. I had about ten haemorrhages that week. Every time they put the bed down I would be bad again.

Then I had another one in Leadenhall market, working in the kitchen there. I'd done something before I came out in the morning. I worked through the day, the whole day, and just as I was going to leave that night, it happened. And this child was fully formed, which really never left me. Because I could see the head, I could see the shape of the child. And the barmaid, she put a black apron over it and put it down the toilet. And I had to go home, walking home, and that's something that I've had to live with. I thought that was dreadful.

Hilda Bennett

Hilda was born in 1897 in Grimsby, one of five children. Her
father was a twine spinner on the docks and her mother worked
as a braider on the trawling nets. Hilda met her husband at the
Hippodrome cinema in Grimsby in 1912. They married in 1915.
During the First World War Hilda's husband served on a mine
sweeper, and then became a fish splitter on the docks. Their first
child, a daughter, was born in 1916. The birth of their son in
1919 was particularly traumatic for Hilda and the doctor who
attended her used forceps to deliver him. Hilda went on to have
two more children in 1920 and 1924. She now has seven grandchildren and ten great-grandchildren.

I started with labour pains on the Thursday night. About six
o'clock I sent for the nurse but she never did anything when
she came. She told me that I didn't need a doctor with it being
my second child. About midnight the matron from the nursing
home came. The baby still wasn't born and I was in such pain
that she said it was about time that she sent for a doctor. So my
husband went and got the doctor but before he even came into
the bedroom we had to put £2 on the table. He gave me chloro-
form and instruments and delivered Charlie. When he was born
he was the ugliest thing you ever saw in your life. He was cut
all round his neck, his eyes was like big black plums, and he had
a scar right down his head. And that's how they left me. They
washed him, bathed him, and left me.

You see, once a baby was born and it had been washed and
put in bed with you, they used to go. That was all their work
was. They used to come in each morning for ten days just to
wash you, like. You used to have to pay a lady to come in
and do your housework and your cooking and looking after the
children and your washing. You'd all that to pay for.

When I used to wash Charlie his eyes used to bleed. I was
absolutely worried stiff. But I'd sooner look after him meself, I

didn't want anyone here telling me how to carry on when I could look after him meself, no. Three weeks after he was born I had a blood-poisoned toe. About six weeks after that, one morning at 6 o'clock I was woke with severe pains in me leg, couldn't move it for pain. I got up, went downstairs, and I had to have the doctor. He said I'd sprained me knee! About a week after that my husband came in from work and he said, 'Oh, there's a terrible smell in here, have you had that knee attended to?' And when he turned the bedclothes down you've never smelt anything like it in your life. My leg was covered with corruption – it had burst. They sent me straight to the hospital, cost me seven and six for the ambulance, and I was in the hospital three weeks. It turned out to be septicaemia. That was because of the birth. You see, it was neglect. The sister said, 'You're a very lucky woman, you could have this leg taken off because that's septicaemia you've had.'

Rose Luttrell

Rose Luttrell was born in 1893 in Victoria. Hong Kong. where her father was working as a civil engineer and architect. Rose and her sister were educated and cared for by a Chinese amah and an English governess until the family returned to England when Rose was fourteen in 1907. The girls continued to be instructed by governesses. Rose did not work and spent much of her time gardening and caring for her pet animals at the family home. When she was twenty-three she met her husband. the manager of a bank in Bath. and they married in the same year. The couple lived at Box in Wiltshire and kept a house with a staff of six servants. Rose had her first child in 1918. The birth was difficult and the doctor used forceps to assist the delivery. The baby was injured and died two days later.

I had rather an elderly monthly nurse at the birth of my first baby. She came a week or ten days before the baby was due to look after me and prepare me for the labour. I was at home at Box and when she sent for the doctor I think he was not really, one could say, quite up to the job. Well, he was my own practitioner, my ordinary doctor, but he wasn't a specialist.

And, of course, there'd been no ante-natal and no X-rays. They never examined you like they do these days. And because of that they didn't know the position the baby was in so I don't think they realized that the baby's head was jammed against my spine and, as I had every pain, instead of the baby coming forward he was being jammed more and more.

During the birth they just dragged me about the room on the bed and I was badly torn. I was in labour for hours and hours and hours and they couldn't deliver the baby because of his head being jammed against me and he was a ten-pound baby as well. Eventually they brought it on with forceps and I was very badly torn, and the baby's skull was injured. I don't know what instruments they used but they crushed his skull, you see.

My son was baptized and he was put in my arms for just once, that was all. I remember that he was shaking all over. And he only lived for two days. It was very sad with the empty nursery. I remember going into the room with all the cot and everything ready. We were all very shattered and upset.

But, of course, one couldn't do anything. You see we were so inexperienced – I don't know whether we ought to have made more enquiries – he was just our ordinary GP and one just took him for granted, but I don't think he had been up to the difficulty of the birth. So the next time I went into a nursing home. My husband said, 'No more doctors at home, you're going into a nursing home', and I went into one in Bath and changed my doctor to dear old Dr Fuller, who was a wonderful gynaecologist, and I had no trouble with my other babies.

Hilda Caldwell

Hilda was born one of twins in Sheffield in 1919. Her father worked for the railway company, repairing wagons and her mother was a machinist. Hilda's father died when she was four and she went to live with her grandmother in Leeds. She was introduced to her husband John (see page 33) by one of his cousins. They knew straight away that they would marry – in fact they met only three times before their wedding in 1942 when she was twenty-three. Unusually, Hilda wanted John with her when their babies were born. They now have four grandchildren and three great-grandchildren.

Oh, God, yes, yeah. Now the thing is that nobody can describe the pain of childbirth. It's one of the most intense things you ever felt. But when it's over, it just goes. It isn't like, say, you cut yourself and, oh, you ache after, you know, you're in pain and then you ache. There's nothing like that with childbirth. When that pain stops, it stops completely. There's nothing afterwards. And you'd get this pain and then you'd go ten minutes and you wouldn't feel a thing and then it would come on again. And it's the most intense pain you ever felt in your life. You can't describe it, really. It's only another woman that's had it that can say, 'I know what you mean.' Oh, yes, and the men couldn't understand it, the intensity. If the men had it there'd be no more children born. They couldn't stand the pain.

Course, I was wanting to get hold of John, my husband, get hold of his hand, you see, and get his strength. But it wasn't the done thing. No, nobody had their husbands there, nobody. You had towels, though, and you were gripping the towels, you see, as you were having the baby. So that's why I wished Dad was there to hold on to his hand. Well, that's an ordinary thing. I mean, if you're in trouble at all, or if you're in pain, you always say, 'Oh, I wish me husband was here.' You know, it's an automatic reaction, that you want your husband there to hold on to, to give you strength, you see. It's a gut feeling, you know. But, of course, then you didn't have any men there. It wasn't thought of. You wouldn't dream of having your husband in the place. Well, the doctors and the nurses and the midwife wouldn't have a fellow there. They said they were too much in the way. The midwife she says, 'Now, get hold of these towels.' And I said, 'Can Dad come and I can grab him?' So she says, 'Oh, no,' she says. 'He can't come up.' I says, 'Why not?' 'No,' she says. 'We don't want any men. He's better down there out of the way, boiling water for you, than being up here with us.' 'Well,' I says, 'I wish he was here.' So she says, 'No, you can't have him. You just grab hold of the towels.' And then, of course, after that you just went on and on with the pain and it got worse and worse and then the baby was born.

So they took the baby down to him and showed him the baby and then he came up to see me. But I was all washed and cleaned and done up then. I was all looking nice again. Well, you don't look so good when you're having a baby, you don't want your picture taken, let's say. Oh, God, love him, he says, 'Thanks, thanks, lovey,' he said. And he cried. There were tears in his eyes. And then he sat, he just sat there nursing the baby, thought it was wonderful. There's just something with that first baby that's different. I think it's the newness, you know, that you've never had a baby before and just seeing, seeing a new-born baby, oh, it's the most wonderful feeling. No, nobody could tell you unless they'd had a baby, that feeling when you see that babby, marvellous thing, marvellous. And he was over the moon.

John Caldwell

John was born in 1908 and brought up in Barrow-in-Furness. His father was a traffic manager in the local steel works. John contracted polio as a child which left his legs permanently weakened. He left school at fourteen and worked as a storeman. After their marriage. he and Hilda shared a house with another couple until they were allotted a council home after five years of marriage. They have two daughters. born in 1943 and 1946. John. like most men of his generation. had no desire to be present at their births.

Well, of course, Hilda was upstairs and the midwife was there and I were sat downstairs, so the midwife says to me, 'We'd like some hot water, boiling water.' So I said, 'Right,' and I started to put the kettles and pans on for sterilization purposes. I'll tell you also what I did, it'd been Christmas and Win had bought me half a bottle of whisky and I was getting a tot or two of whisky down me as well, wasn't I? Giving me courage, yes.

When Hilda asked the midwife if I could go upstairs and be there and help her she said, 'There's no men in this room, only the doctor when he comes. We can't do with men messing about here it's no place for them. He's all right where he is, down there boiling water and messing about and that's all he needs to do.' I was relieved.

I didn't want to see it because I knew she'd be going through pain, in labour, and I didn't want to see her and witness her going through the labour pains. I didn't want to see that. I wanted to see a nice birth with no pains, but of course you've got to have pains so I didn't want to witness it, because I'd see the agony on her face. I thought, 'I'm not going up there, oh, no.' I don't think that I would have gone into that bedroom when she was having a youngster.

Well, I'll tell you what put me off. I always thought, 'Well, a man is a man.' And I was manly. I was big, a tough body on me like a tree trunk and muscles like great branches from that tree trunk. I was very muscular and I thought, 'No, that's no place for me, like,' even though she requested it. I thought, 'That's no place for me, I'm a man, I'm not one of these shilly-shally blokes that want to be in on something that they shouldn't be in on.' And I thought, 'Well, I'm not going to start that silly game.' And that was it. I made me mind up there and then and, of course, when the midwife says, 'There's no room here for your husband,' I thought, 'Well, that'll satisfy me. I'm not wanted up there and I don't want to go up there, so that's it.' 'Cos I'll tell you why in one respect. I've never known any man – mates of mine and pals of mine and men I knew – ever be in the bedroom when the child was born and I thought, 'Well, I'm not going to start that game, oh, no, not me.' Me father had nine and he wasn't at the birth of one of them. No, that wasn't his place, and I suppose I took after him, like. And me brother-in-laws didn't so I thought, 'Why should I break the pattern by going in?' I thought they'd all call me a big sissy that I wanted to be in the bedroom, and so I just brushed it off, no, no place for me.

I didn't hear a thing, thank God, no, I didn't hear a thing. The only thing I heard was the moment she was born and she had a hell of a pair of lungs on her, I heard her crying, but I didn't know whether it was a girl or a boy. I heard this bawling out and I thought, 'Hello, it's here whichever it is, a son or a daughter.' Until me sister brought it down, wrapped in a blanket, and she said, ''Ere, nurse yer baby daughter, Hilda's carried her long enough.' And I looked at her like that and took her on me knee and then I looked at her face and said, 'What's the matter with her face?' And she said, 'Nothing, why?' And I said, 'Well her face is very red.' And she said, 'Well, that's good blood.' And I said, 'Oh, thank God for that.' I breathed a sigh of relief. I filled up, you know, with the relief it was all over and it was a healthy baby.

Betty Dennison

Betty was born in 1914 into a Catholic family in Hull's Old Town. Her father was a merchant seaman. She started working half time at twelve. helping the owners of the fish and chip stalls with odd jobs. Betty met her future husband. a fisherman. when she was seventeen. They married two years later in 1933 and moved into two rooms in a house in Old Town. Her first baby. a daughter. was born in 1935 in Hull infirmary. The birth was a terrifying experience for Betty due to the regimentation and surgical techniques practised by the hospital. She vowed never to have another baby in hospital and their other children. two sons in 1936 and 1939. were both born at home.

I were absolutely thick, thick as a plank. I didn't know where the baby was coming from, and all the nurse said was, 'Oh, well, it'll come, from the same place it went in.'

It was very scaring. You go in there, I don't think anybody went with me, no, just you in this room, it's just like a little gaol cell. A cell, and in there, they take you first into the bath, shove you, push you, get into a bath. Strip, into a bath, strip, into this room, enema, shaving, then, of course, you've got this thick nightgown, split all up the back. And you're told to just get on this bed, well, it's a table, and you're on there while you're examined and they say how far you are on and it'll be another ten or twelve hours. And then they're gone. Your pains are coming more and more, it's kind of gradual but they're coming more. You can get off and walk about but there was nowhere to walk, really. You were just walking and thinking, 'Oh, please God, when's somebody coming? Help, me husband's coming, what time is it?' I don't think you knew the time or anything else. Somebody did come, maybe every hour or something like that, come in just to see what you were doing, examine you again, and every time they came in you thought, 'Oh dear, well, this is it, this is it now, I must be going to have it.' I didn't know about the labour ward or anything. I was there from six o'clock in the morning and I was there all night, then at last, after hours on my own in that little room, they came and took me into the labour ward.

It was bigger and brighter than where I'd been in this little room. And that's where the screaming came from, all these little rooms you see like cells, there was somebody in every one of them all in different stages of labour. And then it was all bright, oh, hundreds of lights and mirrors on the ceilings and them big round lights in the middle of the ceiling. All the ceiling was lit up and everything. That's bright, well, that's frightening, a frightening place to be. You wondered whatever they're going to do in there, and then these stirrups there, your feet hung from the ceiling. What can they do with stirrups?

Oh, God. I'd never known anything like it. I was laid there with my legs up. That is a funny feeling, really, if you don't know what's going on. I think I was feeling panic. I thought, 'Well, I must be dying. They can't get the baby. I don't know what they're doing about it.'

It's just a shocking pain that nobody experiences any more. You don't experience that pain in anything, I don't think.

And all these men's faces you see, 'cause they're up there. Instead of being at the bottom of the bed when you look up they're all on the ceiling, it's like a horror film. You're looking up and there's all these mirrors, with all these faces in and I'm looking at all these faces and if they move, you see the faces move on the ceiling, and oh, good heavens, if you're in a state of shock you don't know if they're up there or down there, do you?

When me waters broke I always remember, 'Oh, thank God,' I said, 'Oh, thank God for that.' 'Oh,' the nurse said. 'Don't thank God yet, that's just your waters broke.' I thought it must be a bit nearer. Then this doctor come over with the mask and he got these forceps and that was when she was born. He pulled her out and the nurse picked her up, hung her on this scale to take its weight on a hook, just hung it up in a bit of rag, six pounds something, and then it's whipped away and then you don't see that no more. You come to, then you're in the bed in the ward with others, like, about six or eight beds. Then maybe, about four hours after, they bring the baby to you wrapped in an old thing like the same as I had on, a bit of old stiff blanket, and they put it to the breast. Then they come and weigh it again, to see how much it's had, you see. Oh, she's had four ounces, so then they'd take her away again.

You wanted to hold it, you wanted to hold it, didn't you, and just look at it. I mean, you've waited all that time for it and you can't hardly see it, can you? They'd take it off you again. Me husband went to see it. He didn't go into the nursery, they just looked through the door with all these cots, and they bring yours to you. And then I say to him, 'What's it like? Is she any bigger, what's she like?' And then he hasn't hardly seen it so he didn't know what the baby looked like either.

Then you could hear them, the babies crying, in the nursery, and I used to think, 'I'm sure that one's mine, I'm sure that's mine. Oh, I wish I could pick it up. I wish I could go get it and pick it up.' 'Cause they all scream alike, they all cry alike so that you always thought it was yours that was crying.

You're dying to get home, you're dying to get home and have your baby on your own and do as you like with it and dress it up and feed it up and do everything that you want to do because, really, it's like a new toy to you, in't it, when you're young and it's your first one, and you want to show her all the love you've got for it. It's really a sad experience for your first experience, in't it, for your first one, like. It makes you think that you'll never, never go in that place again. I said I'd never go in there again, and I didn't.

Dora Wright

Dora was born in 1908 in Stockport. near Manchester. one of eight children. Her father worked in a bakery. Dora left school at fourteen and was apprenticed to a dressmaker. She met her future husband. Albert. in 1931 and married him the same year. Albert had also come from a large family of nine children. He was working as a clerk for a coal merchant although he later became a cinema manager. Determined that Dora should not suffer the constant childbearing and rearing that their mothers had endured. the couple decided to limit their family size. Dora found out about an early birth control clinic in Manchester and was given a cap. She and Albert had one child in 1936. Dora returned to work when their daughter was ten years old. They now have two grand-children.

My mother had eight of us to look after. My father was out at work all the time and, anyway, men didn't help much in those days with the babies. They never took their wives any-where. And so all she had was washing and cooking and running around after us to do, no enjoyment as such. She used to be blackleading the grate, scrubbing floors and that's how she was ill as a result of it. The doctor told her it was just sheer exhaustion. That's why she was bad all the time as she got older. She was just worn out, her general health was terrible. I think it attacked her nerves because I remember when I was in my teens she would always be ill, crying a lot and she looked so tired. But that was her life. Work and us kids. It was a very hard life.

So when I met Albert in 1931 and we decided we would get married I thought about my mother and what kind of life she'd had to deal with and I really decided for myself that I would only have one or two children. I didn't want to wear myself out and get like my mother had. And I wanted to enjoy my children, to give them lots of time and be with them and my new husband. I didn't always want to be scrimping and saving for every penny.

So I talked about it to Albert. I was nervous because you didn't talk about things like that in those days. But I had heard girls at work joking around about how to stop having babies, I knew there were things you could do and so I asked Albert what he thought about it. And so we decided it together, really. We would only have one or two and I could try to get something to stop me having any more. So we could plan our family, wait until we wanted a baby.

It was a performance, really, because neither of us knew where we could go. Things like that weren't advertised then. It was my sister-in-law who found out about this clinic. It was in Manchester and it was run by Dr Marie Stopes. So I went along there with my sister-in-law on the bus.

And after all the nervousness they were really quite nice. Course it was all very hush-hush. There was just this little plaque on the door and so it was quite hard to find. But then when I saw the doctor he asked me whether I was married and for how long and all that and if I had any children. And they gave me a cap. Showed me how to use it and sent me off with that. I was as pleased as punch with myself.

And that's how we went on. I used to take a half-day off work every now and then and toddle off to Manchester and get it changed and get it checked. And it worked, for us, anyway. Because we just had Barbara and then when she was ten I decided I wanted to go back to my job and so we didn't have any more. I was happy with that and I enjoyed every minute of my child, I still do.

Kathleen Davey

Kathleen Davey was born in Hammersmith. London. in 1915 where her father worked as a commercial clerk. She left Fulham Secondary School in 1932 to work as a GPO telephonist. In 1940 Kathleen married a man she had known since childhood and had two daughters. Her husband died of TB meningitis in 1948. She remarried in 1952. She is now widowed and has one grandchild.

When I had Mary, the second one, I wasn't allowed to have her in hospital. They wouldn't let you have second babies in hospital, you had to have them at home. I'd ordered the midwife to come and I also ordered to have gas and air.

When I went into labour the midwife was quite a long time coming, they only came on bikes in those days. I was in the front room because we had to have the bed downstairs and my husband and my mother were waiting in the living room. I was going on for quite a long time because it was a pretty bad labour. And I kept thinking, 'When are they going to give me this gas and air?'

I got to a point where I was really in agony, and I was screaming out. The nurse came over to me and she took up the pillow and she said, 'Would you mind putting this over your mouth when you scream, because the noise might upset your husband in the other room?'

I did think that was the limit, I really did. I didn't forgive them for telling me to shut up when I was screaming. Well, I mean, I thought it was ridiculous because I know it wasn't usual to have your husband with you but I think most men would understand that you were going through a pretty hard time, and they would expect to hear some sort of noise. But actually to try and drown it by putting a pillow over my face, I really did think that was the absolute limit. I was really indignant about that.

But I just had to put up with it. I was only concerned with what I was getting on with. They never gave me gas and air because they said they didn't know I had ordered it. So I had to get on without it. And the midwife said at the end that it was a pity I hadn't got it because I would have had the baby in half the time, as my strength was going.

Gladys Locke

Gladys was born in Bristol in 1919, where her father worked on the Great Western Railway and her mother in a jam factory. Gladys left school at fifteen to work as a shop assistant. She met her future husband, an insurance clerk, when she was seventeen and they courted for three years. While they were on their honeymoon the house they had bought was bombed, so they began married life in rented rooms. Gladys was badly shaken by the Bristol blitz and regularly escaped from the city at night to sleep in fields and under hedges. Her first son, born during the height of the blitz, survived only a few days. She later had a daughter in 1944, a son in 1946 and another daughter in 1954. Gladys has five grandchildren.

I was so terrified of all the bombing, and when I found out I was pregnant I felt even worse because I didn't only have myself to protect, I had that baby. There was this big raid during the blitz and we were trapped in the Colston Hall all night. I went hysterical, because I was pregnant, and a young lady came along and started smacking me face, and shaking me. She didn't realize what was wrong with me. But from that night on I was more than terrified. We were living with my mother at the time and I used to drag her all over the place to get away from the bombing – and my husband, when he was there. We used to walk miles. As long as I was away from Bristol I didn't care where we went. We'd go anywhere, really. Get down in a field, or get behind a hedge. We used to sleep on anything. We used to sleep on hay or in an old barn, or under a hedge. In an open field. Anywhere, but I can't ever say I had a comfortable night. In the winter it was terrible. Used to get wet and cold, thirsty and hungry. But it was more comfortable to me than being back in the shelter. Very often we used to stand and watch what was going on over Bristol.

I was too worried to sleep. I was worried about the baby.

And we used to get cramp. Being pregnant, that made me worse. And we would stay there all night, in the cold and the damp. We didn't get much sleep at all. But I was happy to be away from the city. I was so frightened, I just wanted to get away from Bristol. I don't think I would have been so scared if it was just me but I really, really wanted that child. I really wanted it.

I suppose I was about six months' gone when I woke up one night with terrible indigestion. When my husband went to work next morning he gave me some bicarbonate of soda. He had to go to the centre to work and I was in my dressing gown and nightie, sat in the room. So I just sat there and at six o'clock at night my husband came home and I was in exactly the same position. I hadn't moved and I was in agony. I'd never had any experience at all, and I never thought about a premature birth. But I had been so worried and upset by all the bombing and worn out by trekking out into the country that it had brought the baby on too soon.

My husband got to the nearest phone and phoned up a doctor who came round very quickly, wrapped me up in a blanket, carried me out to his car and took me to Keynsham in what was then the Poor Law Institute, but it was the only place that had room to take me. I couldn't walk and as he was carrying me over the courtyard to go into this place I said, 'Am I going to die?' He said, 'Not if we can help it.' They put me right out with morphine, so I didn't know a thing about the baby.

When I came to they gave me it and it was three pounds. It was a beautiful little baby, though I could only see its little face all wrapped up in a little shawl. They gave me the baby and I fell asleep with it in my arms actually, but of course it died that night. I didn't want to live. My husband was the only one that was allowed in to see me and every time he came in I was lying in the bed with a sheet and I used to pull the sheet over my head. I didn't want to see or talk to anybody. It was a heartbreaking experience.

Violet Ring

Violet was born in 1925 in Teddington. Middlesex. Her father was a florist and her mother looked after Violet and her three brothers. In July 1946 while on holiday in Ramsgate. Violet met her future husband. who was on leave from the Navy. and they were married within the week. Afterwards the couple went to live with Violet's parents in Teddington where her husband found a job as an assistant in a clothes shop. Violet became pregnant quite quickly and on 20 June 1947 she was taken into an annexe of the West Middlesex hospital to have her baby. After an eleven-day labour the baby was born dead. The appalling way in which she was treated illustrates how harsh and uncaring some hospitals were towards women in labour. even in the late 1940s. The trauma of the experience led to the breakdown of the marriage and they had no more children. They were divorced in 1974. Violet has since remarried and lives quietly with her second husband in Cornwall.

I went into hospital on 16 May. I had pains and that but they just put me into bed and the baby didn't come. My husband and my mum came to visit me. It was a terrible place. It was old-fashioned and really vast. I thought I'd be in and out but they just made me lie on this bed and they weren't very nice to you. I laid on that labour bed for eleven days with my legs tied on posts and they used to argue around me about what was best to do with me. But they didn't act at all. The baby was so big that I couldn't have it naturally. They should have given me some help or a Caesarian. I was crying and holding onto things with pain. I was so terrified. When they used to unstrap my legs I used to wander round there trying to find poison. It's as though it happened yesterday.

I only had feelings of hate. The sister used to slap my legs and tell me there was nothing wrong with me, that I wasn't in labour. I nearly went mad. My legs all the time on posts. Then after eleven days the doctor came dressed up all in wellingtons and that and he said he was going to put me out. They put me to sleep for five hours and when I came to all I could hear was my mother's voice saying, 'You call yourself a bloody doctor. My daughter's been in your care for all this time and now you let this happen, I've had two children at home. I could kill you.' All I could think about was my baby and I asked the nurse whether it was a boy or a girl and she said, 'Boy, born dead, lie still.' They'd dragged that baby from me, and they'd ripped me to pieces. It was alive till two minutes before they got it. It suffocated because they left it too long.

I lay there like a dead thing. I had all these cards and presents that I'd taken in with me, 'It's a boy, it's a girl.' They didn't even ask me if I wanted to see my baby. The day after I'd had the baby, they gave me some hard beef and some dried-up cabbage. My mum used to come in and cry and ask what they had done to me.

All I could think of was getting out. I lied and said that I was feeling okay just to get out. I came out and my clothes just fell off me. I looked like I was a hundred and nine. I couldn't pass water or anything, I had fifty-four stitches inside. When my mum brought me home my dad cried like a baby and for weeks and weeks I had to lay on my back. I didn't think I'd ever walk again. The day after I came out of hospital I had a bill for the burial of a stillborn infant. It was buried in a mass grave. My mum went to the burial and she said there were lots of little white coffins.

I had bought a big pram and I knitted things and the neighbours knitted things. People said, 'Oh, don't get rid of your pram, Vi, because you might have another baby.' People used to let me nurse their babies and I used to wish but I knew then that I would never have one ever again. I used to think that perhaps we ought to but then I was too terrified.

The doctor told me that I could have no relations with my husband for six months but I said I was never going to again. So we never did again. Never again. I would never have another one. My husband was funny and nice but we never had sex again in the next twenty-two years of marriage. I swore that I'd never go into hospital or have a baby ever so I couldn't risk it. If that was childbirth, I didn't want it ever again. If ever I'd have been going to have a baby I'd have killed myself.

It would have been Mum's first grandchild, and they were broken-hearted. All my friends were wheeling prams about. To go through that and to come out with nothing . . . I've got photos of all my friends' children but it's left me with nothing. They've got daughters and grandchildren but I've got nothing.

CHAPTER TWO
Baby Care

The first half of the century was the era of the baby care 'expert'. Mothers were bombarded with baby care books and pamphlets; health visitors made routine inspections of the standards of infant care achieved by parents; and clinics and infant welfare centres run by local authorities sprang up all over Britain – there were more than 3,500 by the late 1930s. In Victorian times, baby care had been widely regarded as a private activity best left to the instincts and intuition of the mother. Now it was redefined as a matter of major public and national importance. It was the duty of women to produce strong, obedient citizens upon whom the future strength and stability of the nation depended, and to do their job properly they had to be instructed in the skills of what came to be known as 'mothercraft' – a term that suggests how strongly baby care was seen as an exclusively feminine activity. It was assumed that the father should be a reliable breadwinner and he was given no other role in the new literature.

At the heart of the ideology of motherhood was a 'bonny', well-trained baby. The new breed of experts agreed that the efforts of the mother during the baby's first year or two were of paramount importance in shaping its entire future. As one 'expert' of the time put it: 'The neglected toddler in everyone's way is the material which becomes the disgruntled agitator, while the happy contented child is the pillar of the state' (Gwen St Aubyn, *Family Book*, 1935).

The crusade to improve baby care was, like the movement to make childbirth safer, rooted in a deep fear of national degeneration and 'racial suicide'. The appalling physical condition of many Boer War recruits followed by the mass slaughter of the 'flower of the nation's youth' during the First World War led to an urgent

demand that the government intervene to replenish Britain's stock
in the next generation. This was no easy task. In the first decade
of the century around one in eight babies died before they reached
their first birthday: in 1901, for example, more than 140,000
infant deaths were recorded. Babies of working-class families were
particularly at risk and the death toll was highest in the cities. In
the poorest streets of Liverpool and Glasgow only one in every two
babies survived their first year.

This high infant mortality was widely seen as a failure of
working-class mothers. In fact, the deaths were often due to circumstances beyond their control: most were killed by common
infectious diseases like bronchitis, pneumonia, whooping cough,
diarrhoea and enteritis, closely linked to bad housing, serious
overcrowding, inadequate diet, poor sanitation and contaminated
water supplies. During the summer of 1911 a staggering 32,000
babies died of diarrhoea alone. Diarrhoea – often caused by lack
of hygiene in food preparation and storage – was always rampant
in the summer. It was usually preceded by distressing convulsions
and the baby would die within a week.

Undernourished women often gave birth to weak, sickly babies
which they were unable to breast feed, either because of poor
health or because they had to go out to work. The alternatives
were risky: much of the cow's milk sold early in the century was
contaminated and a major source of infection. Few working-class
mothers used it. The most popular baby food was condensed milk
– especially Nestlé's – first introduced in the 1870s. It was popular
because it was cheap and filling, it lasted longer than fresh milk
before 'going off' and could be bought 'on tick' from corner shops.
However, it lacked the fat content that babies need and many
brought up on tinned milk developed weak bones and rickets.
Early medical researchers also believed that babies brought up on
condensed milk were especially vulnerable to diarrhoea.

As few understood the importance of sterilization, the risk of
infection by bottle-feeding was heightened by the use of germ-
ridden equipment. Bottle feeding had become more widespread
during the mid nineteenth century as bottles with india rubber

Left: Ivy Summers with her husband in the 1940s. The couple had twelve children, the first born in 1920.

Below: A father awaiting the birth of his baby. In the first half of this century it was not considered proper for men to be present at the birth of their child and they were often banned from the delivery room by the midwife or doctor. (*Imperial War Museum*)

Below Left: Nurses preparing a mother for the birth of her baby at home, where until the late 1940s, the vast majority of women had their babies. (*Imperial War Museum*)

Top: Mary Siddall and her husband, pictured with their ten children. Mary's first baby was born at home in 1921.

Above: Rose Luttrell and two of her children. Her first baby was born in 1918.

Middle Right: Mary Morton Hardie with her son, who was born in 1930. Although Mary and her husband tried to limit their family they eventually had eight children.

Right: Hilda Bennett and her husband with their first child, born in 1916.

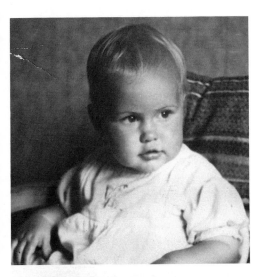

Top Right: John Caldwell (*front row right*), pictured with friends in the 1930s. John and his wife Hilda had their first child in 1943.

Top Left: Kathleen Davey's first child, who was born at home in 1942.

Above: Kathleen Davey and her husband at their wedding in 1940.

Left: Gladys Locke and her husband, pictured during the Second World War. As a result of her experiences in the Bristol Blitz Gladys lost her first child, born in 1941.

Left: Rose Luttrell's three children, pictured in the 1920s.

Below: The municipal baby competition at the Town Hall in South Shields in 1916, when 'bonny baby' competitions, in which weight was equated with good health, were fashionable. (*Beamish*)

Far Bottom: An advertisement for Sunlight Soap in the 1900s. During the first half of the century child care and housework were regarded as strictly the duty of mothers. (*Mary Evans Picture Library*)

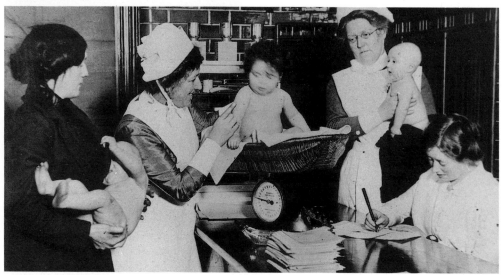

"What is Home without a Mother?"

'Tis a sad, cheerless place. All through the house are to be seen evidences of a mother's absence. Nothing looks right; hardly anything is right. And just as the house is made brighter, happier, and more habitable by a mother's presence, so are the homes made cleaner, sweeter, and healthier by the use of

SUNLIGHT SOAP.

SUNLIGHT SOAP FINE ART PRIZES.

Everyone wishing to possess facsimile copies of the Pictures by Miss DOROTHY TENNANT, entitled "Heads over Tails," and by W. P. FRITH, R.A., entitled "So Clean!" can (until further notice) obtain them **Free of Cost** by sending their Full Name and Address to LEVER BROS., Limited, Port Sunlight, near Birkenhead, together with Sunlight Soap Wrappers as follows—

For 25 Sunlight Soap Wrappers, ONE of the above UNFRAMED.
„ 50 „ „ „ „ THE PAIR UNFRAMED.
„ 150 „ „ „ „ ONE of the above in handsome GILT FRAME.
„ 250 „ „ „ „ THE PAIR in GILT FRAMES.

Top Left: Olive Morgan, in the 1930s, with one of her eight children. She is carrying the baby in her shawl in the popular Welsh nursing fashion of the time.

Top Right: Five of Olive Morgan's six sons in the early 1950s. Two of her eight children died only weeks after they were born.

Above: An East End mother reading to her children from a newspaper in 1932. Working-class families experienced bad health and disease due to poor housing conditions, overcrowding and inadequate diet. (*Topham Picture Library*)

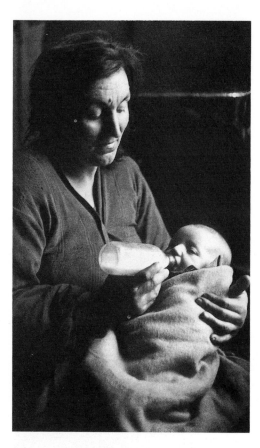

Above: A woman bottle-feeding a baby, pictured in the Glasgow Gorbals in 1948. In poor homes bottle-feeding heightened the risk of infection and disease due to bad sanitation. (*The Hulton-Deutsch Collection*)

Top Right: Betty Dennison, pictured in 1940, shortly after her husband was killed at sea while serving in the Navy.

Right: Betty Dennison, with the three children from her first marriage. After the death of her husband, she was left to bring up the children alone until she remarried in 1947.

Left: Margaret Swanton's first son, who died young of a congenital heart condition.

Below: Kathleen Davy's two daughters, who were born in 1942 and 1944. The younger child, Mary, caught pneumonia due to Kathleen following the regimented Truby King method of childcare.

Below: A nurse bathing a baby, photographed in 1933. Clinics at the time encouraged mothers to adopt the Truby King method with its routines of washing, feeding and toilet-training by the clock. (*Barnaby's Picture Library*)

Right: A health visitor calling on a family in the 1940s. Many mothers resented their advice and preferred to stick to traditional methods of baby care. (*RCN Archives*)

Below: What a baby was thought to need in its first six months in 1947. Mothers were bombarded with books and pamphlets advising them on what they should have to feed and care for their babies. (*Topham Picture Library*)

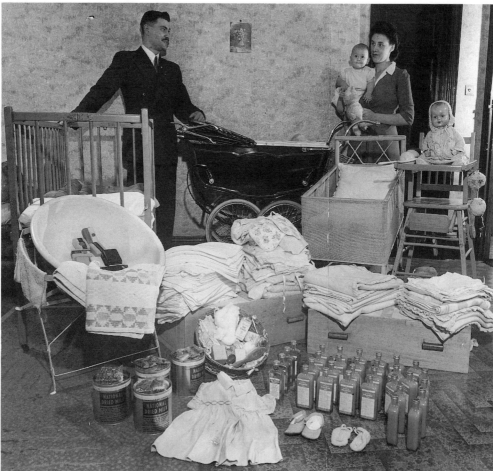

teats – which were easier to use than the old models – were now being mass-produced. In the poorest homes. however. mothers were often forced to feed the baby from any bottle with a narrow neck and a tube of pig's skin or rubber. In the 1900s it was reckoned that bottle-fed babies were fifteen times more likely to die within the first year of their lives than those being breast fed.

In this atmosphere of grave concern about Britain's baby population. experts – or supposed experts – on infant welfare rose to prominence and began to wield extraordinary power. Baby-care manuals were written in a bullying. brow-beating tone. This authoritarianism particularly infused the writings of Dr Frederick Truby King. the guru of baby experts. who established a new 'scientific' approach to baby care which became standard advice to mothers in the new clinics from the 1920s to the late 1940s. After launching a successful movement in New Zealand which encouraged mothers to breast- rather than bottle-feed their babies. in 1917 Truby King established a mothercraft training school in Highgate. North London. With the motto 'Breast fed is best fed'. the Truby King approach became enormously influential in promoting breast feeding. The ambition of many mothers was to have a 'Truby King' baby.

The encouragement of breast feeding undoubtedly brought health benefits to babies and was one factor in the gradual decline in the infant mortality rate during the early part of the century. Breast-feeding routines. however. could become oppressive to mothers for they were the central plank of a new maternal ideology. the broader aim of which was the regimented habit training and discipline of babies. Relentless pressure was applied on mothers by clinics. health visitors and advice books to train their toddlers to conform to a rigid set of rules which governed feeding. crying. playing and potty training. This early psychological conditioning was thought to be essential to the formation of the 'normal'. stable personality that would form the bedrock of a strong nation. As Mabel Liddiard. one of Truby King's great disciples. put it in her best-selling *Mothercraft Manual* of 1928: 'Self control. obedience. the recognition of authority. and later. respect

51

for elders are all the outcome of the first year's training. To train the infant for the first year is comparatively easy but after that the child begins to resent authority.' This medical advice was reminiscent of the religious exhortations given to parents in nineteenth-century evangelical tracts, in which the infant had been seen as a seething mass of sinful, animal instincts, which needed to be controlled or stamped out before they took hold.

Truby King claimed that 'feeding and sleeping by the clock' was the best way to 'establish perfect regularity of habits and is the ultimate foundation of all round obedience'. The good mother was a clock watcher who fed her baby regularly, more or less on the dot, every three or four hours – and never at night. According to Truby King, feeding on demand when baby cried and night-time feeding could have dire consequences on character formation. The child would be spoilt and spineless, a terrible burden on the mother and, later, on society.

A similar routine had to be established in potty training. Mabel Liddiard advised that:

Early training is of great importance; from the third day the nurse should have a small chamber on her knee and the baby should be held with the back against the nurse's chest for not longer than two minutes; the cold rim should just be allowed to touch the child at the back of the anus, and very soon a reflex is established. Many nurses train their babies so that they have no soiled napkins after the first week or so, and very few wet ones.

The Truby King method was geared to 'toughening up' the baby and making it independent of its mother as soon as possible. Fresh air, sunshine and cold water sponge baths were thought to be essential to its physical and psychological growth. The swaddling of babies with layers of clothes was – quite sensibly – rejected in favour of lighter garments or bare skin. Mothers were told to establish a daily routine of putting the baby outside on a rug or in a pram; however, they were also rashly instructed to leave it to brave the elements for long periods, whatever the weather. Charis Frankenburg recommended that 'Infants should hardly be indoors at all between 8 in the morning and 5 at night in the winter. and from 7 a.m. to 10 p.m. in the summer.'

A key element in the 'toughening up' process was the denial of physical comfort and pleasure for babies. If they cried. unless they were in great distress. it was thought best to let them 'cry it out'. providing valuable exercise for their lungs and fostering the development of self-reliance and a stiff upper lip. It was thought inadvisable to kiss or cuddle them. which. it was felt. inevitably led to spoiling and a weak. dependent character. Playing with a baby under six months was not recommended as it created an undesirable state of nervous excitement. which disrupted regular sleeping and feeding patterns. The direst warnings. though. were against thumb-sucking and masturbation: turning a blind eye to instinctive bodily comforts and pleasures like these could spell disaster later in life. Many parents had their babies circumcised in the belief that this would reduce the temptation and danger of masturbation.

The impact of this regimented approach to baby care varied greatly according to the class background and circumstances of the parents. The Truby King method was embraced most fervently by the middle classes. who read most of the official literature on baby care and who took the advice of doctors. clinics and baby experts seriously. Many aspired to a 'perfect baby' and had high expectations of what their child might achieve. The Truby King method. which promised early child development and discipline if its elaborate rules were followed to the letter. held a strong appeal. The 'milestones' of baby development. which stated when a Truby King baby could be expected to smile. stand up. walk. talk and go through the night with a dry nappy. were reassuring and exciting to the young mother. But if babies did not jump the hurdles when they were expected to. the 'failure' created much worry and self-doubt. Some middle-class mothers felt complete failures because they could not achieve the standards expected of them by the clinics and the textbooks. For most. the anxiety and disappoint-ment was greatest when bringing up their first child. Many middle-class mothers applied the Truby King method most vigorously on their first baby, but, as the regime was difficult to follow and often did not deliver all that it promised, became more relaxed about the training of their second baby — and some rejected the advice altogether.

The Truby King method had less impact on working-class mothers. Although widely perceived in official circles as either 'ignorant and feckless' or alternatively as 'over indulgent', young mothers in poorer areas often showed tremendous ingenuity and energy in looking after babies with minimal facilities and little money. They made nappies out of old shirts and sheets; converted boxes and drawers into cots; made baby clothes out of hand-me-downs. Many clung to the traditional practices passed down from mother to daughter. Feeding on demand — by breast if possible — had long been thought the most practical and healthy method among working-class families, and continued largely unabated, despite the efforts of clinics and health visitors to enforce a more regimented routine. Poorer mothers had a more relaxed attitude to potty training and to cuddling their babies. The Truby King recommendation of physically separating a baby from adults, in the cot, playpen and nursery, was impossible in overcrowded working-class homes. Babies were held constantly by different members of the family, were often nursed on demand and included in family and street activities. They frequently shared their parents' bed, a practice which 'experts' constantly denounced as leading to death through suffocation. In fact the incidence and risk of baby deaths of this sort was much exaggerated.

Local baby-care customs also played their part in providing a buffer against the dictates of clinics and health visitors. In the north-west, cinder tea, a popular remedy for baby's wind made by immersing burning hot embers from a coal fire in water and adding sugar, continued to be given to babies in their bottles up to the 1930s. And in Wales many mothers rejected modern 'fresh air' methods in favour of traditional 'Welsh nursing' which involved wrapping the baby in a shawl bound around the mother's body.

Some working-class mothers went regularly to clinics and

instructional classes. Here they learnt some useful information on better hygiene, correct baby foods and health care. But there was widespread resentment towards the new experts, doctors and health visitors, who, it was felt, were patronizing and understood little about the practical problems facing poor mothers. Often they could not afford the items that they were told to use: the banana box cribs recommended by clinics, which, around the time of the First World War cost about one shilling (5p), were too expensive as were many baby foods and medicines.

Between the 1900s and the 1950s the health of babies and infants gradually improved. By the late 1930s the death rate of babies in their first year was reduced to one in forty giving them a four times greater chance of survival than at the turn of the century. The followers of Truby King and other baby care experts claimed this as a victory for their methods, but much more import-ant were the sustained improvements in diet, housing, health care and the standard of living in Britain. Mothers and babies were better fed; families were generally smaller, enabling more care and attention to be given to babies; many poor families were moved out from city slums to suburban council estates where they enjoyed better facilities; milk and baby-food products became safer and more nutritious; and protective vaccines were developed against the fatal infections of the past. 'Black spots' of high infant mor-tality remained into the 1930s, but these tended to be restricted to the old industrial heartlands where there was high unemploy-ment and severe poverty, for example in South Wales and the north-west.

The Second World War led to more state intervention in health care for mothers and babies than ever before. There were a number of improvements: clinics, for example, offered mothers free orange juice and cod liver oil. It was all part of an effort to boost the health and morale of the nation in a time of crisis. But there was also a downside to this intervention. In an atmosphere of regimentation and increasing state control of many aspects of life, mothers of all classes began dutifully to follow the Truby King style baby-care methods of the clinics. During the war many more mothers than ever before 'did as they were told' by doctors. nurses and health visitors. Oral testimony graphically reveals how these routines often added to the problems and pressures faced by young mothers.

When the war was over a new approach to baby care began to come into vogue. Mothers were told to form close. warm and loving relationships with their babies. The motto was 'enjoy your baby' and 'have fun'. The new guru of this more permissive approach was Dr Benjamin Spock whose *Common Sense Book of Baby and Child Care*. published in 1946. became a best seller outsold only by the Bible. The old rigid rules which mothers broke at their peril were replaced by friendly advice and more relaxed attitudes to feeding and potty training. although older health workers still clung to the Truby King method. The new approach fitted the democratic mood. the demand for greater individual freedom and the emergence of the welfare state. Mothers wanted to enjoy their babies and their families after the horror of the war: many were no longer prepared to put up with the regimentation of the past.

Mary Siddall

See also Chapter One. page 17. Mary had ten children. all of whom survived − a remarkable feat considering her stature (she stands four foot ten inches tall) and that she could not breastfeed any of them. She had her children in 1921 (girl). 1924 (boy). 1926 (girl). 1930 (girl). 1932 (girl). 1937 (boy). 1938 (girl). 1940 (boy). 1941 (girl). 1944 (boy). Mary has eleven grandsons and eleven granddaughters. eleven great-grandsons. twelve great-grand-daughters and one great-great-grandson.

My husband, he weren't very affectionate with children, you know. He never took mine out, like some do. I used to say, 'Fred, will you take baby out in the pram while I make the dinner?' No way, no. So I did all that, one in the cot, one in the pram. I don't think he honestly wanted any children, to tell you the truth, because you never saw him play with them or anything like that. I had to do that. He'd never read a story to them or he'd never have a little game with them, even as babies. It were all left to me, you know.

I were always there and always seeing to them. He'd never think of them at all, he'd never think of saying, 'Come on, I'll take you for a little walk.' Never. I don't think he should have been married or had any children. He hadn't much patience with children and I think he had to be jealous of his own children, I hadn't the same time to see to him as what I had before having the children, you see. I used to get annoyed with him, but I were never bitter, I never detested him. He were still my husband and the father of my children. But I would have liked him more if he'd have done a bit more for me. As the older ones got older they helped me a lot with the other half.

He just said, 'Well, I'm not like that. I can't be taking the babies in the prams,' he says. 'I weren't born to be like that.' And I said, 'No, but you were born to make 'em.'

I had ten altogether. I coped with them all. But it were hard.

It were very hard to bring them up, but I pulled through. We did without ourselves, to see to the children. We did without for ourselves and any furniture, we didn't buy nothing.

I'd be too tired to sleep sometimes. And then I had to wash 'em, and they had ringlets, long ringlets in them days, used to comb their hair, keep their heads clean, put the ringlets up at night. You know, it took me a long time to get 'em ready for bed anyway, so they went to bed and they'd sing and sing and I thought, 'My God, I wish they'd shut up.' But anyway, when the last song come I thought, 'Thank God for that, they're going to sleep.'

I think I went once to the clinic and that were enough. Because I hadn't time to go. They told me I had to feed the babies at a certain time every three or four hours. Well, I didn't take any notice of that, I fed them when I thought they were hungry. When they cried, of course, the babies, I used to go upstairs and see to them and settle them and change them and they'd sleep again. But when I bathed them at the night and put them in their cot and they settled down I used to go two or three times to see if they were all right. And then in the night I used to sit and sew these nappies out of the shirt laps – had to make ever so many of them, you know.

I had an oak dolly tub. I used to get hold of the little one and put him in the tub. I used to put him near the door to see the traffic passing through near the house. He'd play hours in that tub. So that's what learnt him to walk as well, 'cause he couldn't bend down so much, you know, in a tub. I used to throw him one or two little bits of toys and his little bread tin and a paper.

And then when I was baking at home, and when I'd done the tin, the bread tins, I used to bring one or two bread tins and sit them on the road with a tea cake. I'd give them the pegs to play with, he'd play drums, you know. And then I used to make a rag doll for the little girl and a little shoe box. I'd put the doll in, cover it up, you see, then it kept them quiet for me when I did me washing and, you know, baking or whatever I were doing.

If they had earache I literally used to boil a potato, just a whole potato, put it in a stocking, in a sock, and put it round her neck. And then one of them had a carbuncle in his arm, oh, it was a big one. So anyway the doctor kept coming and coming, but this Friday he was coming to lance this here carbuncle. So before he came I got some Epsom salts and I kept bathing it and bathing it. And it burst. And when doctor came on the Friday he says, 'Oh, it's burst.' And I didn't tell him what I'd done.

When they were tiny babies and they had wind I put 'em on me shoulder. They used to sell the red rose gripe water in them days, too dear for me to buy so I used to make cinder tea. You take a cinder out of the fire, a red-hot cinder, put it in a cup of cold water, let it stand a few seconds and then put some sugar in, and let it stand. And then you sieve it in another cup, then it'd cool off a bit, pour it in a feeding bottle, or a spoon, then they could take it. When they've had the cinder tea, you pick up your baby, put your baby on your shoulder, and you just pat the little back like that, and they get their wind up. They were all right after. And that were cheap enough, weren't it?

Ivy Summers

See also Chapter One. page 13. After her first baby in 1920 Ivy
had a child almost every year or two until 1942. She had her
second daughter in 1921. followed by a boy (1922). a girl (1923).
a boy (1926). a girl (1928). a boy (1931). a boy (1932). a girl
(1934). a boy (1935). a girl (1941) and finally another boy in
1942.

Ivy now has forty-nine grandchildren. one hundred and thirty
great-grandchildren and seventeen great-great-grandchildren.
Most of her family still live in Grimsby where they were brought
up.

The second one that I had, she was born with a hare lip and
a cleft palate and when the nurse saw her she said, 'Oh, my
God, Ivy.' I said, 'What's the matter – is there two?' She said,
'No, it would be better if there was two.' And when the baby
was born the doctor came. He said, 'Is this your first baby?' And
I said, 'No, I've a little girl a year old. Why?' So he said, 'Well,
this baby won't live.' He said, 'She might live an hour or she
might live the clock round but put her in a back bedroom, just
wet her lips and don't bother with her.' So when he'd gone the
nurse, she said, 'Shall I put her in the back bedroom, Ivy?' I said,
'No, you shouldn't. Give her to me.' And me sister was there
and I says to her, 'Go to the chemist and bring a bottle and bring
a tin of Nestlé's milk and go round to the church and bring the
vicar. Ask him if he will come and christen the baby because she's
not going to live and I want her christened.' And the priest came
with his surplice on and the holy water and he knelt at the side
of the bed and he said, 'What are you going to call her?' I said,
'Call her May.' That was after me sister. So when he'd gone I
said to me sister, 'Go down, put a spoonful of milk in some water
and fetch it upstairs and fetch a pair of scissors.' I just cut the end
off the dummy teat and let the milk trickle down her throat. She
was so lovely. She weighed nine pound and a half and she was

60

such a lovely bairn, you know. Black curly hair and big dark eyes and I kept her on milk and that kept her going. And we kept her going a year like that. We daren't give her nothing to eat 'cos she'd got this big hole in the roof of her mouth. And any road one day me father, he'd come off dock and he'd brought some sole and I was sitting having me dinner and I just peeled a bit of the sole off like that and she just grabbed hold of it, put it in her mouth and ate it. And after that we fed her. She was seventy-one in May. Well, she was important because she was mine and I didn't want to think she was going to die through my hands. It was funny thing for a doctor to say, wasn't it? It was as good as saying, 'Put her in the back bedroom and leave her to die.' 'Cos I dare say in two or three days, if you didn't give her nothing she would die.

I used to love them and kiss them and cuddle them up and that. And I never left them to cry, if they was crying I used to pick 'em up and I used to do me work when they was asleep. But I never let them cry. Mind you, they was very contented.

All my babies had a bone dummy from being born to about three year old and I never took them off until they give them up themselves. Put a dummy in their mouth, they'd suck it and be as quiet as anything. It used to sort of soothe them. It must have done. They had them on a piece of string and put them in their mouth when they wanted them. On a bit of ribbon. Yes, they was lost without their dummy tits, the babes was.

But they didn't believe in them at the clinics. They'd sooner let them suck their thumbs. I took one of them to the clinic one day and, of course, he had his dummy pinned on and the nurse just unpinned it and threw it in the wastepaper basket. So I said, 'Just take it out of there and put it back on him where you got it from because he does need it.' I says, 'Wash it first.' So she said, 'I don't believe in them.' And I says, 'Well, perhaps you don't believe in them but I do.' I mean, you couldn't have kept them quiet otherwise. They'd some queer ideas at the clinic. They had queer ideas of stripping a baby and laying him on a cold scales to weigh him. I said, 'Put a bit of blanket on there, they'll get cold.' They was full of ideas that was daft but I never took any notice of them. I never went to the clinic no more after that and when she came to the house she said to me, 'You haven't been to the clinic.' I said, 'No, and I'm not coming no more.'

The clinics used to say the baby shouldn't sleep with you and I told them, I said, 'My babies have all slept with me until they've been a year old from being born.' I said, 'And they're still going to sleep with me 'cos it keeps them warm.' You see, I slept with mine in my arms and as I turned over I took him over with me and then I left them in bed while I come down and see to the others – put a pillow in front of them so they wouldn't fall out of bed, and that's how I used to do with them when they was babies. And they didn't agree with that and they also didn't agree with how you fed them. 'Cos I used to feed mine with arrowroot biscuits with Nestlé's milk. They said a bottle of Ostermilk was enough. I said, 'Well, it isn't because they're hungry and you've got to feed them before you give them the bottle of milk.' And I was always in their black books.

Their father used to make them. He used to make a little box in a toilet, we had a pot underneath it, and they used to go and sit on there – till they was eighteen months old. Then a proper little toilet seat with a pot under it and when you fed them you'd sit them in there. Then you'd take 'em out when they'd done their business, but you trained them like that. Some of them, they was trained early, you see, they used to go and sit on the toilet, think they was clever 'cos they could sit on the toilet. You didn't have a lot of mess with them.

And you had your napkins. I used to wash about two dozen napkins every day, and boil them and hang them out on the line for them to dry. You had the proper napkin squares. If you was well off you bought napkins, you bought a dozen. Me mother used to save her sheets, cotton sheets. If they'd started to go she used to say, 'Well, you can take that home, cut it up and make napkins.' So I used to make squares and sew them around the edges and they used to make nice soft napkins, 'cos you couldn't always afford to buy the towelling ones, 'cos they was expensive. You'd perhaps get a dozen out of one sheet.

Well, you was tired getting up in the morning; you was tired going to bed, because you was working all day. In the winter I used to take washing in every day. We had to for money. And I used to do a dozen clothes for two shillings for people along the street. That was big things or little things and, believe me, you got more sheets and shirts and tablecloths than you got little things and you had to wash them. I used to have two dolly tubs and a scrubbing tub. You blued them first, then you starched them, then you hung them out, you fetched them in, you folded them up and you ironed them and you got tuppence for each one you did. So I had to do dozens and dozens before I earnt owt. To earn about fifteen shillings a week you was working nearly all day.

And as I was doing me washing, as soon as I used to start with the hot water I used to sit little one, who'd p'raps be about eight months old, I used to tie him in the chair, put a pillow at the back and sit him on a pillow and fasten him in with a scarf. And the other one I'd sit in the armchair, he'd be about two year old or two and a half. I'd sit him there, give him something to play with and then I used to get on with me washing. I had a bucket on the fire and a bucket on a gas ring on the table 'cos there were no coppers in them days and I used to be boiling a sheet in one and p'raps table cloths in another, what I used to take in, and I used to sit them in there. Then, when I took the things off the boil I took the babies out and let them play in the yard. And their father used to put a board across the door so they wouldn't come out. They used to stand up against there and watch me in the yard. Yeah, that's how I used to cope with them. Nowt never happened to mine. I could always see things happen before they did. I used to think, well, if I don't shift that it'll fall over, or something. I never left anything where my babies would get by it. I always had a fireguard round the fire, so they never had a chance of anything happening to them. And I can honestly say that my kids never had one thing through an accident when they was little. I always looked after them.

You never had no money for toys in them days. But they was very contented, my bairns, I will say that. I used to have a bottom drawer and I used to have chopped wood in there 'cos we had coal fires in them days, so what I used to do, I'd sit them against there and they used to make stacks with wood, play with the wood and that, you know, and they played hours like that, and their father used to make them all sorts to amuse them. He used to sing to them and play the mouth organ to them and his one-string fiddle. He used to amuse them while I was at work at night.

Well, you hadn't time to sit down, no time at all. But you never thought nowt about it, you just go on with it. You had it to do. I used to blacklead me grate every morning and I had a red brick floor I used to scrub. I used to come home from work at twelve o'clock at night, scrub me floor before I went to bed. Harry used to say to me, 'What are you scrubbing the floor tonight for?' I said, 'Well, you never know what's going to happen in the night.' If owt happened in the night, you had to fetch the doctor in a clean house. Everything was clean before I went to bed at night. Kids clean in bed, it was just a way of life, how you worked.

I had my tenth in 1935 but then when he was about two he got ill. It was about five o'clock at night and he was real warm, you know, and I sent for the doctor and when the doctor come he said, 'Oh, he's just got a slight chill, put him to bed. We're just starting with M & B tablets.' They just looked like saccharine, little tablets. He said, 'Give him half a one in his bottle of milk.' So I put half a one in his bottle of milk – and don't forget he was a beautiful baby, fat, beautiful, and I sat on the rocking chair and was singing to him. He fell asleep and I just laid him down and he stopped breathing. Me husband walked in the room – he'd just come home from work. Well, it upset him. I never seen anybody cry in me life – he broke his heart, 'cos he thought the world of his kids. He was a lovely babe, rosy cheeks, lovely fair curly hair. He'd only been ill for about an hour and that was M & B tablets.

And when the doctor come I said to him, 'It's that tablet that you gave me. I just give him half a one what you told me to give him in his bottle of milk and it killed him. He just stopped breathing, just went to sleep.' And that's how he died. Two year and two months old. 'Well, we're just learning with them,' he said. 'It's just like misadventure, it's one of them things that you can't – there's nothing you can do about it. We're just learning with them,' he said. Well, I don't know how I felt but every drop of blood drained from me. I can't cry – I go cold inside as though I'm dead and I just have no feelings at all. That's how it upsets me, like that you see. The shock. I just walked about like a zombie, as though I was dead.

We didn't have any money. You see, he died on the Thursday night and my husband got paid on the Friday and he only had two pounds seven so I went to the undertaker and I said to him, 'I wonder if you could bury my baby? I've no money to bury him but I'll pay you so much a week.' So he said he would and he charged me two pounds ten in them days, two pounds fifty now, and I paid him half a crown a week till it was finished.

Eleven of the twelve children that I had survived and now I've got forty-nine grandchildren and there's about a hundred and, I should say, thirty-something great-grandchildren and there's seventeen of the fifth generation, and there's still more to come. There's about four of them expecting. Me great-grandkids. They're springing up all over. I have no regret about having the kids at all, and I've all the grandkids, they all come round and the oldest of the fifth generation is twelve. There's worse things than having families.

Rose Luttrell

See also Chapter One. page 29. After the death of her first son in 1918 Rose went on to have three more children. a boy in 1919. another in 1921 and a girl in 1923. As was often the case in more upper-class families the children were brought up by a nanny. leaving Rose free to continue the pursuits she had enjoyed. like gardening and letter-writing. before her children were born. Rose has two granddaughters and five great-grandchildren.

I didn't look after the babies, I had a nurse. After the monthly nurse left I had a nanny and she looked after them for me. In those days mothers never looked after their own babies. The first nanny we had was a very nice girl, very well trained but we discovered that she was having a young man up in the nursery in the evenings so we had to get rid of her and then we engaged another dear old nanny who I had for nine years.

Oh, I used to go into the nursery and play with the baby whenever I wanted to and, of course, when you were feeding it you saw it and it used to be brought down after tea and I used to go and watch Nanny put him to bed. I had access to the nursery whenever I wanted but you didn't do anything actually with the baby – Nanny did everything. My bedroom was quite a long way from the nursery so I wouldn't hear them crying at all. You didn't interfere with Nanny. If you had a good nanny she wouldn't have put up with being interfered with. You left it entirely to her.

I did used to push the pram to the station at Box to meet my husband. One in the pram and the other walking beside me. That I did on my own, without Nanny – gave Nanny a little bit of a rest. I used to love it, being allowed to have the pram and the baby.

I think sometimes we used to go up and have tea in the nursery with them. It wasn't the done thing for them to come and eat downstairs. None of your friends were doing it, d'you see? It wasn't the custom. So they had all their meals up in the nursery and we had our meals in the dining room.

I never did any cooking at all for the babies. You see, I had a full staff. I had a cook and a kitchenmaid, a housemaid and a parlourmaid and, of course, Nanny and the nurserymaid. I had six servants, you see, so I never did any housework or any domestic work at all. I saw the cook in the morning and ordered the meals for the day and I never went near the kitchen. Oh, on the odd day that Nanny went out, I used to warm the bottle – she showed me how to do it and I did it under her instructions – but otherwise I never did anything for the children. Well, you don't want to pay somebody to do the job and then do it yourself, do you?

Of course, Nanny and I were great disciplinarians. If you said, 'No', you meant no. No nonsense about that. I can see them now. If they wanted to chew their bonnet strings Nanny used to tap them on the hand and their little faces used to drop. They knew exactly what they'd done wrong, just a little tap on the hand like that and she used to say, 'You're not to do that', and they knew it.

Edith Broadway

Edith was born in 1907 in North London where her father owned a tobacconist's shop. She left school when she was fourteen and started work a year later as an apprentice to a milliner. She met her husband when she was sixteen at a tennis dance. He was twenty and worked as a cashier in an oil company. They married four years later in 1928. Edith gave up her work as a milliner and the couple moved to their first home, a large three-bedroomed house in Seven Kings, Essex. Her first daughter was born seven years later, the second in 1939 and her son was born in 1946. Edith brought her first daughter up using the Truby King method. She became disillusioned with the harshness of the techniques and was more relaxed and liberal in her handling of her two other babies.

I had waited so long to have a child and because I wanted the best for my baby we thought that the Truby King method was the answer to what literally with your first baby is an experiment. It sounds harsh, I suppose, but nevertheless I bought the book. That was going to be my guidelines. I used to take her as I was told to do to the clinic every Monday. They instructed me in what really was a rigid system whereby you didn't feed them at all except when you were meant to, that was four-hourly, and certainly not in the night. At home we had a room made especially for her as a nursery so she wasn't allowed in our bedroom or allowed in my bed.

It left the mother reasonably free between times but at the same time it was too regimented, four-hourly. All you did was pick her up and feed her and change her nappy, pat her back and put her back in the pram. There was no cuddles, nothing like that, and, according to Truby King, you should not feed her at all in between times.

We were told to potty train them almost from the time they were born and that was what I did, automatically. As a tiny wee baby after she was fed she was potted. That was the system. And it was rigid, it was to the minute of the clock almost.

When she was about six months old there was a manifestation which frightened me and worried me with her tummy. So I sent her to the Truby King clinic because I wanted to see what was happening to my daughter. They put her on a diet and they gave me a regimented programme. They didn't tell me what was wrong and unfortunately the diet and the regimentation were imbalanced. Basically she had acute acidosis and the method that Truby King used for her was sensible to a degree, vegetables and fruit, but my little girl didn't care for either. I used to spend hours peeling grapes, throwing away the pips and then presenting it to her as tempting as I knew how. She'd have a mouthful and that was it, and of course there was no protein. So we went on and I kept to the diet.

And I kept to the strict rigid routine of not cuddling her when I wanted to – you fed her, changed her, winded her and put her in her pram, and pushed her up to the end of the garden and that was it. And you really didn't give the cuddles and the love and affection. If I kissed her it was on the back of the neck and nobody else was allowed to kiss her. That was something that we did bar, was kissing. I kissed her little body and I kissed her neck, but never kissing her as such.

And I wouldn't allow anybody else to cuddle and nurse her. I used to let her, as she got older, sit on her granny's lap, but not for long. I mean, just a little nurse and a little cuddle and that was it, but she was getting on then, she was nearly a year, maybe, before anybody else was allowed to hold her or play with her. It was naughty, wasn't it, when you come to think of it. I not only deprived my baby of the love and the cuddles and the fun we could have had, I deprived myself as well. I suppose my compensation was that I did used to sing, 'Rock-a-bye baby on the treetop' and all the little nursery rhymes. She loved that, she really did. But as a tiny baby you laid her on the rug and you'd say 'Piggy Went to Market', and all those sort of little things, and probably you'd tickle her and we used to have laughs and fun. That I did enjoy. But the only time we really had to play was an hour before bedtime and then we'd have an hour on the floor when she was tiny and that followed all the way through, of course, we had an hour on the floor for playing and then her bath and then her bed and we didn't expect to hear any more from her all night until about six next morning, and we expected that and because of the rigid regime we got that.

Choosing the Truby King method meant that I didn't want a spoilt child, I didn't want a baby that was screaming every so often and expecting to be cuddled and nursed, and I wanted her to grow up to be obedient and to do as she was told. I suppose that is one's idea of a perfect child and it's wrong. It's wrong, you're not allowing a child to be a child and that in itself is wrong but, yes, perfection was doing as you're told and no nonsense and that's how it was. I wasn't a tough person, that's the funny part about it all, I wasn't hard and I wasn't tough and I wanted to love my baby, but this regime was very much against my desires and I'm sure loads of other mothers must have done and felt the same thing.

It had a bad effect on her because she grew up withdrawn. I think the diet and the programme had taken things to the extreme. Shirley wasn't progressing. She looked pale and ill and worried me to death. It left her under-nourished and therefore it left her vulnerable. She was withdrawn, very withdrawn, until she was five. She never cuddled me, she was not demonstrative in any way and then it surprised me when we were out shopping one day and a little hand came into mine and I began to feel that at long last, you know, we were sort of being able to approach each other.

She was a very, very good child. She was stoical. If she had pain she never complained but, of course, I felt as time went by that a lot of this was basically suppression. I couldn't help feeling that. She still isn't spontaneous but she is a perfectionist. And I think this stems right back to what I wanted her to be as a baby and I aimed for that.

I would say that, bless her, she still has a reserve which I

70

think actually has been caused by the way we brought her up then. Shirley is in her own way much more reserved in that she often seems to me rather bottled up, and I would say that is as a direct result of the training she had as a baby.

Olive Morgan

Olive was born in Llanelli in 1914. Her father worked in the local tin mines. She left school at the age of fourteen to work in a shop and help with the shopkeeper's children. Olive met her husband, who was a bricklayer, just before her sixteenth birthday. They courted for four years while saving up to get married. Their first baby was born in 1934, and lived only three months. A second son was born in 1935, a healthy eight-pound baby. Her only daughter, Carol, who was born on Christmas Day in 1940, died a week later. Olive then had five more sons, born in 1942, 1944, 1947, 1949 and 1950. She now has fourteen grandchildren, and two great-grandchildren.

My first son couldn't keep his food down at all when he was born. He was really tiny, about three and a half pounds. We tried several different types of food but nothing seemed to agree with him. He cried all night from the time that he was born. Nothing would keep him quiet. The doctor told me to keep him warm, but there was no way. There was no heating in the bedroom and I couldn't leave him downstairs all night because there were cockroaches that came out in the dark. He just kept crying and he didn't gain any weight and he died when he was three months old. I was heartbroken. I thought I'd never get over it. But I shall never forget him.

I had eight in the end. And even after I had just given birth to a baby, I'd still have to work to look after the others. They'd bring their shoes to the bed for me to clean, for them to go to school. I remember that three hours after I'd given birth to one, I had to bath the little toddler, he was only crawling. And he used to get so dirty crawling about. I had to bath him to go to bed, and that was only hours after giving birth, until I was really exhausted.

The mother was expected to do all the work at that time. The father never helped at all. If the baby cried all night, the mother nursed the baby all night. I was so tired in the day time, sitting down to feed the baby. I would sit on the settee with the baby on my lap, and the bottle would often drop from my hand to the floor. I was so whacked.

I had lots of ways of trying to keep them quiet when they were small. One was to sing to them, what voice I had. They used to like that. Nothing special, just the song of the day, such as, 'Teddy Bears Picnic' or some of the Welsh verses that I knew.

I didn't think much of the clinics. Why walk a mile, with a small baby, undress him down to his nappy, and weigh him in cold scales? I was supposed to keep him warm. So, how can you keep a baby warm, if you strip him in the clinic?

Of course, the clinics had their fancy ideas of the way of bringing a baby up, but we had our own way in Wales, and nursing the baby Welsh fashion, with the shawl wrapped around the baby, then around the mother and underneath the mother's arm was our way. The baby was close to the mother then and could hear the mother's heart beating. And they were curled up then. They loved that, they'd go to sleep that way. It always worked, it always kept my babies quiet.

Kathleen Davey

See also Chapter One. page 40. Kathleen adopted the Truby King regime with her two daughters who were born in 1942 and 1944. She was especially conscientious about putting her baby outside in the fresh air every day. Her second baby. as a consequence. caught pneumonia and had to be admitted to hospital.

W e were always told that you should leave the baby out in the garden, for at least half an hour every day. Except, of course, if it was foggy or something. So, I religiously stuck to that and I used to let them go out in all weathers. I used to put hot water bottles in the pram and they used to stay out.

Well, Sally survived it without any trouble at all. But Mary was more delicate, even though she was a bigger baby when she was born. She didn't thrive as well as Sally but I was still told to put her out.

One day, it was bitterly cold but the sun was shining and it was a nice day, but frosty, you know. I wrapped her up and put her outside in the pram. I left her out there, not long, I'd been out shopping and left her there for a little while in the sun until she was asleep. Of course, I should have brought her in before. It was too cold for her and she caught pneumonia. And that's when she went to hospital.

She was in hospital for a fortnight and I wasn't allowed to see her. All you were allowed to do when you visited was to look at her through the glass doors. And she was crying her eyes out. I would have given anything to have gone in and comforted her but they wouldn't allow it, they said seeing the parents upset the children. As though she wasn't upset enough. I even had to plead with them to let her have a little counterpane, a little cover that she had, that she used to hold when she slept, and suck her thumb. They didn't want to do that, but I said she would never go to sleep unless she had it. So, the sister let her have it, but she had to hide it underneath the other covers so it wasn't seen, or it would spoil the whole effect.

I thought it was terrible not to be allowed to see the baby. All I wanted to do was to see her, and cuddle her and make sure she was all right. But all I could see was that she was crying and crying, and she was in a strange ward and she didn't know anybody. She was eighteen months and she was just beginning to recognize people and that sort of thing, and it was awful to see her just crying. We had to go away and be satisfied that we had seen that she was still alive. I felt terrible, absolutely dreadful. I didn't really blame anybody. I thought, 'Well, I was told and they must know, they're the experts or supposed to be the experts.'

It was a terrible time because when she came back from hospital she was still terribly ill. It was terribly cold weather and so I had to sleep downstairs with her because we only had one room that was warm with a fire, so I had to bring a bed downstairs and her cot downstairs. She nearly died actually.

I put it all down to the fact that she was allowed to go out in the cold and got pneumonia. I suppose if I'd have been sensible and not been so conscientious I wouldn't have let her go out in the cold weather. But I felt guilty if I didn't. I used to think, 'She's got to go out once a day.' They said all babies should go out once a day. 'If you keep them indoors then when they do go out they catch a cold.'

I was very stupid and naïve then. I didn't know anything about babies. I had nothing to do with them until I had my own. And I just took the people at the clinic word for word, what they said must be right.

Margaret Swanton

Margaret was born in 1924 and brought up in Bayswater, West London. Her father was an advertising agent. Her parents divorced when she was eight and she was sent to boarding school. She left school during her sixth-form year to do a secretarial course. When the war started Margaret joined the ATS where she met her husband, an engineer. They courted for six months, marrying in 1944. Their first son was born in 1945 and Margaret brought him up as a Truby King baby. He died from a congenital heart condition at the age of five. They had their second son in 1947, and after the agonies and disappointments of following the Truby King method, they decided to bring him up by the more liberal Spock technique. Margaret embarked on a second career in her early forties working as a probation officer until she retired. She now has five grandchildren.

I was quite nervous about how to handle my baby when I got him home from the hospital. They had actually given us a demonstration of how to bath a baby with a doll. But when I got home – it's a big difference bathing a real baby from bathing a doll and I can't tell you how nervous I was all the time when he was very tiny. All we'd been told at the hospital was a lot of rules and regulations. First of all he must be breast-fed and he must not be picked up between feeds. If he cried, never mind, let him cry, he must only be picked up about every three hours to begin with. Then, as he got a bit bigger, it would be every four hours. I found that really, really, very upsetting. He was a very crying baby so I found that quite worrying that I wasn't allowed to pick him up or comfort him. And on no account were we to have him in bed with us. And I did once or twice, when I'd fed him, keep him in bed with me, and I was petrified then. I thought, 'Oh, supposing I roll over in the night and smother him?' That used to make me feel very guilty.

The nurses in the hospital made it clear that I should go to the clinic for any further advice I needed. The emphasis really was on seeking professional information and advice all the way along the line. And I think I went along with that because I felt that I really didn't know anything about how to handle a baby, and that these people, the nurses, the medical staff and so forth, people in the clinic, were the authority.

There was a big chart on the wall in the clinic about milestones. It showed what he was expected to be doing at certain stages. And it was pointed out that it was very important. There were problems inherent in that because all of us together with young children, would tend to compare notes, and of course we didn't realize that children vary. I mean, not all babies grow at the same speed, they don't all develop at the same time. But because of this chart we all thought every baby should be walking or every baby should have two teeth or four teeth by a certain time. It made no allowance for individual development and was a bit unnerving because you were always thinking there was something wrong or that you were not doing things right. Your baby'd got to reach this point at such and such a time or he was left behind.

I was told to hold him out over the pot after every feed when he was only a few months old. The rim of the pot had to just about barely touch his bottom, meaning that the poor little baby could feel that chill underneath him and presumably, if he didn't perform he'd get a really cold bottom altogether. Well, of course, he never did anything at all, maybe a little wee-wee, and then you put a nice clean nappy on and about five or ten minutes later you'd see this little face all scrunched up and straining and red in the face, and you knew he'd done a great big packet in his nappy. But they kept saying, 'No, you must get him potty trained, that's the only way he will behave properly, otherwise you will have a dirty little baby boy who will be dirtying his pants until he's five or six.' I got the impression that he would turn into some kind of sexual deviant. I think that was basically what it was all about, and that to be potty trained engendered self-control. I sometimes wonder if this whole regime wasn't part and parcel of the fears one had about sexuality, and especially sexuality in a child and that it must be stamped out at all costs. Don't let your baby play with himself, he shouldn't get any pleasures from his body. I mean, I can remember thumb-sucking was totally taboo and any form of quite mild masturbation was considered very sinful, you know. I think there was a very strong repressive element to any form of express sexuality.

One of the main fears engendered in me was that if I showed him too much affection then he would be spoiled. Spare the rod and spoil the child. It mustn't be picked up when it cried, it must be out in the cold, a lot of musts and oughts about it. If you were too demonstrative too, you know bouncing them and cradling them and holding them too much of the time, that was bad for them. It was very inhibiting to a warm, outgoing mum. When I was holding him I felt great warmth and love and affection towards him, but then, once he'd gone to sleep I must put him down, let him go to sleep and not disturb him in any way.

Well, the crying in the night-time was very disturbing to me. The nurse at the clinic used to say you should be able to get something like five hours' sleep straight through. It never seemed to work like that with me, mind you. They didn't tell you what to do if the baby wouldn't stop crying. Once I even shook him quite violently, which was ridiculous because it didn't stop him crying, it made him cry even more. I sort of threw him face down on the cot, not from any great height, but about a foot, and I felt terrible afterwards, I really felt dreadful. But that was the sort of frustration that built up.

I didn't know until my baby was about seven or eight months old that he'd got a hole in the heart, he had an ailment congenitally. He was born with it, and this caused him to be in discomfort rather more often than a perfectly normal, healthy child. And that poor little boy really got no response from me. Instead of getting comfort when he should have done, he was just ignored and left and put in cold places.

By the time he was about four or five years old I felt he'd become quite a withdrawn little boy in a sense, and I'm sure with hindsight now it was because I didn't treat him spontaneously or respond to his crying in a more natural and normal way.

All the rigid methods from the clinic totally lacked any kind of spontaneity or any feeling that a mother instinctively has about what's wrong with her child. The mother was, in my estimation, a somewhat inferior, silly creature, who had to do what the medical authorities told her. I could almost describe it as a reign of terror, that's how powerful it was or it seemed to be to me. The Truby King regime on the whole made me feel I was just an instrument to produce a child for their benefit and that my child would become whatever the country needed at the time, to maintain this tremendous empire which we still had, of course, just before the war. To rear good old strong English boys to go out and become district commissioners, you know, get shot at. And there was a sort of class distinction about it, which I think was predominantly middle class. 'Let's keep England for the English and let's make sure that we have true blue British men to go out and keep our Empire for us.' I was of very little account, apart from producing a son and then sticking to the rules and all.

A couple of years later when my second son was born I got hold of a book by a Dr Spock and I just sort of leapt up in the air with glee. Here was somebody else who was saying that all this regimentation was nonsense and rubbish. He said that mothers must trust their instinct and they must not follow rules too rigidly. It was wonderful to be told that I, as a mother, had some sort of right or claim to understand my child, whereas I'd been told all along that I was basically ignorant and that if I didn't do what I was told, my child would be a disaster.

So my second baby was brought up in a totally different way to the first and I didn't have any problems. He was allowed to express himself and be free, to crawl across the room, climb on furniture, all this kind of thing. It made me feel better about myself . . . trust my own judgement as to when it was appropriate to feed him or when to ignore it if he was crying.

I would love to have had the opportunity to bring my first son up in the same way. The fact that he was a child with a disease, who subsequently died, made things even worse and I regret bitterly that I could not give him the kind of affection that I feel he should have had. Instead of which I stuck to these ridiculous rules and regulations far too long.

CHAPTER THREE

Happy Families

A new ideal of parenting and family life emerged during the first half the century. largely pioneered by suburban middle-class couples. Their dream was of a small family and a much more private and home-based lifestyle. It was built around mothers who never went out to work and who were totally dedicated to their children and home. This ideal of the 'happy family' set a mould for parenting and family life in Britain and established a trend which was widely aspired to by all social classes.

The 'modern' ideal of parenting broke with some fundamental principles which had underpinned family life in the past. The well-to-do had traditionally employed servants to do much of the hard labour of looking after the home and bringing up the children. In the 1900s there were more than 2 million domestic servants including around a quarter of a million nannies: 'service' was the single biggest employer of female labour. To have a servant was an essential badge of social status and even a humble clerk and his wife would sometimes employ a young 'maid of all work' for housework and childminding. But the rise of employment opportunities for young women in the new factories and offices meant that fewer and fewer were prepared to put up with the drudgery and low pay of a domestic's life. By the 1930s there were less than half a million domestic servants in Britain. The 'servant problem' and the difficulty of getting 'staff' provided a big push for the idea of a private. servantless home.

What made this new kind of home appear so attractive was the development of a mass of labour-saving machines. made possible by technological advances in gas and. its great competitor. electricity. The inter-war years were the era of the vacuum cleaner. the washing machine. the gas cooker. the electric fire and the gas or electric iron, gadgets which promised to take the drudgery out of housework and turn it into a skilled and fulfilling job. The ideology of modern housewifery and suburban motherhood was promoted in a rash of new mass-circulation women's magazines which replaced those which had earlier catered for the Victorian lady administering a household staff. The leader in the field was *Good Housekeeping* (1922), followed by *Woman and Home* (1926), *Wife and Home* (1929), *Woman's Own* (1932), *Woman's Illustrated* (1936) and *Woman* (1937).

The setting for this new family lifestyle was typically the interwar suburb. During the 1920s and 1930s large numbers of young middle-class couples left inner Victorian areas for the suburban fringes of towns and cities. Their aim was to own a modern semidetached or detached home, wired for electricity, on the edge of the countryside. A boom in home ownership resulted, fuelled by massive lending from building societies: whereas in 1920 only 10 per cent of families owned their homes, by 1939 it was 30 per cent. A parallel migration of working-class families into the interwar suburbs also took place. Most were rehoused by local authorities on council estates, where they were provided – in a scaled-down form – with some of the modern conveniences enjoyed by their social superiors. Many had come from large families and had been brought up in a strongly communal atmosphere in overcrowded inner city areas but now aspired to a smaller family and a more private family life.

The 'new' mother and housewife was the key figure in this series of social changes. Her 'professional' role involved raising the standards of comfort, convenience and child care in the home and she was encouraged by the magazines to develop the skills of nurse, needlewoman, teacher, nutritionist, chef, beautician, amateur psychologist and design expert, as well as to understand the workings of all her new gas and electric gadgets. According to *Good Housekeeping* she was 'the craft worker of today'. The father, however, was a distant figure in this popular literature on the ideal home. The division of labour was simple: he was the breadwinner and could not be expected to help much, or at all, with looking after children or the house when he came home tired from work. Most fathers we interviewed conformed to this stereotype and had little practical involvement in the day-to-day running of the home and the upbringing of their sons and daughters. Those who worked long hours and commuted long distances to work often had no choice. but few 'absent' fathers felt that they had missed out on something important. The minority of fathers who played an important domestic role often had their duties thrust upon them: either they were widowers or were dependent on their wives going out to work because they were themselves disabled or unemployed. Even then men were usually embarrassed and uncomfortable about the threat that this domesticity posed to their 'manliness'. Unemployed men in Lancashire who cooked. did the housework and looked after the children while their wives worked in the textile mills were sneeringly referred to as 'Mary Annes'. The overwhelming consensus was that the home was the woman's domain and that child-rearing – especially with younger children – was women's work.

For many women the new ideal of motherhood offered an exciting challenge – at least to begin with. They bought magazines in their millions. became avid consumers of household goods in the new department stores and joined organizations like the Electrical Association for Women. formed in 1924. which gave practical instruction in how to use all the latest appliances. For those who moved out from the slums to council houses the opportunity to become a 'modern mother' was a dream come true.

But most soon discovered the downside to the dream of aspiring to be a perfect parent. With little or no help from their partner many found their new role exhausting. soul-destroying and isolating. To make matters worse. most married women could not return to work outside the home. A widely imposed bar on the employment of married women existed in many professions. in education and in the civil service during the inter-war years. Married working-class women also found it difficult to find full- or part-time jobs in factories or offices. In the 1930s 95 per cent of all married women with children did not work outside the home. Justification for the ban was couched in terms of the need for women to raise a family and keep the home happy. And among middle-class and respectable working-class men it became a matter of pride and status that their wife did not got out to work. The women who badly wanted to return to their jobs or careers and who felt trapped at home were the most likely to suffer from the nervous disorders and breakdowns that doctors began to describe as the 'suburban' or 'housewife's' neurosis.

The 'new parenthood' was underpinned by traditional and 'old-fashioned' attitudes towards children and their upbringing. One of the main concerns of parents continued to be with the discipline and control of their children. Obedience. habit-training. respect for elders. cleanliness. tidiness and good manners were all encouraged as prime virtues by magazines and child-care manuals. The disciplined behaviour of one's children was an important source of parental pride and family respectability among all classes; conversely children who were 'rude' or 'rough' were seen as a sign of weak. failed parents. Stern Victorian attitudes and the moralistic approach of 'spare the rod' had softened a little by the 1920s and 1930s but they still remained influential in most homes. When Father was at home – especially at mealtimes – his word was law. with no room for discussion or questioning as to why a decision had been made. The practice. common in Victorian homes. of hanging a cane or a strap above the fireplace as a warning against bad behaviour. continued in a few families into the inter-war years. This 'seen and not heard' approach was based on the evangelical idea of original sin and the need to break the child's will. Usually it was the mother. responsible for most discipline. who inflicted punishment. Most physical ones were minor – a smacked bottom. hands or legs were most common. But occasionally the overriding concern with discipline led to child-beating. often by the father. By 1914 the NSPCC (formed in 1883) had 258 inspectors investigating more than 50.000 cases of parental abuse every year.

Even older children. out at work. were often expected to obey their parents absolutely. They handed over the wage packet to their mother and were given pocket money in return. Parents exerted immense influence over their teenage children's courting partners until around 1939. They tried – often successfully – to control where the couple went. what they did. and when they returned home. Girls. in particular. could expect severe sanctions and punishments – often from their father – if they were late home or suspected of some sexual 'misdemeanour'.

For middle- and upper-class parents one other important concern was the maintenance or improvement of the family's superior social position through the career success and marriage of the children. This preoccupation shaped many of the attitudes of well-to-do parents: they stressed the importance of education and paid for their children to go to private schools; encouraged them to adopt the 'correct' types of speech. dress and manners thought fitting to their class; and tried to prevent them from being 'damaged' through mixing with working-class children. The freedom of the informal street culture of working-class children was seen as a particular threat by many middle-class parents, who preferred their children to play at home or in the garden and to spend as much time as possible doing homework. Only rarely did mixing between the social groups pose a problem as most cities. towns and even villages were sharply divided into working-class and middle-class districts – but sometimes working-class children came too close for comfort. One form of action taken to prevent intermixing in several towns and cities during the inter-war years was the building of walls to segregate one area from another. The most celebrated example occurred in Oxford in 1934: middle-class parents on a new. private housing development in the suburb of Cutteslowe were so concerned that their children might be 'corrupted' by the children on the neighbouring council estate that they built what came to be known as the 'Cutteslowe Walls'. eight feet high with spikes along the top. across the middle of the roads that connected the two areas. Many working-class families objected strongly but the better-off vigorously defended the walls and they were not demolished until 1959.

Over the decade. however. a new. more indulgent and intense

relationship between parents and children began to become more widespread. softening the traditional concern with discipline. obedience and social class. The reduction in family size enabled parents to devote more attention to the care of each child. and the enjoyment of more leisure time as a consequence of shorter working hours and labour-saving devices at home meant that parents could spend longer playing with their children. Fathers began to form closer relationships with their children and the booming toy industry supplied at least the middle class with a host of popular playthings – board games. books. train sets – which were based on the concept of 'family fun'. At weekends the traditional middle-class family Sunday. once dominated by church and Sunday School. started to become more 'fun' oriented. the highlight perhaps being a motor-car trip into the countryside for a picnic. Between 1920 and 1939 the number of cars increased from 500,000 to 3 million. most of them bought by middle-class family men. This was the era when droves of suburban families motored out into the countryside to enjoy picnics. rambles. and to explore remote villages.

Working-class fathers. enjoying a little more leisure time and. for the more fortunate. paid holidays. also came to feature more in their children's lives. The annual week-long family holiday at the seaside – a time to get to know Dad – became well established. Railways. motor coaches and charabancs became cheap and easy ways to get to the coast and. by the late 1930s. 5 million people – or one in six of the population – were spending at least a week's holiday away from home. By the outbreak of the Second World War. 7 million people were going to Blackpool every year and half a million went to one of over a hundred holiday camps in different parts of the country.

Working-class fathers also came to play a more important role in their children's lives at home. Before the First World War most working-class homes were so small and overcrowded that there was little or no space to play with children indoors. Parents naturally encouraged them to play outside in the street so that they might enjoy a little peace and privacy. However. from the 1920s. local authority provision on a mass scale of relatively spacious and comfortable council houses with gardens for the working classes began to change the pattern of family leisure activities. Fathers played with their children at home or in the back garden and children spent less time on the streets. This trend was reinforced by the rapid growth in motor traffic between the wars, which made the streets increasingly dangerous for children.

Mass-produced wireless sets were bought by many parents: by 1939 9 million British families had one and listening to the wireless became a popular family activity. Some radio programmes like the BBC's *Listen with Mother* or Radio Luxembourg's *The Ovaltineys*, encouraged a suburban, home-based idea of play involving both parents and children. From the 1950s this became even more pronounced with the mass ownership of television sets. It was estimated in the mid 1950s that the average British child spent around two hours every day watching television.

The increasing privatization of family life and the development of more indulgent attitudes towards children is most graphically illustrated by the phenomenal spread of Christmas as a great family festival in all social classes during the first half of the century. The rituals of the Christmas tree, Father Christmas, presents for the children and the family Christmas meal complete with roast turkey, plum pudding and crackers were the 'invention' of the relatively well-to-do Victorian middle classes in the mid nineteenth century. Behind them lay a worship of the family and a desire to protect children from the harshness of the real world. But well into this century Christmas was not an important time for most families. Many working-class people, especially domestic servants, had to work on Christmas Day; if they had a day off many chose to spend part of it going to a soccer or rugby match or to the greyhound stadium; many could not afford to buy special food or presents and the biggest celebrations often took place in a communal setting, usually the pub, the club or the workplace, away from the family. All this gradually changed as the century progressed and more people were given holidays on Christmas Day and Boxing Day; with the rise in wages and living standards families had more money to spend on the trappings of Christmas; and the growing toy industry persuaded many parents to 'be' Father Christmas and spend as much as – if not more than – they could afford on presents for their children. The wireless and then television also provided powerful means of turning Christmas into a national family festival. From the late 1950s two-thirds of all British families would watch the same Christmas Day programmes in their sitting rooms. This big, sentimental day – looked forward to eagerly by everyone – expressed many of the changes in relationships between parents and children in the first half of the century. Underneath it all lay an ideal of snug domestic bliss and an aspiration towards a happy family in which Mum, Dad and the kids were the centre of each other's world.

Rose Luttrell

See also Chapter One, page 29 and Chapter Two, page 66. After her marriage in 1916 Rose lived with her bank manager husband at Box in Wiltshire. They kept a house with a staff of six servants. Rose had three children who were cared for by nannies and governesses and she and her husband had little to do with the daily care of their children and their home. While her husband was at work, Rose spent much of her time gardening or letter writing.

I can't think what we did with ourselves, because we had our breakfast about nine. I had a full staff: I had a cook and a kitchenmaid, a housemaid and a parlourmaid, and a nanny and a nurserymaid. I had six servants, you see, so I never did any housework or any domestic work at all. I saw the cook in the morning and ordered the meals for the day and I never went near the kitchen. You didn't go interfering. The cook would have given you notice and left you.

And as for the children, really it was Nanny who took charge there. I was happy and confident to leave her to look after them. They loved it in the nursery and they loved their nanny. Of course, I did see them in the garden or after tea but mainly the children were my nanny's responsibility and it really worked out very well indeed.

If they were in any trouble, if they fell down 'I want to go to Nanny.' They looked upon their nursery as a sort of haven. Nanny and the nursery – they had that wonderful feeling of security, there was always Nanny there to give them a welcome if anything happened in the garden. If they hurt themselves or they were unhappy about something, they went back to Nanny.

Oh yes, my children would often rather go to Nanny than go to their parents. A lot of children saw more of their nanny than they did of their parents. The nanny was a much more important person. But I wasn't jealous of her a bit. I put my absolute faith in her. I remember Nanny used to get rather cross because one sent the children back to the nursery in a filthy condition because they'd been gardening. 'Oh, you do make a mess of these children,' I remember Nanny chastizing me. One was quite ruled by one's nanny and I don't think I ever queried it. I think the children probably loved their nanny more than me and their father when they were quite tiny.

Of course, my husband didn't come back till, oh, about four o'clock from the bank. He left the house at ten o'clock in the morning and he was back again by four o'clock. So he did nothing at all with the children. He used to have them on his lap sometimes but he never did a thing with them. Never fed them or did anything – he wouldn't have known how to. He'd be much too frightened. He'd never seen a man do it. He'd never been fed by his own father so – it wasn't done. All he did was to enjoy them, he loved the children. He used to play – he wouldn't stand any nonsense – but they could do anything they liked with him. I never remember him speaking roughly to them or chastizing them at all. They loved him.

Naturally, one played in the garden with the children and one used to go out with them more as they got older.

Of course, it was a great age for letter-writing, everybody wrote a tremendous amount of letters, and then you went out in the garden and you did the flowers. We went for a walk. Of course, the people who hunted and people who had their hobbies did their hobbies. I always had a dog, took the dog for a walk. I had a tremendous lot of animals, rabbits and guinea pigs. I was also a great gardener all my life. I used to show at the local shows and I took first prize in all the annuals.

I used to suffer with what they call migraine. It used to be called bilious attacks. I used to have terrible headaches and was sick. It was, 'Oh, you've been greedy, you've been eating too much. Eating too many chocolates or something.'

And my husband and I had a tremendous lot of friends in the neighbourhood and we used to go away for weekends. My husband used to go deer-stalking. And, of course, my husband's home was at Dunster Castle and we used to go down there a lot for weekends, leaving Nanny with the children.

I learnt to drive in 1923. We used to go for drives. We used to go for picnics. I remember driving over to Bath with Nanny and having picnics. Life was much quieter in those days. You weren't rushing and tearing from one thing to another, took whatever little fun came along. The children used to love going on picnics. Of course, they used to go to dancing classes and to gym classes. And in the winter lovely children's parties in the big houses all round Chippenham.

Well, we used to go down to Dunster Castle for Christmas. Mrs Geofrey Luttrell used to invite us and Nanny and I and the three children used to motor down. My husband used to follow by train and we used to go down to the Castle laden with presents. We all went down to church at Dunster. I don't think Nanny and the younger children did. Then we all had lunch together in the dining room – that was the great thing of the day. After that we just went for a walk. There was a Christmas tree, of course, in the hall. My nanny found it rather hard work because it was a long way carrying the children up from the front hall, front door to the nursery up a big staircase. She found it very hard work because she was quite an elderly woman.

You just moved among your own friends or your own contemporaries and they were all leading the same sort of life. I don't think we did have much to do with other people. Except, as I say, the cricket matches, the village cricket match, but my children never had any chance of mixing, there was never any contact, there was never a question of mixing. It never crossed my mind that they should. But, of course, one read about them and one saw them and one lived among them but one had nothing in common because, you see, one was living a different life, our interests were so different. I always remember my daughter saying the first time she really mixed with a different class to what our own was, it was when she went into the Wrens. She always said it was a wonderful experience and she wouldn't have missed it for anything.

My husband and I once took the children down to Bude for a holiday. We thought we'd try and do it on our own and we found it very hard work. We realized what Nanny had to go through and I remember my little girl sitting on my lap, she had her hand on the car and my eldest boy thought he'd try and help by banging the car door and banged it right on her finger and nearly took the top of her finger off – had an awful job. I put it under the tap and her finger's never been right. We said, 'Never again.' We had to do everything and we'd never looked after children by ourselves before, you see. We thoroughly enjoyed it but we said it was jolly hard work because there were three of them. Fathers in those days did nothing for the children. We were in lodgings, we didn't have any cooking to do or anything like that. We spent the day on the beach with the children, helping them to paddle, and I used to bathe with them because they were only small.

There was one thing in particular one disliked rather in having to look after the children. And it was having to get up early. I remember dreading hearing them start moving about because, you see, I never had anything to do with them until about ten o'clock. They had all their meals in the nursery at home. We had our meals in the dining room. No, the children never came down till they were quite big. Because it wasn't the done thing. One was just rather glad to see Nanny back again, to feel that next morning you hadn't to get up early, get them out of bed and give them their breakfast.

Edith Broadway

See also Chapter Two, page 68. After Edith married in 1928 she became a full-time housewife and mother. She soon found herself feeling frustrated and depressed with the narrowness of her daily life and as a result began to suffer from nervous illnesses, described then as 'housewife's neurosis'. Edith had three children, the first two in 1935 and 1939, but it was not until her son was born in 1946 that she received the medical help she needed to overcome her illness.

Well, I was a millinery designer and when I got married of course I gave my job up. I was in a new house, a new home, with a husband who went out to work every morning at half past six and didn't get back until seven o'clock in the evening. I had nothing to do, all day long stretching in front of me. What do you do with yourself when you've done all the housework and the things that you've got to do and there's nothing and nobody, when you've been used to a life full of people, which I was? Finally I said to my husband that I wanted to go back and do my job. I'd have to go back under my maiden name because they wouldn't take you if you were married and I went on about how much better it would be if I went back. We needed the money in those days, too, because, well, things were just as difficult and we were buying our own house, and he listened to me and he said, 'Yes, that's right, darling, all right, you go back to work and I'll give up my job.' I thought he meant it – in fact, I believed he meant it – and I thought, 'Oh dear, I'm out, there's nothing I can do.' So I couldn't go back to my job, which was very sad, really.

He didn't want me to go out to work, no way. If I went out to work I wouldn't be able to wait on him – men were very much owners, you know. 'I married you to look after you but you've also got to look after me.' And that's the way it was. If the wife went out to work that wasn't the case, he wasn't keeping her, and it went against the grain. They wanted to be the boss. He was not going to be subjected to bringing his pay packet home and giving it to me so I was allocated a certain amount for housekeeping and if I wanted more and he couldn't give it he'd say, 'No.' He wasn't mean, he was reasonably generous, but he didn't like me having so much that I could afford to be independent of him. No way. That would never have worked. I had been earning about twice the amount that my husband was earning but the fact that I could earn that didn't interest him at all. He wanted me to be, from the word go, dependent on him. And I was, all my life, financially. I just took the threat and swallowed it.

I almost went behind his back. I thought, 'Well, he goes out in the morning, doesn't get home until seven, and in between I could go back to my job and he wouldn't even know I'd gone.' I was a little afraid of how he would react. And I didn't want to deceive him, so there it is again, you see.

What it led to was a nervous breakdown. They called it housewife's neurosis. It was very frightening and it took me a long time to get over it – about fourteen years. It was really a result of my not having enough to occupy my mind. My husband never ever realized it, the fact that I needed just more than dusting chairs and washing up and washing, he didn't recognize that fact. We really complied with the order of the day and that was that married women did not go out to work, they had large families and devoted themselves to the house and husband and the babies.

Kissing him goodbye at half past six in the morning, going back to the chores and getting the house right. As time goes by one gets adjusted but I'd never done it before I was married and washing was a nightmare, because we didn't have anything like the equipment you've got today. Everything you did was done by hand. I can remember the tears falling into the sink when I was doing the washing, filling the sink more than the tap, I think. There were the sheets and pillowcases and shirts and I hadn't got a clue where to start. You see, I was creative and housework isn't very creative. Household chores were an absolute bore.

I liked to see it looking beautiful but I really didn't want to do it. He did get me a resident person and that was a great help. He tried to supply me with the help he thought I needed in the house but by that time it was too late. It does just get you by the throat and it isn't very easy to come to terms with.

I used to feel that there was so much outside and here was I, trapped in this little street with this little narrow house. It wasn't enough for me, I wanted more, I wanted to be on the move and I felt every day was deadly. I'd been used to earning money that I could spend *ad lib*, the first week's money I got from my husband was twenty-five shillings and I went out and spent eleven on flowers. I had no sense, not money-wise, and then, of course, I had to ask him if he would give me some more money.

It started with an illness. I had an ear infection and I was very ill. I went out in the street and the street ran away from me and that started panic stations and the panic grew and I couldn't cope with the panic. That went on for a very long time. They all thought it was my heart but it wasn't. It was a nervous disorder that they didn't know how to handle in those days.

I had no horizon, that's what it really boiled down to. I wasn't free to come and go as I pleased. I think my husband's temperament was part and parcel of that. He wanted me where he wanted me. I felt that I was suppressed at every turn because he was the dominant factor. He didn't interfere with the children, with the way I brought them up, though there were other areas which I wasn't allowed to indulge in. It was the deadly monotony of everyday living. I'd lived a very varied, interesting life and suddenly it was all taken away from me and there was not a hope of me being able to recapture that.

I felt I had to achieve something because I wasn't achieving an awful lot as a housewife. I really wanted children – I couldn't pass a baby in the street – and I just loved the thought of having my own. But when the children came that was pretty traumatic. I didn't really cope – I wasn't happy – I lived in a state of extreme fear. The responsibility was the thing that really bothered me because I was trapped. I was in a trapped situation. It's difficult, because I loved my children and I was happy with my babies. It was this other thing, this monster, that I was battling with that was the problem. I think I resented the fact that I felt like that because it was spoiling my life. It was colouring my life and I wasn't enjoying my children.

It wasn't until my son was born and the whole thing blew that I had to go to a psychiatrist and, by the grace of God, he was excellent. He told me I would see a long dark tunnel with a tiny light at the end and every day that light would get bigger until one day there'd be no tunnel and that's exactly how it worked.

I think I had built up a resentment but as time went by, of course, and I got well, I did enjoy my children. I think the children helped me in a sense because I loved them and I was determined not to let this thing get the better of me for their sake.

But I can still remember that feeling and think about things I would have liked to have had. I'd like to have travelled – I'd like to have gone with my husband and I would have liked to have gone to Switzerland and skiing and the other side of the world. I loved boats – I loved ships.

Robert Williamson

Robert was born in Bradford in 1910. the son of a tram driver. He had four sisters. He met his wife. Hetty. at the Pavilion DeLuxe Picture House and they married in 1931. Robert was working for the Bradford Dyers Association and the couple rented a one-up-one-down house in Shipley. near Bradford. Their daughter. Norma. was born in 1932. In 1934 Robert was made redundant and spent the next five years trying to find work and earning money caddying on Bradford golf course. In 1938 the family moved to a council house on a new estate in Shipley. Robert was an unusual father in that he spent a great deal of time with his daughter and helped his wife with her domestic chores. This was partly due to his unemployment – he had time on his hands. Robert has three grandchildren and five great-grandchildren.

I think I was considered a bit different because I didn't go home drunk. Fellows have done that night after night and spent much-needed family money at the bar. I was always considered different in that respect and I don't feel any worse for it.

I never had a mate as such, during my family life, during my married life. I were considered out of step but it's them that were out of step. They were robbing home to do other things.

I'd help with the washing and mangling when you had these wringing machines, which was horse-work using them. Biggest problem is when you've got nappies to contend with and you've got to boil them in an iron pan on an open fire to keep them white. They were terry-towelling in those days and that was the only way to keep them white. Big iron pan, some Rinso and big tablets of Fairy green soap. Me wife used to take a bit of washing in to earn a bit of extra money, a bit of laundering, and she went out cleaning. So I backed her up because that was grist to the mill, always helping the family exchequer, nothing wrong with that.

In the olden days we used to peg out washing in the street

between the opposite houses and put the prop up. I used to do that. You'd get it all out and then the coal man would come down with a big cart of coal and we'd have to lift the prop up for him to get by. The streets were always dirty. They never paved them. They'd pulled the houses down before they'd paved them. The middens were at the top and I used to go up to the middens with refuse, wouldn't let her do that. There were no dustbins you see, people didn't have them then.

And I used to like to go shopping because I used to shop better than her. Not because I could choose the right things but because I could get things that didn't cost so much. It's as simple as that.

My wife was the best cook, I never done any cooking. I used to make me own breakfast every morning, always did do before I went to work. I wasn't one of these chappies who had to get their wife up first and then when the hubby got his cup of tea and that was ready, then he'd get up. I'd just shout up to her, 'I'm off.' And she'd come down and lock the door. If she wanted a cup many a time I'd take one up to her as well.

She'd do the cooking of the evening meals and that. But I'd do the washing up, you know the labouring job. That was her forte cooking and that was my forte. And I was happy with that.

I never got embarrassed to do chores or anything. The way I looked at it was that you had to share all the chores in a happy successful married life, epecially the menial ones. Don't interfere with the cooking. If she's a good cook let her carry on being a good cook but you be a good washer-upper and you'll have a happy life.

It enabled my wife to do extra jobs which brought extra revenue into the home. We could both help each other to work at these little jobs to make ends meet which had to be a good thing. Maybe some people thought I was a sissy or a bit of a pansy but I think a woman's job is quite hard enough looking after the children. If any of the other blokes did laugh at me they did it behind my back because if they'd said it I would have fit them up, not physically, but by word of mouth and pointed out where they were going wrong. I could hold me head up that I was doing the right thing.

Women have done the housework and washing and that from time immemorial, haven't they? This is what they think their job is but no, I think everything should be shared in family life, especially in that environment that we were living in, you know, a very working-class environment. They're born to the other type in the highest echelons to have servants and things like that to do these menial tasks. Well, I don't believe in that, never have done.

Every morning I would take my daughter to school and then in the afternoon I'd pick her up. My wife was probably doing a bit of charring while I was doing this. In the evenings I would play cards with her, Snap and simple games. Or draughts.

She was the type of girl who never needed disciplining. I never laid a finger on her in anger. I never laid down the law with the flat of me hand or me fist like some fellows did. Some fathers would smack their children really hard, but not in this household. If there was a little tantrum cropped up I'd pick her up, put her on me knee and tell her a nursery rhyme, kissing her or telling her a story or something and that would do the trick.

She went to bed quite early. Six in the winter and nine in the summer. But we thought she was better off in bed than playing out in the streets. I used to croon a bedtime tune to her. Every night when she had her bath before bed I used to sing to her. My wife would shout me up and I'd go in and splash Norma in the bath. Then I would read to her a lot, too. Always read her a bedtime story till she nodded off and she'd settle down for the night.

101

Barbara Ruck

Barbara was born in 1913 in Witney. Oxfordshire where her father owned a blanket mill. She had two younger brothers. She was sent to boarding school in Bexhill. Barbara met her husband when she was twenty-three. and they married in 1938. They were keen tennis players and both of them played for the Oxfordshire county team. Barbara was a teacher and her husband worked for Lloyds bank. They moved to Wentworth Road in Cutteslowe. North Oxford. in 1938: their house was on a private estate which was divided from the nearby council estate by the Cutteslowe Walls. The couple adopted a son in 1951 and Barbara now has five grandchildren.

I lived in a house just four doors from the wall. It was an ordinary plain brick wall that went across the road from one side to the other. It was red brick and about ten feet tall. It had spikes on because some people used to climb from the other side.

They were nice houses here. They had slightly higher rent and they had built these houses to be a residential district. Then Oxford council decided to build a council estate and they built it right bang up against this residential complex. Obviously it made the houses less worthwhile renting. You weren't going to have a nice little quiet enclave, as it were, you were going to have a lot of people walking through to shops and schools and all sorts of things and so they decided they would build a wall across. Oxford council had been rather undiplomatic, shall we say, by building the council estate right close to the other. If they'd only left a little gap in between.

We actually got our house because the man who was in it had heard that the wall was going to be demolished and he didn't like the thought of it. We were just going to get married and we needed a house very badly.

Well, we didn't have anything to do with the people on the other side of the wall, partly because we were busy, and we had no occasion to. I never really, I think, ever met anyone from the other side of the wall, as far as I remember. I mean, I may have met them in the street or something but you see they were miles away, really, because there was all this distance between us that they had to walk round.

And the children from either side wouldn't meet because the children from that side would go to the local school and I would think that the children that lived round here would go to one of the others. There were a lot of small schools in Oxford then, you see. They were good schools, most of them, but they only had very few pupils. Graham had these little friends but the other side of the wall no, not really. The general feeling was that they could have been better brought up. The parents the other side of the wall, they would bring children up slightly differently and the children would go to the local schools and I would think the local schools in those days perhaps weren't quite so involved with manners and behaviour as perhaps the private schools were. In those days most people who earned a respectable amount of money would send their child to a private school, small and costly possibly, but they would like them to be brought up that way I would think.

You can't expect people the other side really to have liked it very much, can you? And I suppose in those days when you're young you don't think so much, do you, about other things? I was busy with my little crowd and didn't really have time to worry about them. The wall was built because of the difference in class. If you worked hard or got enough money you could lift yourself upwards, as it were. Then you wouldn't want your children to mix, partly because some of the other children may have been dirty, because there was more dirtiness in that time, partly because they wouldn't have such nice manners, perhaps dropped their aitches, not washed so well, certainly not so well mannered and partly because they perhaps thought they would be rougher. There was much more of a gulf between one side and the other and generally they would have a bad influence on their children. They would be much keener for their children to have a good education. I think the people the other side of the wall they weren't so interested in education. I mean, they sent their children to school because they had to go to school.

We were quite pleased on the whole that we were not bothered with lots of people walking through and past our houses. We were living in a quiet place, you see, without a lot of children. We had enough on our plate without bothering very much about the wall. We had a nice house and we were thankful to have it.

And when the walls did come down, we had two beautiful apple trees in the front and when the children came round past the school they stripped the trees of apples. It was rather distressing.

The people the other side of the wall, I think, must have been quite poor. They felt that they were being treated like lepers. They were shut away and they had to walk round miles to get to the schools and the shops and I think to start with there weren't any buses. They felt that we thought we were too good for them but at the time I was just glad I had a house. I was married and I was happy. The people the other side couldn't really do much about it, though they climbed the wall occasionally – it was one of the sort of daring things to do. What they thought they were going to find the other side, I don't know.

Elsie Cherril

Elsie was born in 1910 in Banbury near Oxford. She had two sisters and a brother, and their father was a french polisher. Elsie married a gardener in 1932 and they moved to Oxford where she was working as a college servant at the university. They had four children in 1933, 1935, 1938 and 1941. The family lived in a house on the council estate side of the Cutteslowe Wall in North Oxford. Elsie has ten grandchildren and ten great-grandchildren.

I lived near to the wall. It was ridiculous, right bang in the middle of the road, so that everybody just had to go right round the by-pass to get anywhere. We all thought it should never have been there. But the people on the other side just thought they were better than us. They didn't want to be seen living in the same place as us so they built the wall.

I think it was all wrong, just because we lived in council houses. A lot of them on that side had their own houses – they even had motor cars, a few of them. We had to rent ours and I suppose they weren't quite so comfy as the houses they had. Our husbands didn't get as much money, maybe, as theirs did but we had to work hard for the money. We kept our places as well as we could with the money we had. Perhaps we didn't have lots of things, or cars and that, but we were just as good as them on the private side.

I think they thought our kids would be running riot over the estate but we brought them up as well as they brought theirs up. Of course, there were a few terrors on our side, but if they were naughty it was only devilment, and find me the child who doesn't get up to some mischief at some time, whether he lives in a council house or on the posh side. No, our children were like any normal ones. Course, they thought the wall was stupid like we all did, but that was to be expected, wasn't it? Great big wall slap in the road which they knew that they shouldn't go near. They used to play football against it, they used it as a goal. The children on the other side did too, both playing the same game but never together. It was stupid, really. Naturally some of the kids would try to climb over, to see what was on the other side, like, even though we did tell them that the other side was no different to our side, only more stuck up.

The main thing about it, though, was that you had to go all the way around the by-pass to get to the other side where a lot of us worked. Some of the men, if they had odd jobs to do in the houses on the private side, would get over by using a ladder. They used to heave a ladder over once they were on top and get over that way. Sometimes the postman would see them doing that and he would ask them to help him over, too, because he had to go all the way around, see?

I had a cleaning job in one of the private houses so at first I had to walk all the way around and it really took so much longer. But then I happened to talk to one of the people who had the house nearest to the wall and they said I could get over from their garden. So after that I used to do that. It was a bit difficult because the wall was that high even going over from somebody's garden but it saved all that time, walking all round the by-pass.

The wall should never have been put up in the first place. They were no better than us and we were no worse than them. The only thing was the different houses. I was glad when it came down, great ugly thing in the way. But I know the private side weren't very pleased.

Alfred Short

Alfred was born in Ashington in Sussex in 1903. His father was a rose-grower and his mother died when Alfred was ten years old. He had two sisters. Alfred married Enid in 1928. He worked as a bus driver in Sussex and the south from the age of twenty-four for over forty years. They had a son in 1930 and a daughter in 1933. Because of his long working hours Alfred was unable to spend much time with his children. He looked forward to his rare days off when the family could go out together.

I missed out on my children all through their young years. I was working all the time so really it was up to Enid to look after them. I wish I could have been at home more. But I had a job and that was the important thing in those days and, really, with overtime and that, I brought home quite good money.

I was up early in the morning before they got up and I was out driving the bus all day, sometimes on a double shift till they was tucked up in bed. They used to know when I was passing the end of the road in the bus and the two of them used to stand at the gate and wave at me as I drove past. So I used to see them, but never to talk to, see? Then after my shift I used to get home, dinner in the oven and that. And I'd always creep in to see the two of them was OK. Sleeping quietly, they would be, but I'd always have to be sneaky because they woke up quite easily. Never missed peeping in at them to see them asleep.

Because I was generally not at home and their mother would be doing things around the house they used to go next door a lot. He used to take them out for walks and that to take them off Enid's hands for an hour or so. I would get home in the night and if they were still up they often used to tell me that they'd been out with him next door – Uncle, they called him. Really, I suppose you could say I was jealous. They used to think an awful lot of him. More than they did of me, I think. Well, I didn't have the time to spend with my own, working all the hours God sent.

I missed out and that was the sad part of it. I didn't get many kisses and cuddles off them when they were young.

It was the Saturdays or Sundays that I had off that I would look forward to. They were something for my family, when I could help Enid get them out of bed and dress them up all nice, like, and take them off for a walk. We used to walk for miles on Sundays. Sometimes we'd go on the bus 'cause I could get quarter fares for us. Then we'd go into town and go and see a picture that they liked, Abbott and Costello or something funny. And then fish and chips and into a pub with them – lemonade and crisps while me and my wife had a couple of drinks. And we used to think that was such a treat, all being together, having a day out with the children. And you'd have change out of a ten-bob note.

But that was something quite rare because I could only have time off when my boss saw fit. So all year round I used to look forward to Christmas. Then I would have a whole day with them at home. I used to look out in the different places I went to in the bus for toy shops and things I could save up and buy them for Christmas. I would see, say, a train set for my boy and I'd keep my eye on it for months till I'd saved up enough to get it and put it away for December. I suppose I thought that with working so much I wanted to buy them special treats, like.

I remember packing all their presents up with the wife in the evening and creeping up to put them in their stockings they'd have at the end of the bed. And you had to be so silent, creeping around. One year they did wake up and I don't know whether they believed in Father Christmas still or not but I pretended that I was doing something and that if they didn't go back to sleep Father Christmas wouldn't come . . . We did have a laugh, though. Having to be quiet and not knowing whether they were asleep or not. And it always seemed to snow at Christmas then. We'd get all excited. 'You will take us out for a walk in the snow, won't you, Dad?' And we'd go whilst Enid was making the dinner. Play snowballs or make a snowman. It was my only really family time. I missed so much of their growing up. I used to

108

treasure those odd days and always look forward to Christmas. Now I dread it. It's not the same without children. I just try and remember back all those years to the time I spent with children, all the excitement and presents and that. Seeing their little faces all happy and smiley, it was really like a novelty for me to be with them, see.

Annie Watson

Annie was born in Burnley, Lancashire, in 1910. Her father was a steam lorry driver. She had one brother and one sister. Annie met her future husband when she was seventeen. They married when she was twenty-two in 1932 and moved to Colne where they took over the running of a Singer sewing-machine shop. Annie's husband became the manager and salesman while Annie demonstrated the machines in the shop. They had two children, a boy, Brian, born in 1936, and a daughter, Irene, born six years later. Annie and her husband went to the first Butlin's holiday camp at Skegness in 1936, taking Brian when he was only six weeks old, and the family continued to go there for years afterwards. Annie has two grandchildren and three great-grandchildren.

We always had a holiday every year. My husband was a sewing-machine salesman so we had a car which made it easy to get to places. Normally we would go to the beach, Blackpool mainly, and stay in boarding houses. That was lovely, except when it rained. You'd have to be out of the place all day, that was one of the rules, and there wasn't much to do with a child if you couldn't be on the beach.

In fact, there was more rules and regulations in boarding houses than there were in gaols! You name it, there would be a rule about it, written on the back of the door. 'No noise, breakfast at seven, no visitors, be in at a certain time at night, be careful with the hot water.' They went on and on.

And you even had to pay for the use of the cruet. At the end of the week you'd have a bill which said, 'Salt, sixpence'. Well, that was a bit much.

That was one of the reasons my husband suggested Butlin's. He'd heard about this new place at Skegness and thought we'd give it a try and he booked us in for a week. It was one of the first holiday camps and you had a chalet for each family. We thought it might give us that bit more freedom than taking Brian to boarding houses all the time. I wasn't keen to go at first but he got it all ready, even everything for our little boy, and packed the car up and we set off.

I liked it as soon as we arrived. We had a little wooden hut to stay in, nothing grand, mind, just two single beds. I wasn't used to fancy places anyway, we could never afford to stay in a hotel, so I thought Butlin's was lovely.

There was just so much to do. The Redcoats were marvellous, they really organized everything, there was never a dull moment. I remember the loudspeaker in the morning, 'Wakey wakey, rise and shine.' Not that you needed it, you'd have woken up already with the noise of the people going past your chalet. Then they would let you know when breakfast was ready through the loud-hailer. There was a great big dining room with several sittings to accommodate all the people.

After breakfast you'd look in your Butlin's brochure and see what was on that day, there'd be so much to choose from. Competitions for everything and prizes for all sorts. It was ideal for families, there were nurseries for the children. If you went out in the evening and left your children back in the chalet they would keep an ear out and announce over the loudspeaker, 'Baby crying in chalet forty-two.' So you had nothing to worry about.

It was so well organized, you could please yourself all day. The Redcoats would be there all the time to keep the party spirit going, getting people to join in all the competitions. Not that I needed much encouragement, I used to enter everything! I was always keen on sport so I used to go in for all the swimming competitions. I remember one year I won the lot, ladies high-diving, crawl, freestyle. My husband felt a bit left out, what with me winning everything, so he thought he'd better have a go himself. He went in for the bowling but he didn't win. I entered my son in the fancy dress too, there was a shop on the site where you could hire costumes. He was a cowboy one year and a jockey the next. It really was like a party all day long.

Some people I knew were snobbish about Butlin's. They'd

say, 'What do you want to go there for, mixing with all those people?' But I've always been one for company so I loved it, I really did.

James Hardie

See also Chapter One. page 21. James Hardie bought his family's first car in 1938. Like many fathers at that time James was beginning to enjoy more spare time with his wife and children. The car offered his family much greater freedom. privacy and choice of what to do and where to go during their leisure time.

The first car we had was an Austin Seven. Now I'd never driven a car at that time, that was the first car I'd driven. I knew how to drive but I'd never actually driven, so the chappie said, 'There's the car – on your way.' He says, 'All you got to do . . . ' And he got a piece of chalk, and chalked on the floor of the garage and says, 'That'll be your first, second gear and third gear and fourth gear and off you go.' You didn't have to pass a driving test in those days. And I had to drive it back home about ten miles. Just like that. Oh, it was nice, it was lovely. The roads were nice.

I can remember bringing the first car home and leaving it at the door of the house and, of course, all the people were round, your surrounding neighbours. 'Oh, Jim Hardie's got a car.' They were peeping out from behind their curtains and that. I was showing off a bit, you know, being quite happy with it and, yes, it was quite exciting and, of course, the family were very excited about it. All they wanted to do was sit in it and go running in it so it was a case of taking them all on runs round the area. It was a novelty.

Of course, they weren't as reliable as they are now. You had one windscreen wiper in the middle and you pulled a little lever out and then it went, but sometimes if it conked out we'd fall back on the old remedy of a potato. You cut it in slices to get the moisture of the potato and rubbed it on the outside of the screen, just all over the bit where you're looking through and the droplets didn't hang about then they just sort of went into overall water and you could see through it.

You were thought to be quite fortunate if you had the car, otherwise you had to depend on buses, you see, and you didn't get so far away. And it gave you a lot of privacy, having the car. It was so nice to get away up in the hills, away from home and away from other people, just your own family around you, to get away from the busy town. It was just the pleasure of being together. In those days, the cars were small so you were quite tightly packed in it. But we were just a nice family party.

I was working in a shop and I had a half-day Wednesday and that used to be picnic day. We lived in Motherwell. Twelve miles away we were right up into the Clyde valley which is a very nice area and you come on to the hills. What we call the Tintoe is the highest hill in the southern uplands in Scotland. We used to take the picnic up there – fruit, biscuits, flask of tea and sometimes we'd make a fire and boil a kettle, get a lot of little twigs, and have a real camp fire, and all the kids used to enjoy that, playing about with the fire.

You could gather the little trout in when you just leaned over the bank and put your hand in the water, it was so clear, and you just left it there and if a trout sort of swam over that way you just pulled it out the water, threw it up on the bank and you could catch them up to maybe five or six inches. So the kids used to get a lot of fun with this. When they first come out the water they was wriggling all over the place and they all used to scream and squeak to see this fish. Sometimes, we kept them out and sometimes we put them back in. We just let the children run wild more or less and you kept your eye on them so they didn't fall in the water. We had a lot of fun running around, climbing the hills, lovely country. That was on sunny days.

Right: Alfred Short with his son, born in 1930, and his daughter, born in 1933.

Below: A family tea-time during the 1940s. Most fathers had little practical involvement in the cooking, cleaning and day-to-day upbringing of their children. (*Topham Picture Library*)

Above: A mother and father playing with their children in the late 1930s. The booming toy industry provided middle-class parents with many games to play at home with their children. (*Barnaby's Picture Library*)

Right: Hilda Caldwell with her children and some of their friends, who used to watch the Caldwells' television when it was a novelty.

Below: Annie Watson (*left*) and her son, Brian, at the Butlin's Holiday Camp in Skegness in 1938.

Far Bottom: A mother reading a bedtime story to her children in the 1930s. (*The Hulton-Deutsch Picture Library*)

Right: Annie Watson's son, Brian, photographed in 1938.

Below: A family at the seaside in 1909. In Edwardian Britain few families could afford a holiday, but by the late 1930s the annual week at the seaside was well established. (*The Mansell Collection*)

Top Left: Esther Peel, pictured in the 1920s. Her second husband was an alcoholic so she was forced into menial farm work to feed her children.

Top Right: Doris Bailey, *right*, and her brothers and sisters in 1921, outside their house in the East End of London. Her youngest sister, Rosie, in the pram, died at the age of four.

Above: Parr's yard, Nottingham, pictured in 1931. Slum housing like this was widespread in Britain during the 1930s. (*Nottinghamshire County Council*)

Top: A Northumberland miner's wife and child, photographed outside their cottage in the 1930s. Parents in mining villages often had no running water, no electric light and appalling sanitation. (*Popperfoto*)

Above: A posed scene in an East End home in London in 1912, depicting a mother and her children crying because they have no food for dinner. Hunger and malnutrition among poor families were becoming a major cause for concern in Edwardian Britain. (*Hulton-Deutsch Collection*)

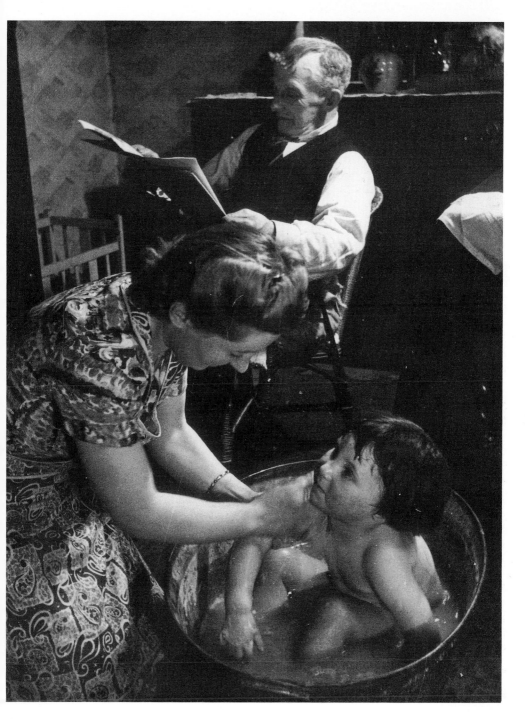

Above: A mother bathing her child in a tin bath in their living room in the 1930s. Despite these cramped and difficult conditions many mothers worked obsessively to keep their homes and children clean. (*Imperial War Museum*)

Top Right: Edie Jones, pictured in 1930. Edie's husband was unemployed and she brought up her family on the dole.

Top Left: Verna Brennan in the back yard of her house in Dock Street, Port Talbot, in the 1930s. The whole street stole from coal trains – they could not afford to buy the coal.

Above: A mother and her child hop-picking in Kent in the 1930s. Every Autumn a quarter of a million East Enders from London would travel to the hop fields to enjoy a working holiday away from the London smog. (*Popperfoto*)

Hilda Caldwell

See also Chapter One. page 31. Hilda and her husband John moved into their first house in 1949 on the Moortown Estate in Leeds. It was a brand-new housing estate with lots of young couples and there were plenty of children for their two daughters to play with. In 1953 the Caldwells bought their first television set. which soon became the major source of their family's home entertainment.

They'd come home from school and I'd give them something to eat, then they'd be straight out to play again. There wasn't the traffic in those days so you didn't worry about them and there were so many kids on the estate that they went round in, like, a big gang. They used to go right down to the golf course and play there or on the street outside or up against the house in the garden.

There was seasons for games and all the children round about would be playing the same thing. All of a sudden in the shops it would be skipping-rope time and that's all you'd see, kids playing skipping games. Then there was kite-flying, marbles, whip and tops, 'tig' and two ball and one ball up against the house wall. They used to draw out hopscotch on the pavements and play for hours on them. They had different fads of games.

Course sometimes it was raining and they had to be indoors and then they'd be playing cards, Snap and all that. Or we used to play dominoes. And they used to draw me and Dad pictures, or paint.

Then when the television came in, Father says, 'Now, we're having a television.' So we got a little nine-inch Bush. We paid two and six a week for it, to buy it. We had it in the room and our kids says, ooh, the first time it was on, 'Can Barbara come?' 'Yes, Barbara can come.' After school, we finished up with about twelve kids. Every tea-time, straight from school they'd go home, get washed and changed, after tea, straight round. *Muffin the Mule* and all this kind of thing, I think *The Wooden Tops*. Oh, the kids

115

used to love it. And when Father came home from work, he used to get home about quarter, half past five and he used to say, 'What are all the kids doing?'

Every Saturday night we had four neighbours and they used to all come in. On a Saturday night, there was a play on, live plays, and you'd take it in turns to bring sandwiches and cakes. That was the night out. You couldn't afford to go anywhere and you couldn't go with the kids, you see, you couldn't leave the kids. It was really something, you know. Nobody had television then. It was one of these status symbols. But we got a cover that went on, and it made it into a twelve-inch. And we only had it on at certain times because we didn't want to wear it out. We thought if we used it too much, it would wear out.

They used to look in the papers to see what was on television. We had more friends than we had anything else. Oh, when you had a television, everybody came, all the gang. It was more communal spirit then. But you used to say, 'We'll only have it on so long.' Dad used to say, 'Turn it off, it's been on long enough. You'll wear it out.'

Well, as each of the families got their own televisions, that kiddie never come, so at the finish they all had their own, like, private little watching, and we were just left with our two kids and us. I felt lost. I used to love having the kids there, you know. They used to be drinking pop and eating crisps. Well, it used to be like a party every day. You missed it. All in their own little groups in their own family, it made it more private, you see. The thing was that you lost the community spirit. They'd got their own so the kids stayed home.

CHAPTER FOUR

Staying Alive

At the bottom of the social scale, family life was a daily battle for survival. During the first half of the century a large section of society lived on or below the poverty line: these parents struggled to house, feed and clothe themselves and their children at the most basic, subsistence level. Early poverty surveys, like those of Charles Booth in London and Seebohm Rowntree in York, estimated that at the turn of the century around 30 per cent of the population of Britain were living in poverty. Although social investigators in the inter-war years noted a gradual improvement in the standard of living and in housing conditions, it was estimated in the late 1930s that around 10 to 15 per cent of the population still lived below the poverty line, teetering on the verge of destitution.

The factors that led to the impoverishment of families remained remarkably consistent throughout the period. Unemployment, low wages, widowhood and single parenthood, the chronic ill-health or disability of the breadwinner, and large numbers of children could drag a family down to the breadline. The worst poverty was often concentrated in areas of high unemployment like Tyneside, Lancashire and South Wales, whose staple industries of shipbuilding, cotton and coal were in serious decline. During the inter-war years Britain suffered mass unemployment on an unprecedented scale with almost 3 million out of work in the early 1930s. Although alleviated by various forms of unemployment insurance, parish relief or payments from the Unemployed Assistance Board, the absence of paid work often meant chronic hardship. Under the notorious Means Test families had to sell all non-essential household items to be eligible for benefit. However, unemployment was not always the most important factor leading to poverty: in rural areas, for example, it was largely due to the low wages of agricultural labourers. Pockets of poverty, often concentrated in 'slum' streets or neighbourhoods, persisted all over Britain.

Most of the families that were forced to eke out a poverty-stricken existence were not simply passive victims, ignorant, uncaring and brutalized by want, as they were so often represented at the time. They developed many skills and strategies – some of them illegal – in 'staying alive'. In the forefront of this battle, usually, was the mother. Dedicated to the care of her children, she was the mainstay of the lower-working-class family. With little or no money to hand, it was her tireless effort, skill and ingenuity which kept the family going from one week to the next. She had to play the roles of mother, wife, cook, cleaner, nurse, household manager, wage earner and family protector in appalling conditions. The skills she developed made all the difference between a family which survived and one which became destitute, with the children taken into institutional care. These strong women of the slums enjoyed high status and influence in their own communities. They were an altogether different breed from the new respectable, suburban mothers who did as their husbands told them and kept house. A hidden matriarchy dominated the family life of the poor in Britain.

The main problem facing these women was that of feeding their families: hunger and malnutrition were endemic among poor Edwardian families. Even in the late 1930s official surveys estimated that almost 8 million people – 17.5 per cent of the population – spent less on food than was regarded as the minimum by the British Medical Association. Many poor families spent all that they could on food but the main difficulty was lack of money to buy what they needed. Although much maligned at the time for their 'dietary inefficiency', most poor mothers did their best to fill the stomachs of their husbands and children. They bought vast quantities of cheap carbohydrate foods like bread and potatoes, made more appetizing by being smeared with dripping, treacle or margarine, which were washed down with innumerable cups of

120

tea. and there was the weekly treat of fish and chips from the local 'chippy'. This was a highly effective way of providing energy and avoiding hunger.

Their main aim was to put a hot meal on the table every day. To do this often meant buying the cheapest. throwaway items from the butcher or fishmonger. like pig's head. sheep's head. cod's head or a bag of bones. From these ingredients. they ingeniously produced a variety of different dishes that often became family favourites. The diet was supplemented by stale cakes and broken biscuits. bought cheaply from the baker. with over-ripe fruit and vegetables 'on the turn'. which were practically given away by greengrocers and at markets. Any fresh vegetables were most likely to come from the family allotment. or the back garden if there was one. grown by the father. Food was normally bought daily in very small quantities. sometimes from the corner shop 'on tick'. not just because money was short but also because there was no cool place to store it at home. Despite their economies. poor women often found that they did not have enough money to buy food all week. To raise desperately needed cash they would go regularly to the pawn shop armed with bundles of the family's best clothing. which would be redeemed at the end of the week when the wage packet or 'dole' money arrived.

Occasionally food might be stolen by the husband or children: a bird or rabbit that was poached. a tin of meat taken from a shop. vegetables 'pilfered' from the market or a farmer's field. Often. mothers seem to have turned a blind eye to this practice of 'stealing to survive'. In particularly hard times a few mothers themselves would steal to feed the family. Much more commonly. they would half starve so that the rest of the family could eat. At mealtimes they would take the smallest portion or. if necessary. nothing at all. and were the most likely members of the family to suffer from malnutrition.

Another major worry of the poorest parents – especially mothers – was illness. Despite their tireless efforts to nourish the family. they and their children were vulnerable to serious ill-health. disease and disability. One factor in this was dietary

121

deficiency but probably even more important were the appalling housing conditions they endured. The poorest families often gravitated to slum areas with the cheapest rents where they lived in damp, overcrowded, sunless and insanitary homes, often without running water. These families were ravaged by childhood diseases like diphtheria, scarlet fever, tuberculosis, whooping cough and measles which, in the days before immunization, often led to disability or death. Those who survived might develop a host of other infections or diseases: rickets, ringworm, pneumonia, bronchitis, severe dental decay and ear or eye infections. Overcrowding and shared beds meant that diseases spread quickly to most other family members. One survey of Newcastle-upon-Tyne, published in 1933, showed that poorer children suffered from eight times as much pneumonia, ten times as much bronchitis and five times as much rickets as children of professional families.

The parents were also frequently in poor health. A study of working-class wives in 1939 found that almost half suffered from 'bad' or 'very grave' health problems. They reported debilitating illnesses like anaemia, constipation, haemorrhoids, headaches, persistent toothache, rheumatism, varicose veins, severe backache and kidney disorders. Social investigators were horrified by how quickly worry and ill health aged poverty-stricken working-class parents. In 1913 Mrs Pember Reeves commented in her classic survey of Lambeth wives, *Round About A Pound A Week*, how young mothers looked as if they were 'in the dull middle of middle age'. The poor died younger too, sometimes in their thirties or forties. In the 1900s the life expectancy of a working-class woman aged twenty was just forty-six years. As the century progressed, however, both men and women increasingly survived into their fifties or sixties. In this sense, the mothers whose voices we hear in this chapter are remarkable survivors, having lived into their eighties or nineties.

Mothers did what they could to keep their families healthy, to prevent illness and to provide as much homely comfort as possible on a shoestring budget. Much time was spent sewing, patching and recycling clothes passed down through the family. Most could

122

not afford to buy new so second- or third-hand garments were bought at market stalls or jumble sales. Expensive items like boots and shoes were often obtained free from local charities. To help them last longer. in summer the children were sometimes allowed to take off their boots — which rarely fitted properly. anyway — and play barefoot in the streets. Mothers whose husbands were unemployed conspired with neighbours to avoid the worst penalties of the Means Test by hiding any furniture or domestic items that would have been confiscated as 'non-essential' by the authorities.

Warmth at home was seen as a priority. Most poor families were dependent on coal fires for heating and cooking and in especially hard times stealing coal from slag heaps. trains or coal-yards was one of the most common crimes. often committed by all members of the family. in poor working-class communities. But it was usually not seen as a crime by the families. In the struggle for survival they saw it as their 'right' to have fuel. especially if they lived or worked in a mining area like South Wales or Yorkshire.

Many parents were aware of a close link between dirt and disease and poor mothers often worked obsessively to keep their homes and children clean and tidy. They waged a constant war against the plagues of bugs and other vermin which infested the poorest areas. A clean home and children who did not smell sig-nalled a mother who took the care and welfare of her family seriously. Although the passion for cleanliness sometimes led to unnecessary and time-wasting routines. like the daily donkey-stoning of the front step in many working-class areas. had there not been such an obsession with cleanliness the toll of death and disease in poorer families would have been even higher.

Little health care was provided to help poor mothers in their struggle to look after their families. In pre-welfare state Britain the responsibility was left to local councils and charities. Although in the inter-war years a few pioneering councils. such as Bermond-sey in South London. tried to build 'mini welfare states' for local people — the centrepiece of which was often a health centre and a solarium to treat children with TB — most. especially in rural areas.

123

did little. Under the National Insurance scheme the father was normally the only member of the family entitled to free health care. When the children fell ill. poor mothers continued to treat them with traditional folk medicines and quack cures to avoid the crippling expense of paying for the doctor. Brown-paper poultices were often plastered on the chest at the first sign of a cold. and children with bronchial complaints were often taken to new road-works to inhale tar fumes which were thought to help them breathe more easily. The best chance most poor children had for health care was through the school medical service which expanded from Edwardian times: by 1935 2.300 doctors. 5.300 school nurses and 1.650 school clinics provided treatment for children. The level of care was basic but it was more than many poor mothers could afford elsewhere. Most soldiered on. perhaps with the help of medicine from the chemist. however bad they felt. aware that the family simply could not afford for anyone to be ill or to stay in bed.

Perhaps the greatest fear of many poor parents was that they would become homeless and end up with the thousands of destitute families that begged in the streets by day and slept rough by night in fields. lodging houses or – in the winter – in the hated work-house. Every week there was rent to pay and if families fell too far behind with it they were evicted. To help make ends meet some mothers took in homework – most often washing – or did a part-time cleaning job. Many fathers on the dole illicitly took part-time jobs. like caddying on golf courses. to earn a few extra shillings a week to help keep a roof over the family's heads. The last resort of the poorest families to avoid being turned out on the streets was to do a 'moonlight flit' and start again in a new area with a clean rent book. This was easier in big cities where families could 'disappear' for a time and where there was often a surplus of cheap rented accommodation. than in villages where everyone knew everyone else's business.

Poor families enjoyed a few pleasures together: walks into the countryside: occasional parties and festive celebrations: and singing round the piano. But pleasure usually had to be combined with work and earning extra money. On country walks the children would help their parents collect berries and other foods for free to be turned into jams and wines; at festive celebrations in the spring or at Christmas and New Year children were often dressed up by parents to collect money from door to door; and musical families would occasionally put on small shows or concerts, usually in the street or at the back of a tenement block, during which they would take up a collection. The classic example of this was the mass exodus every autumn of a quarter of a million East Enders from London to the hopfields of Kent. The six-week stay on the farms in the hoppers' huts was the nearest thing to a holiday that most such families would ever get. It was a welcome escape from London smog and gave families – often extended families – the opportunity to enjoy themselves together in the countryside. But the main point was to earn money from the farmers and most days were spent working hard. It was a way of buying a new set of clothes for the family to last another year, and at the end of the season the hop pickers ritually burned the old clothes they had worn on huge bonfires in the fields.

It is important not to romanticize the struggle for survival in the slums. The cost in terms of the health and happiness of the families forced to live this life was enormous. Some mothers could not cope with the immense burden and their children were placed in institutions. A few ended up in mental handicap hospitals, broken by stress. Other mothers, usually of single-parent families with no other means of support, turned to casual, part-time prostitution to feed the children and pay the rent. Some, driven to distraction by cramped living conditions, worry and ill-health showed little love for their children. Family life for them was blighted by constant arguments, fights and severe physical punishment of the children.

But it was fathers – often angry and frustrated by a life of poverty and unemployment – who were the main child-beaters in slum streets. In the first decades of the century many of the prosecutions of the newly formed NSPCC were of fathers. Drink, the main escape and entertainment of the poor, made some even more violent and their aggression might also be turned on their wives. In the poorest parts of cities like Glasgow and Liverpool, the weekends, when most heavy drinking took place, were well known for attacks by husbands on wives. Social investigators were shocked to see women going to the shops on Saturday or to church on Sunday covering up a bruised face or a black eye.

Even children brought up in poor but happy families who survived the diseases rife in the slums paid a price in that they were frequently kept away from school, deprived of a decent education, because their labour was needed at home. Truancy was particularly prevalent among the eldest and second eldest daughters in big families of the poorest class, who were often required to help with washing, cleaning, looking after younger brothers and sisters, or to baby-sit while their mother did the shopping or a cleaning job. In the 1900s, absenteeism was as high as 20 per cent in the poorest parts of some big cities. When a child from a poor family reached school-leaving age it had little or no chance of continuing its education or taking up a scholarship. Children were put out to work as soon as possible and their wage packet handed over to their mother unopened. This was one of the main ways in which a poor family might lift itself out of the poverty trap and live in relative comfort and security at least for a few years. At the same time it meant that there was little upward social mobility from the poorest families and that when they became parents the sons and daughters would also find themselves at the bottom of the pile, struggling to make ends meet.

The biggest uplift for the poorest families occurred during the inter-war years and was initiated by the state: a massive slum clearance programme and the building of cottage estates on the outskirts of towns and cities, creating 4 million new homes to rent for working-class families − the 'homes for heroes' promised in return for the sacrifices of the First World War. To many mothers who had struggled to keep their families alive in run-down city tenements, the new homes with modern conveniences, like a bathroom, living room, kitchen with running water and a back garden, were a dream come true, releasing them from some of the drudgery of slum life. The mass export of poor families into the suburbs was a key factor in improving the health and welfare of working-class families during the 1920s and 1930s. But it was not without its drawbacks: some parents did not like the new, more private family life of these suburban council estates. In the old inner-city areas whole families -- mothers, grandparents, uncles, aunts, cousins – lived within walking distance and would see each other almost every day. The physical closeness of life in the slums generated communal bonds, looking after neighbours' children, borrowing sugar, running errands and even collective defiance of the law, all of which added up to a mutual support system for the poor. Built up over many years, the network was quickly severed, for most councils had little concern with keeping extended families and communities together when they rehoused them. A real sense of loss prevailed, which partly explains the 'poor but happy' nostalgia of some elderly people for life in the slums.

Esther Peel

Esther was born in the village of Woodford. Northamptonshire. in 1907. Her father was a pit labourer and she had one older brother. Her three younger brothers died of malnutrition when they were only infants. Esther's first marriage. to a labourer in 1930. ended unhappily and she was left alone with a son born in 1933. She remarried in 1937. to a painter and decorator. and they had a daughter in 1938. Esther's husband was an alcoholic and spent what little money the family earned on drink. but despite his cruelty and violence towards her and the children Esther had nowhere else to go and was forced to remain with her husband for fifteen years. The marriage finally ended in 1953. She now has three granddaughters and one great-grandchild.

I can just remember my mother sending my brother to school and I used to have to stay at home to mind the baby. My mother used to say, 'There's a cup of sop in the oven for the baby.' All it consisted of was bread, water and a sparkle of sugar. And she'd be out all day and I would have to feed the baby. I was hungry too so I used to have a spoonful of it. Then my mother would come home with sixpence, after a day's washing, and send me to the shops. I'd get a penny herring and a penny loaf. I would have ha'penny-worth of sugar and tea and a penny-worth of Virol. And if there was a ha'penny left I used to go to the dairy and get a ha'porth of milk. And that was the lot. My dad used to have the herring. And my brother and I had a slice of bread each dipped in this horrible fat and that was our lot. I was always hungry. We were lucky if we got a slice of bread.

When you're hungry you'll eat anything. But, of course, the husband always had to be fed first. I was nine before I had an egg. If my dad had an egg, you know, he used to cut the bread in soldiers and he'd dip one soldier in for me and one soldier in for my brother and that was the most we ever had of an egg.

The mother was the last. 'Well, you haven't got any, Mum.' 'No, I don't feel like it.' That was always the excuse.

There was nothing else to do. If she cut up some meat she'd give us the meat and she'd probably just have the bits that fell by the wayside and that was her lot. But you always got the excuse that she wasn't hungry.

We were very poverty-stricken. Really, my baby brothers starved to death. They just faded. There was no food for them. I can remember the doctor coming to see them and he told my mother they had to have Virol every day. That was kind of a thick, sticky malt stuff. But, well, we didn't have pennies every day to give to the babies.

I remember when my last brother died, the one I used to look after. I think I looked on him as a doll. Because I never had a doll, I never had a toy. And one day they said he'd died. When I went to bed at night he was in a coffin in my bedroom. And my mother said, 'Say goodnight to him, won't you?' I did. I used to kiss him goodnight and he looked lovely. I did say to my mother one night, 'He's ever so cold, shall I take him in bed with me?' And she said, 'No, you mustn't disturb him.' I used to feel sorry that he was there on his own and I used to think, 'They're going to take him away.' There was some bubbles of spittle at the corner of his mouth and I thought, 'Well, if he was ill, if I take those and put them in my mouth I'll probably die and go with him and so I can look after him again.' I missed him, missed his coughing when he'd gone. I remember the day he went. Someone gave my mother and my grandma a lift because she sat in this pony-trap with this coffin on her lap.

To try to get us extra food Dad used to take me with him rabbiting. He taught me how to make snares. He'd take me to a place called Three Hills and sit me down and say, 'You make some daisy chains . . . ' And he'd eventually come back with a dead rabbit in his poacher's pocket. It went all the way round and I thought it was lovely and warm. It was just fun to me.

He'd got a friend in the next lane and he used to go there where they'd got an outside shed with a copper that you boiled with sticks. And I think that's where they used to get rid of the evidence, you know, they used to cut it up and I suppose he shared it with this friend of his. I do remember saying, 'Are we going to have rabbit pie or stewed rabbit?' And he used to say, 'We'll see when we get home.' I think everyone was doing it. No thought of getting caught. I mean, you got a higher punishment for riding a bike without a light than catching a rabbit. We had a very understanding policeman. If he thought there was something going on he used to say, 'Hello, me duck, where's your dad?' 'I dunno.' That's about as far as he'd go. He had to know because a lot of people would have starved to death if they didn't go poaching. He probably had a rabbit as well.

My brother taught me how to catch birds. He used to fix up a sieve, fine mesh on a stick, put crumbs or corn in there and we'd sit indoors and watch. And when there was sufficient birds in there we'd pull the stick away and we'd kill the birds and have sparrow pie.

And they used to go netting. They'd go in the daytime and find rabbit runs and then in the evening rabbits always come out to feed. Well, they would go round and put nets right along where the rabbit holes were then go away, leave it, and after about half an hour or an hour they'd go back and walk up the middle of the field and frighten the rabbits back, and of course the rabbits would run to get in their holes only they couldn't because the net would be there and that's how they caught their rabbits.

And when I was married we were very poor. We didn't get much money 'cause my husband had had to take this farm job. So I thought of my dad and poaching and it was one way of having a free meal. There were so many rabbits down the field so I got some wire and I knew how to cut a piece of hazel to make a peg to knock it in the ground. I slipped out that evening. September is a hunter's moon and that's the time to go. And I went and set in a field three snares, and I went half an hour later and I had two rabbits and the fox had taken one. Sometimes we hadn't a saucer in the house because when you set a snare you go when it's dark and you put something white near a snare so that you can find it in the dark.

130

I could skin, gut a rabbit. I could do it with hares, anything. Knew how to cook them. I loved doing it. I think I was more frightened of going out in the dusk. But my husband didn't know I did it. So whenever I got rabbits I used to think, 'What the devil am I going to do with them?' So I arranged a story with my mother that my stepfather had caught them and that he gave me one and kept one for themselves. That's the only way I could get out of it.

I used to have to go to work. I'd worked in the fields. I've done field work – potato picking, pea picking, fruit picking, anything. And I've gone out doing housework. As soon as the kids had gone to school I'd go and do cleaning. I had to because what money we had my husband spent on drink.

He liked his drink and as long as he had his drink that was it. There was a lot of unkindness. I think once you are married you become a possession with some people. They think that's what you are and they can do as they want with you. He used to knock me about and knock my son about. My son was frightened of him. I had to put up with a lot, for the sake of John and Jacqueline. It kept a roof over our heads and gave us a bed. With a man like that there's nothing else you can do. You was open to sexual blackmail but you just had to put up with it.

He'd come home and count his money and think, I suppose, what a fool he'd been to spend so much but he was always one of the lads, first to treat anyone. I said the money should have been in my pocket instead of the publican's, but it used to be, 'I do as I like with my own so-and-so money.' It always finished up with a bashing. It was usually a weekend occurrence. And I suppose, in a way, it was jealousy because I was probably protective of my son, which any mother would be, because he was cruel to him. He'd smash his toys. My son had a golliwog that he adored, took it everywhere, and in a fit of temper, when he came home from the pub one night, he smacked John round the face and he had hand marks for a fortnight. I daren't let him go to school. And he ripped John's golliwog to bits. And then I mended it but he wouldn't have it any more. 'I don't want it any more, Mum.'

131

I thought to myself, 'You're not a fool, you're fairly well educated, for God's sake, don't let him get away with it.' I couldn't stand the smell of beer. As soon as they've had a drink they want sex, and that's their pleasure. Pub. Sex. I hated weekends, when he'd got the money. I was powerless. Well, it was rape, wasn't it? I wish it had been law then. It was force to have sex.

I'd go to bed, feign sleep, but, of course, he used to come to bed and expect sex straight away. So, of course, there'd be a battle royal. You'd keep quiet quite a bit because you don't want the children to know. I was sexually attacked. He abused me, unnatural sex actually. It was a very unhappy life.

I do remember that to curb his sexual tendencies I made myself pyjamas, instead of a nightdress. But it didn't do a lot of good. There was just more to rip. I fought like hell! There was nothing else to do, only fight. Bedroom used to look like a bomb had dropped.

But you've got roof over your head, you've got a couple of kids, and so you put up with it. You see, I was young for my age. And I couldn't go back to my mother. You were too ashamed, really. I was a fool. You'd give in for the sake of peace.

One day he started bashing me and he had lovely curly hair and we were right in the door jamb, so I grabbed his hair and I bashed his head, bang, bang, bang against that door. And he'd had rather a lot to drink and I bashed him and I said, 'You touch me once more I'll kill you, I'll cut your throat, I'll stab you, I'll do anything, I'll kill you.' You see I was always rather strong-willed and I'd stand so much.

But it wasn't until I realized that I was a woman within my own right, that I had as much right to refuse sex as he had a right to demand it. And after that I went into my daughter's bedroom.

You see, when the children are small you have to put up with it because that's the only way you've got a roof and a meal. Because you're protecting them, and also pride, because you don't like to admit to all and sundry. I used to like to walk out with

132

my head high. But once they were older and they were leaving home I decided I'd had enough and I sent him packing. From then on I was my own boss.

Doris Bailey

Doris was born in 1916 in Bethnal Green. East London. Her father worked as a french polisher and she had three sisters. Her youngest sister. Rosie. died in 1925 from meningitis when she was four years old. Doris first met the man she would marry at the age of fifteen: he was dressed as Father Christmas at a Sunday School party. They married in 1940 and had three children. a girl in 1943. and boys in 1945 and 1948. They now have nine grandchildren and two great-grandchildren.

Now Rosie was the youngest of us four sisters. She was my baby sister and we all loved her very much. When she was four years old, one day she wasn't very well, she wasn't ill but she wasn't very well, and my dad, when he came in from work, he said, 'I think we'd better take her to the doctor's.' So they did and when they brought her home again she seemed a bit brighter and so they let her sit up and when they had their supper she was sitting at the table trying to spear pickled onions, and every time she speared one she was really excited and then Dad said she'd better sleep with them tonight as she's not well. So we three children went to our beds and Rosie went to sleep in Mum and Dad's room.

The next morning I woke up early and I could hear the most unusual noise and it was a man crying. I'd never heard such a thing and I got out of bed, opened the door and went and stood on the landing and I could hear my dad crying and as I stood there my auntie came along and she said, 'Dot, Rosie's very ill, go back to bed.' So I did and we lay there for a little while and I got out of bed again and this time I opened the door and I saw my poor mum standing there in her nightie with her old brown overall over her nightie and she wasn't dressed and I said, 'Mum, is Rosie very ill?' And my mum said, 'She's dead.' Just like that. She said, 'Get yourselves ready for school.' And we went off to school and when I got to the infants' door I stopped for a minute because Rosie had just started at the infants and I usually took her in, but I thought I'd better not because if I went in and tried to tell them I would cry, and my sister always called me watercart anyway, so I didn't want to cry in front of the teacher. So I went straight up to my class and after a while the headmistress of the infants came in and spoke to the teacher and they called me out to the front and my teacher said, 'Rosie's not at school today, Doris.' And I said, 'No, she's not coming any more, she's dead.' And the teacher said, 'Oh, my God.' Then I went and sat down.

When I got home from school it was so quiet and then I realized that other days my mum was always singing when she got the dinner ready, but she didn't sing, and when Dad came home he didn't whistle. It was so very quiet and they took me into the front room to show me Rosie – she was laid out on a table, a round table it was, and she had a white nightie on with lace all round the neck and round the sleeves, and her long golden curls were hanging down and her face was so white – she looked so beautiful. I said to Mum, 'P'raps she's not dead, Mum, p'raps she's only asleep.' And then my mum burst into tears again. I wished I hadn't said it. And then we went out into the garden and Mum never sang and Dad never whistled, it was all so very quiet. We took her toy box out and, d'you know, we shared her little things out between us.

Lily Felstead

Lily was born in Northwich, Cheshire, in 1907, the daughter of a gamekeeper. She was one of eleven children, of which eight survived. Lily met her future husband at the age of eighteen while she was working in a pub for six months. When the job finished Lily moved away, and the couple did not get back together until she returned to Cheshire to nurse her sick mother five years later. They married in March 1929 and settled in Northwich. On the day of the wedding Lily's husband told her that he had lost his job. From then on he picked up work where he could, usually manual labouring jobs. His health was poor and he suffered his first heart attack two months after their marriage. He died nine years later, leaving Lily with four children to bring up alone. Their first son had been born prematurely in October 1929, followed by another in 1931, and daughters in 1935 and 1938. Lily found it difficult to cope, receiving almost no help from her family or neighbours so she decided to remarry in 1941. She now has twenty-two grandchildren and twenty-four great-grandchildren.

The first few months I was married dole money was seventeen shillings. Out of nine years my husband only ever worked six months. We never had any money. My husband couldn't get a job so I used to go charring. There was no money for coal so we went cinder picking. You picked them, then you had to carry them half a mile back again.

You'd go to a second-hand shop for clothes and I did all my own knitting. I took in washing for two families and it was a case of washing and ironing, probably for one and sixpence, and then you'd go charring. You'd probably do a bit of knitting for someone, a bit of sewing for someone, and for two shillings, but that helped to pay for your bread.

You went into the allotment or the garden and picked some rhubarb, so you'd sell probably two pennyworth of rhubarb, you'd sell the cabbage, you'd sell the chicken for one and sixpence.

136

You had to go scrounging round the place to see whether you could find that other ha'penny to go and buy a loaf.

But I could always manage to manufacture a meal out of very, very little – turnips were easy to get hold of, carrots were, and you could always make stew with sixpennyworth of stew meat from the butcher's and a few bones thrown in. I used to buy shin bones, put them in the fish kettle, cook them so you had some very good stock for stews, and I used it in most gravies and everything, so they were nourished. You were the person that was hungry, never the children, because at times you'd be too sick to want to eat – oh, no, if there was two pieces of bread that was divided in four, the kids had it.

One day we had a runt pig give to us, nobody wanted it so they gave it to us. We fed that pig with scraps from the people around us, peelings and all. Then we sold it for five pounds, but hardly had we got the money in our hands before somebody had reported it to the dole people and our dole was stopped for a month.

I had three kids already when I realized I was pregnant again. I was so ashamed because, quite honestly, they gave you hell if you were pregnant on the dole. The rude, horrid remarks that was passed to you. You were ashamed to go out so I didn't go out. You couldn't hide it and it was like a crime.

And then my husband would probably get another fortnight's work so you were reimbursed again to do a bit of spending. You could go to town and you could fill a basket for five shillings. Always this spasmodical working of a week or so, whichever he could do, and then nothing again. What are we going to do? We'll cope. Always we could cope . . .

My husband was proud, though, a very proud man. One day he come in and I was doing all this washing that people had given me. He said, 'Let them do their own washing.' He'd been out looking for work and he had never really seen me doing this washing. You'd do this while he was out because he hated to feel you were having to work to keep children that were also his. And this particular day he got hold of the dolly tub, he tipped it in the yard.

The time came when he'd the chance of a regular job and the doctor was visiting at the time because my husband was bad with chronic bronchitis and the doctor suggested that there was no way that he could let him take that job. But all my husband could think about was that Hazel had seen a doll in a window in town, and, 'Think of all the things, Lil, that we could buy for Christmas if I get this regular job. Something to look forward to after all this out of work business.' And he got out of bed and he went.

It was to the salt works. They'd got a boiler that wanted picking from inside and unfortunately the man that was the care-taker of the works didn't realize my husband was in that boiler and lit a fire under it and it gave him a back draught of sulphur. Well, he come home that Saturday afternoon as black as the ace of spades. I didn't want him to go to work again, I'd rather have had him at home living than working. Because we could manage – we'd managed for such a long time that it didn't really matter much. But, anyway, he went back again to work on Monday and I used to cook a meal and take it to save him coming back home.

Well, on the Friday, the following Friday, he went along to get some money that was owing out to him for dole, and when he come back again he was so cold he couldn't even hold a cup. He couldn't keep from shaking so I got him to bed on the couch, and then I got the bed downstairs. He lay there until he died on 7 March. Because he'd had rheumatic fever there was no compensation for that, as you could call a freak accident. He just coughed and he coughed and he coughed his lungs away with this sulphur that had burned him. I just looked at him one day and that was it, he was dead. I just didn't know what to do. You never think it will happen and then suddenly you realize that he's dead, and, of course, then when the body's laid out and you take a look you just begin to wonder how are you going to carry on. How d'you feel? How the hell d'you feel? When something like that happens to you you're so numb you don't really know what to do so I prayed that we would all die. I'm not ashamed of

138

telling you all this 'cos there didn't seem to be any prospects at all for any of us, and with him not working there was to be no pension for me.

I did feel I couldn't carry on. You couldn't discuss these things because nobody wants to know, not really. They're all right if you're always laughing, but you mustn't be in trouble because you've got no friends then. The anguish that you kind of had to endure of thinking that there you were, with four children, and you hadn't got two ha'pennies for a penny. How are you going to cope? So gradually you've got to do something about it. So, as I say, I marshalled all me resources and came to the conclusion that my sister would housekeep for me and I would go to the Blue Cap pub to work. I'd leave the children at half past six in the morning and they wouldn't see me until half past five at night, because you couldn't leave off in the dinner hour because you didn't have any dinner hour properly.

It was nothing, only stress and overwork, because many a time you would have to stay longer. The landlady was very good, she gave me a lot of things to bring home for the kids. I'd been there about five or six weeks and she was getting a bit concerned because I was losing so much weight. Well, you couldn't eat, you couldn't do anything, all you were was churned up inside. Your muscles knot with anxiety of wondering what your family's doing at home. You should be at home, but you can't afford to be at home – as simple as all that. And the result of that anxiety is the loss of appetite. But I never have told my kids this. They were important – they were my sacred trust. Those kids had to be both looked after and fed. That was pre-dominant in my mind, that those kids should get a chance in life and I tried to give it them in every way, keeping them tidy, working for them.

How can you settle down to do these jobs when your mind is at home all the time? And then one day I'm coming back from work and I couldn't even see the kerb. I just lost my sight, but even that, I just couldn't let it go because I couldn't afford to stop, so I carried on until April of 1939. It would be then when

I was forced to go to see the doctor and he demanded that I stop work and rest my heart. I weighed five stone two. That was it.

Then my next-door neighbour told me the children were suffering through having to look after themselves, wash in cold water in the winter time. They would have to light the fire themselves. My sister wasn't taking care of them at all. It was all wrong and I didn't know. They never ever let me know that they were suffering or I would have packed my job up just like that. Actually my daughter had been scalded – I was working and the kettle was boiling on the job and of course it had to be reported, this burn, this scald. She was taken to hospital and the doctor wouldn't even allow me to visit her. I think one of the nosy neighbours had reported it. The next thing this woman come and she said that there was no way I was a fit mother who would go out and leave children. So I said, 'What do you want me to do, do like other people do? I am not bringing them up on charity.' And it was then that I decided that I was going to find a job where I could work and yet be at home to see them to school and be there when they come back. So I went sick visiting.

I had to just try to do anything to keep those kids at home, to keep them with me. That was really what forced me into marrying again and that first twelve months was hell, because I didn't really want to be married again. But if anything happened to me I thought I'd have someone to take over the responsibility. He really was jealous of the kids. 'Get this done, get that done, get the other done. The fire wants feeding.' So many things had to be done and then he would use his belt on those boys. Their stepfather was unkind to them, especially the boys. That first twelve months I caught him with a belt in his hand and then I found my youngest girl bruised. When I went to bath her and I saw all the bruises on her I know why women kill men, because I could have killed him right then and there. I just wanted to be sick at the side of the bath when I saw that child. I couldn't wait for him to come home from work and said, 'If ever you lay your

hands on my children again, as God's my judge, I'll kill you.'
And he never did. But I always felt guilty because I'd been forced
into marrying. I just had to find a way of keeping the children.

Maria Davis

Maria Davis was born in 1917 in Cardiff. She was married in 1935 when she was eighteen. Her husband was a dock worker but he was constantly out of work. Maria worked in a sweet shop until she had their first child, a daughter, in 1936. When her baby was only a year old Maria decided to leave her husband in Cardiff and moved to London. Destitute and without any means to keep herself and her daughter she became a prostitute.

I just decided I would have to leave so I went to the station, there's a little park outside there and I sat there crying with my baby. I had nothing at all. A girl came up to me and started talking to me, sort of felt sorry for me, I suppose. She told me I should go to London and get a job there. And she paid my fare to London and came with me. She looked after me very good for quite a time. When I came to London I was really destitute. I had nothing, nothing, nothing at all. Nowhere to go. Nowhere to stay. And then I decided I couldn't live off her all the time so I found this lodging house. I had to get money for the baby but I had no social security, no nothing then. Had no curtains. I had no food. All I had was a bed settee which the girl had given me and I had the baby's cot and the pram and an old cooker that was left in there, and I had nothing else.

Then I met this neighbour. I got friendly with her. And she suggested I did one day's work. She told me it was prostitution. But it came very hard. I didn't know how to do it. I told her I couldn't do it. But I did need the money. The Social wouldn't give you anything for furniture them days. Or help. So I just had to do it. I was a very poor single family. I was really forced to do it. I didn't want to.

She said she'd help me. So she came with me and she showed me and told me a lot of things. 'You just don't lay down and have sex, you've got to do other things,' she said. 'You'll never get no money like that.' I just had to do it but I felt terrible. I felt dirty. I felt ashamed. The first person that come I didn't know what to do. I just felt awful, disgusted, horrible. And he was one of the upper crust as it happens, and he was really brutal. I just couldn't take my clothes off. He didn't want to pay me any money. He wanted everything and – he wanted everything for the least money, and he was a horrible man. He started shouting, 'I'm not going to pay money if you don't take your clothes off.' He wasn't the only one. There was lots like that.

I'd never undressed in front of men before. Especially sex and mauling me all over. You're expected to maul them all over. It wasn't nice. It was awful. I used to dread every day for months. Well, I didn't think about nothing really. A blank most of the time. In the end I just done it and shut my eyes sometimes till I got used to it.

Some of the customers were awful. You see the state of the people, how they used to come up. Some spotless and others were, you know, you'd take their clothes off and they used to be smelly. It was the worst. And whippings, using different instruments on them. One man came up and asked me to strap his bottom with a pair of kippers.

I used to wait until I went home and I had the baby there. My friend used to look after her. Then eventually I got the flat, you know. I used to get about a dozen, maybe more, a day. About ten minutes, fifteen minutes. No more unless they paid for more time.

You had nice people and you had upper crust. They used to think you were dirty, you know. You had to do this and do that and the upper crust wasn't very nice. I used to hate the aristocrats. But I had to go in for the money. They used to possess you. Very demanding. Talked to you dirty and all. Sometimes I used to say, 'Well, why do you go with somebody like me if you don't like people like us? Why doesn't your wife satisfy you? Why do you come to us? Nobody asks you to come up here.' And they'd get annoyed, you know. And I told them I was forced to do it. I said otherwise I wouldn't be going with them.

After I set up my own flat in Compton Street the customers

used to come up and see my name on the door. But I was earning my own money then and I was getting a little bit on my feet. I had to do it. I needed furniture. I needed clothes. I needed for the baby. They came to the door. They rung the bell and walked up. You just put your name up on the door and if there's a red light they know what it is. It says 'Model'. That was all they needed. The rest they soon found out. And the regulars used to come up. They used to bring a bottle of wine and ask you to go for a drink. And I became very friendly with some of them.

There was nice people come up and you got a drink and they'd spend an hour with you and talk – talk about their life, you know. They keep chatting to you about their life. Even when you're having sex they were chatting about their wives. And asked you what you did. Could they take me out. But I never went out with anybody.

I had no man at the back of me, just my baby. No pimps. You had a couple of fellows occasionally asking you if you wanted protection and I said, 'I already got one.' I was independent. Oh, I had a baby, that was enough. I was living on my own. I didn't want any more men. No, no.

I was brought up in a big family. I had a chapel background. What I was doing I knew was wrong. I didn't think I was wrong, I knew I was doing wrong. And that went against me, it made it much harder. But I had to do it and there was no – no other way. I still had my home to get and my baby to keep. It was providing me with the things I wanted most for my daughter or myself. But mainly my daughter. I had to bring her up properly. And give her the things that I couldn't give her otherwise. I had no home to start off with, just a settee, two orange boxes and a cooker. And so I had to really work hard for the first several months to get what I needed. Got my daughter new clothes. Myself new clothes. I was very happy. Bad days were worth it. But I don't know how I got over it now. Well, I felt really bad, really bad.

Even though I learnt to accept people – it's still horrible. It wasn't so bad as it was in the beginning. But you still have awful people. And no one knew. I never told anyone. I didn't know anybody. Only just my friend and she was a good friend. And she helped me when I went to work. She looked after my little girl. My daughter, she never found out then but I told her years later. You see, I never thought of myself as a prostitute. I just got the money because I had to for my daughter. I know I was, but I never thought of myself like that.

Edie Jones

Edie was born in Hampstead, North London, in 1912. Her father was a maintenance man for the Gas, Light and Coke Company. Her mother also worked, taking in washing and doing cleaning jobs. Edie had one sister and three brothers. She spent three years of her childhood living with an aunt and uncle while her mother was looking after a premature baby. Edie met her husband while working in a tool shop when she was sixteen. He was made redundant from his job in a shipping office when he was eighteen and then worked on the railways for several years. They married in 1932 and went to live in Islington. He found work in the building trade as a painter and decorator, but as this was seasonal during the 1930s, he was frequently unemployed and returned to the railways. They had two children, a daughter in 1933 and a son in 1939 who was killed in a road accident in 1942. Edie has two grandchildren.

I was always hungry. Very often the money run out by Monday and I can remember walking to the Unemployment Exchange on Thursday morning, when we got the money, pushing my small daughter in a pram, walking with my husband, when I used to wait outside the Labour Exchange, and when I saw him coming down the stairs knowing he'd got the dole in his pocket, I used to rush into the baker's which was next door and get three ha'penny rolls, give one to the baby, one to myself and wait for him to come in the baker's to pay for them. By the time we got to the door we'd eaten half of it. I only used to weigh seven stone. I was five foot eight and a half.

We always made sure that we got something every day for the babies. There was always a meal for them and we would say, you know, 'Not hungry, we'll have ours later.' I suppose you got used to going without. The doctor said, 'What are you feeding her on?' 'Nestlé's Milk.' 'That's no good for a baby, her bones won't set, you must get her some cod liver oil and malt.' 'Oh, how much will that cost?' 'You can get a bottle in the chemist for one and ninepence.' 'But my husband's unemployed. Can't afford one and nine.' And they said, 'Well, get it out of your dole money!' I don't know where they thought the dole money went, we didn't have five shillings a week left for food. Well, we couldn't spend more than sixpence a day on a dinner. If you got up to the baker's by seven o'clock in the morning, the price of a loaf was fourpence ha'penny, but the stale ones from yesterday you got for thruppence, and we lived on bread. But perhaps you'd only be able to get one of those loaves a week and that had to last you the week. Toast made from a stale loaf and an Oxo cube was quite a standard meal for unemployed people.

If you were unemployed you took a paper bag and you stood close outside one of the big shops where all the crates were laid on end with all their supplies in. And there was a young boy up there looking after them, you stood as near to the crates that was marked twenty-four for a shilling as you could get, and you had thruppence in your hand. You sort of aimlessly shook it and you sort of waggled your paper bag, like, and sure enough a woman would sidle up to you and say, 'Eggs? How many? Three pen-n'orth?' Sometimes you might have to wait as long as an hour before you got your three penn'orth of eggs – six for thruppence. One of you went around and collected up the thruppences and all the rest gathered around the door to make sure you didn't make a quick getaway. Then it would be sharing them round. The twenty-four eggs. You know, six for you, six for you, and so on. I've often taken six eggs home in my hat.

Butchers didn't have refrigerated rooms to keep their meat in, so they brought a stall and fixed up outside their shop. Put all the meat that was left on it and auctioned it. You'd pick up perhaps a joint of meat, he'd slap half a thing of sausages on the top and perhaps a couple of chops and then they'd say, 'Who'll give me half a crown?' The thrill, waiting to get him down until he said perhaps one and six. 'I'll have it, I'll have it!' Course, it helped if you were young and cheeky and managed to get to the front of the queue.

147

And sheep's heads, we used to have, and cod's heads. My aunt, she sent me a pig's head and told me it cost fourpence, and told me what to do with it, and you could live for nearly a week on a pig's head. They used to be enormous, just the head, where they'd chop the head off. Used to be about that big. And you took the eyes out and once you got the eyes out you boiled it. And we made brawn, we took the tongue out and boiled that and made cold tongue to eat. You made pea soup, you took the brains out, tied them up in muslin and boiled them and spread them on mashed potatoes.

Well, as the dole money was all we had to live on, you had to pay your rent, otherwise you would've been out on the street because in those days they didn't have to get a court order, they just gave you a week's notice and you were out. So you had to pay your rent to keep a roof over your head. However few bits of food you had you had to have money to put in the gas meter and your light meter, so a certain amount had to be set aside for that.

You had so much benefit and then you had to apply for further benefit and they applied to you this thing they called the Means Test which meant that an official came to your house and poked his nose into everything – they opened cupboards and drawers and even went out in the garden and opened the coal shed to see what you'd got in there in case you 'dark-holed'.

My husband was a very good piano player and his mother had a piano – he was the only one that could play it – and so she gave it to him, and we'd only had it about three months when his benefit ran out and we knew that when the man from the Means Test – Mr Meanie we used to call him – we knew that when Mr Meanie came the piano would be the first thing that would have to go. And I knew that it would break his heart and I was very upset and was crying, when the milkman knocked at the door. Course, he asked me what was the matter, and I told him and of course I suppose he heard stories like that all the way round his round in those days. He thought about it, went out to his cart and he came back with a luggage label, handed it to my husband and said, 'Tie that round the leg of the piano and I'll help you shift it out into the passage and when Meanie comes, it's not your piano, you've taken it in for Mrs Pike next door.' So we thought it might work and we did that. It was an awful job to get up and down the passage with the piano there, we had to wait four or five days before old Meanie turned up. 'What's this doing here?' 'Well, it was delivered for next door and the lady's away so we took it in.'

It was a case of, 'How many in the family – three? Well, you've got four wooden chairs in your kitchen, get rid of one of them.' He went round there, we had to get rid of one of the kitchen chairs, we had to get rid of my husband's armchair. He even counted the cups. I was sure he was dying to say, you know, 'You've got six cups, get rid of three of them.' But he went off eventually, and later that evening the woman that lived in the flat next door came and knocked and she said that he'd went to her house and asked her if Mrs Pike was there. 'No, she's away.' 'Was she expecting a piano, do you know?' 'How do I know? I don't enquire into her business.' And twice our piano went down the back garden path, along and up into her house so that we kept it.

Ray Rochford

Ray was born in 1925 in Salford, Manchester. His father, a slaughterman for the Co-op, died when Ray was seven so his mother took on cleaning jobs to try to keep the family together. Ray had one brother and one sister. He started work as a mill hand when he was fourteen, and left to join the Navy at seventeen. He spent most of the Second World War serving in the Far East. When the war ended he returned to Salford, and married in 1947. He has five children, born in 1948, 1949, 1952, 1960 and 1967. He also has fourteen grandchildren and five great-grandchildren.

In 1933 when the old fella died, things got a bit rough in our family. The old girl was left with three kids on twenty-one shillings a week, so we fell behind with the rent and we had to do a moonlight flit.

I was in school one day at St Mary's and the teacher said, 'You're wanted in the school playground, Raymond.' So I went outside and me mother was there and she gave me a note and said, 'Go round to Wood Street, go to this address.' Course I accepted that so I went to this place in Peel Green, two rooms it was. When we got there she said, 'Now don't tell anybody where we live.' 'Cos we owed that much money. Now when I went back to play down Wood Street, down Lane End, playing with the kids, they asked me where I was – I daren't tell them where I lived in case they told their mothers. When I finished playing I used to stop on the street corner and look behind me to see if I was being followed in case they was following me home. And that's how it was in those days.

I used to go out nicking from the shops with the other lads. We used to go in in twos and ask him to get something off the top shelf and he used to get these ladders and go up to the top shelf and, while he was up there, he used to have these biscuits in glass-fronted cases, and we used to open the lids and dive in.

150

I always made for the chunks because I loved chunks, large tins of salmon, and when I got home I'd say to Mother, 'Mrs So-and-So bought this and she didn't want it.' 'Oh, thank you very much.' Daren't tell her I'd nicked it. Otherwise she'd have got me to church and to confession. I think a tin of chunks was worth five Hail Marys then, and that was what we used to do. Go in these shops and nick things, take 'em home. Always took 'em home to us mothers whatever we took.

Well, the parents knew that the kids were thieving because they'd fetch things home that they knew bloody well they couldn't buy. And they'd go and sell them, or they'd go and help a neighbour out. They'd go and give a neighbour a couple of blankets that had been knocked off, or they'd go and take some tins of corned beef – they knew – and if their son got caught, well, they just accepted that. It was part of the game, getting caught. But without it they couldn't survive and sometimes they used to tell their sons what they wanted. They'd give them a shopping list. 'Can you nick this, can you nick that? Yer Dad needs some working boots.' Well, they used to have working boots hanging outside pawn shops – big string of them – and as you passed you got yer penknife out and cut a pair off the bottom. Johnny Owens used to look at the size of the boots to fit his old fella and then he'd cut a pair off, size ten.

When the Means Test came out there'd be a dawn raid. They always came early in the morning to catch you out. There'd be one bailiff, the treasurer and sometimes a policeman if the area was rough, and they'd come in the house and they'd assess the value of your grandfather clock if you had one, three-piece suite if you had one, or the Welsh dresser, even the carpet, and then they'd total the value and they'd say, 'Now sell all this and when you've sold it we'll start yer benefits again.' Now to avoid that we got some inside information from a fella that worked at the council, and he'd tip 'em off which streets were being visited and so they'd carry the furniture from there into this backyard. Everything, strip the house, and when the bailiffs come the house would be empty, and then when this street was due for a visit

151

they'd be tipped off and then they'd carry the furniture into there, and that's the way they used to avoid the penalties of the Means Test.

Rose Townsend

Rose was born in 1912 in Bristol. Her father was a first-class plumber and she had three brothers and three sisters. Rose met her husband. a builder. when she was out cycling with a friend. They courted for eighteen months. and married in 1933. They stayed in their first home. rooms over a butcher's shop. for a couple of months before renting a small cottage close to Rose's mother in St Paul's in central Bristol. Rose's first daughter was born in 1933. followed by a son in 1935 and another daughter in 1938. The family moved to a new council house on the Southmead Estate in 1938. Rose now has twenty grandchildren and twenty-two great-grandchildren.

We lived in this old cottage together, we 'ad the one full size bed upstairs 'cos the other bedroom wa'nt too good to live in. And we used to have terrible cockroaches running around the floor because it was a horse's stable next door. And I found them on the bed in the sheets, so I used to look every night 'fore I put the children to bed and see there was no cockroaches. We only had one bed so the children had to sleep with us in the middle of the bed with my husband one side and me the other side. I put them to bed early 'fore me and my husband went up. So my brother came down and he suggested we Vaseline the legs of the bed so they wouldn't climb up onto the children while we were downstairs. I used to wash the floors with Jeyes Fluid, 'cos there was bugs on the wall. I used to go round every night with a cloth, to make sure there was none and get a mop and go up the tops to make sure there was none to fall on the children while they were in the bed.

I had the two young children then when I was in the cottage. I used to have to go to get me some water from the taps six 'ouses up the path and brought it back and I used to put it in the boiler outside, and boil it up, bring it in and pour it into the tin bath before the fire, the range. I used to put the children in two at a time. Well, it used to be very difficult. We used to have to be carrying water all the time, for different jobs and things that we had to do. And then the boiling it up and no facilities whatever, my husband used to have to light the oil lamp so that I could see.

We used to buy sacks or somebody used to give us some and I used to rip 'em down the sides then we'd cut up all different coats and woollies, different colours, I used to sharpen sticks, make it to a point so that we made holes in it and they used to put the cloth through the holes and two ends used to come out then we used to make a loop and pull them tight to make like a pattern and make a rug. My children used to sit and help me make it, two one side and one the other and me the other side and we were sat by the fire, and we had the radio on. Then I backed it with another sack.

I used to think to myself, 'Oh, whatever women have to put up with.' It was so monotonous. We had to put up with this when people had nice houses and running water and we 'adn't even got a light to write, only a lamp and the children were crying, 'Oh, Mummy, I'm cold, I'm cold.' But it was terrible.

It used to get me down as well because we never had much food, we didn't know where the next meal was coming from 'cos my husband had been out of work. So I had to give what I had to them and go without myself. And my husband used to go down his mother's. That's how we managed. As long as I got the children something nourishing for their tea and their breakfast I didn't mind.

I bought pig's head. The butcher'd clean it for me, take the eyes out and the brains, and I used to bring it 'ome. Then we had a big saucepan and put it in the saucepan, filled it with cold water and took it to the stove let it boil, and left it for three hours, all the bones had come out. And when it was drained I put it on a tin plate, took all the bones away, put another tin plate on top and put the flat on top of that and left it for three or four hours to cool down. We was able to cut it up into lovely slices. That's how I fed my children. You could make the pig's

cheek last, we used to make it last as long as we could 'cos it was
so nice, and then they used to say, 'Mum, get another pig's cheek,
will you?' So I says, 'Yeah, all right, later on in the week we'll
have another pig's cheek.'

I really think I was close to a nervous breakdown. I never had
the things to look after the children. The place was getting me
down, you couldn't make it look nice. The health visitor used to
come an' she used to sit there and say, 'Have you done this today,
have you done that today?' 'I've done everything,' I said. 'You
can go upstairs and see it all up there. I've done the best I can
with old cottage like this.' She used to say, 'Have you swept that
this morning?' And my husband got real mad with 'er. She wasn't
married. She didn't understand.

When my children had whooping cough my mother told me
to take them down the road because the men were tar spraying
and it would help them. So I put them in the pram, the two
youngest, and the eldest one walked with me and they said,
'Where we going, Mummy?' I stayed on the pavement. They
open the top and all the tar comes out and you can smell it really
strong. I took them down every day regular. They loved it, they
loved the smell of it. They was enjoying themselves watching the
men, you know, spraying the roads and all the fires going there.
The man said, 'You really ought to have a tar rope round their
necks.' I said, 'I can't really put a tar rope round their necks
because they'll get all dirtied.'

When they had sore throats my mother used to say, 'Put yer
husband's sock that he been wearing, sweating sock round their
necks, and that'll help with their sore throats and mumps.' They
didn't like it very much but I said, 'It'll get your colds and
everything you've got better.' When they had such bad colds my
mother used to say to me, 'Your best thing, Rose, is some brown
paper and get somebody that cooked a goose to give you some
goose grease, cut them a brown paper vest out. Get a long piece
of brown paper, fold it in 'alf, cut a neck out for the children and
leave it open at the sides and just slip it over their heads, grease
it well, front and back and leave it on for two weeks, don't take

155

it off, don't wash them.' It was marvellous. About a fortnight I let them stay on, so I used to wash their legs and everything, but never touched the brown paper vest. At night when they went to bed with their pyjamas on they were so hot and it used to go right into their chests and make them overheated, so I used to say to 'em, 'Well, I'll pull the bedclothes back for you.'

I don't think I could really have coped if my mum hadn't helped me. She used to cook our Sunday joint and in the week she used to cook little things for the children, make sure we had a cooked tea. She used to say, 'Bring the children up, Rose, and then you can go up to Co-op.' I used to go up to my mum and talk to her and ask her advice about certain things, about the children and everything. I used to say to my mum, 'It's very difficult, Mum, I don't know what to give them to eat from day to day with such small money.' She used to say to me, 'It's a hard job to cope with them, Rose. You'll have to learn to do it for yourself and try and cope and get little things at a time. That's what I used to do.' We used to make a cup o' tea and my sisters used to be there and my brother and we all used to sit round and have a chat, you know, and I used to take the children up and they used to sit on their uncle's lap and he'd give 'em something to play with on the floor. My brother used to buy me groceries so that I could manage in the week. He'd buy me some butter and sugar and tea out of his own money and bring it down every week in a little box. He used to buy the children sweets and chocolate. I used to have quite a nice hour up at my mum's. I used to enjoy that. I depended on my family. So I used to enjoy going up there to see them, just up the road, where they lived, to have a cup of tea.

When my little girl was ill once she was that bad we had to call the doctor out. He came and he said, 'What terrible conditions. The council is coming round inspecting cottages, thinking about moving people out to Southmead Estate and I'll get them to call on you.' And the inspector came and he said, 'Oh, terrible, will you be ready within a fortnight to move to the new houses at Southmead? We've got some houses being finished in Ashburton

Road.' Within about a fortnight we were glad to get out of there, away from all that, the bugs and the gnats and the cockroaches.

When I moved down Southmead Estate, to the new house I went into, I couldn't believe my eyes. I did enjoy it, moving to that house, after being in an old cottage like that. I was only twenty-five when I moved to Southmead. I walked from room to room looking to see what there was, what I had. There was a bathroom and I seen what a lovely bath there was as well, I was amazed. And a nice larder in the corner with a stone slab on the bottom all cold to put anything, like a fridge. We had the 'lectric light, see, that was nice, so we had the wireless then. I had such good luck to go into such a nice council house.

And the children, they were that excited. They were dancing about with me upstairs and downstairs looking at the bedrooms. They said, 'Which is mine, Mum?' They were as pleased as anything, that they'd have their own bedrooms.

We had a nice front room and kitchen, a nice kitchen, we had the bedrooms for the children, three bedrooms. They had a bedroom each, we had our bedroom, I liked that. Downstairs we could all sit together in the front room, at night. I bought all the furniture on the weekly.

I used to bath them on Saturday nights, all of 'em. And before I bathed them I used to mix up a cake with currants and fruits and our boy, he used to say, 'Put it in the oven, Mum, while we're having our baths.' We had the boiler in the corner and I used to fill it with cold water, put a light under the gas to boil it up. We used to have a pump and I used to jerk it backwards and forwards to make the water run into the bath. Then they used to play about in the bath and dry themselves by the fire. And when they were all dried, and in their pyjamas and that, we sat by the fire and I used to get the cake and turn it out on a plate and get all the paper away from it and then I'd take it in and our boy used to say, 'Mum, I've got the kettle on, we'll have a cup of tea and you cut my slice and your slice 'cos we likes it hot and June and Pat can have it cold.' Every Saturday night, I always bathed them every Saturday night.

It was wonderful to have a garden, so the children could go out there and play. They used to help me grow the vegetables and help me dig the garden. I used to dig but they used to rake it for me and put the seeds and the beans in. And then my husband used to dig it up and put the potatoes in for us. And that was one side of the garden. The other side we reserved for the children. We put grass all down the side so that I could take 'em out there and we could have a picnic. We used to sit out there, and they'd say, 'Mum, get the chairs out.' Two deckchairs we used to have.

The children liked it, we had our own fields at the back. We used to have cooking apples and eating apples and plums, we used to go up there and run round the field picking blackberries, make blackberry and apple jam for the children. They had all the fields to play in because they never built on them till after the war. They used to love that.

Verna Brennan

Verna was born in Dock Street. Port Talbot. in 1918. Her father worked on the docks for the Great Western Railway. She had four sisters and two brothers. Verna met her future husband when she was nineteen: she was a keen football fan and he played for the local team. They married in 1939 and moved into rooms in Dock Street a few doors away from Verna's parents. Her husband John's job on the blast furnaces at the steelworks was a reserved occupation. so when the war started they were able to move into an empty house in Dock Street together. Their first daughter was born in 1940; they had another in 1948 and a son in 1954. Despite the harsh conditions and poverty of the time the people of Dock Street formed a strong community. helping each other as best they could – even resorting to stealing in order to survive. Verna and her family were forced to move from Dock Street when it was demolished in 1954. She has five grandchildren and one great-grandchild.

Well, we lived in Dock Street, which was a row of twenty-five houes which had no electric or gas. We had to have coal for heating the house and for cooking on. We had to have coal to survive. If I didn't have the coal, as I say, now to light the fire, well, no way could I bath the baby in cold water. Without the fire I was finished, without the coal I was finished, so we had to steal it. We had to steal it to survive, it's as simple as that. That's why we done it – because we needed it. We needed the coal. We couldn't afford the coal, I think it was half a crown a week, we didn't have the money to do it, simple as that.

There was a railway track ran all at the back of Dock Street and the coal company sent coal wagons along there. All we had to do was get up on the wagons and get it. So, well, it was a bad thing we were doing 'cos we were stealing the coal, but it was a necessity anyway. It had to be done otherwise our kids would go cold.

159

I'd be out in the garden 'cos I'd be pegging out clothes on the line and someone would shout that a coal train was coming. It used to pick up speed when it was coming to the street because they knew what we were going to do, so the boys then would go up on the tracks and they greased the lines and, course, the wagon wheels were spinning around fast but the wagon was hardly moving because of the grease. So we had time to climb up on the wagon, throw the coal down and put it in the coal house. After we finished throwing the coal down, of course, there'd be a mess with all small coal and dust on the floor, so we'd all go in and get our brushes and sweep all the lane and put it in the big square dust pans. It was in the back lane and we'd just sweep that all into this big rubbish bin, see, cover it over then with whatever was thrown in before and then we'd a lovely and clean back lane so they couldn't catch us with any signs that the coal had come from the wagons. We'd be right then for about a week, so when a week come we'd be up again doing the same thing.

I remember once when I did it I was pregnant. Somebody said there was a train coming. I didn't have far to go before the baby was born. This was on a Monday and on the Wednesday my daughter was born, but I had to get some coal. It was even more desperate with another baby coming. And I suffered for that. Through going up for that coal I was really ill through the birth and after.

I didn't think I was doing a bad thing. I knew it was something I had to do. It had to be done. We needed coal and that's the only place we could get it from.

But once I got caught on one of the wagons and I had to go to court and I was really petrified. But we had a man living down Dock Street, we called him the Philadelphia Lawyer because he was brilliant. Well, he come down to the house and he said to me, 'Verna, now don't be afraid going up the court,' he said. 'Don't forget to tell them you passed a full row of wagons and you went into the empty wagon.' So I goes up into the court and the magistrate he give me the lecture about stealing and all that business. So I said, 'Well, I were in an empty wagon and I didn't think I were doing any harm by being in the empty wagon.' And I got off scot free!

With times being so hard everybody would 'elp everybody else in Dock Street in those days, and, well, we made these parties for the children. I think we were the only ones in the town that did it. Those whose husbands were still working would lend it to them who was out of a job, would be glad to lend it to 'em because they knew they might be out of work themselves soon enough.

Well, sometimes now we wouldn't have any money, we were broke. Waiting for pay day and we'd wonder, 'Now, who can I borrow off? Who'd have money?' I could always borrow off my mother or my sister Joyce, 'cos, I mean, she used to do sewing and she always had a few bob, so I could always borrow money off them. Practically the whole street was in that position but everybody would lend everybody else. We'd never be afraid to ask for anything, you'd always have it. If you'd run out of marge, you'd go to the neighbour or to friends. Whether it was money, food or even clothes they'd lend it. They were a fantastic lot of people living in Dock Street, wonderful people.

Then we started hearing rumours 'cos the councillors were coming down there, which they never did before. Couldn't care less whether or not the kids went to school, or what have you, they wasn't bothered before.

Then they started coming down the street and telling us about the benefits. 'Why don't we go and live in a council house?' The benefits of living in a council house. 'You'd have gas, you'd have electric and what have you.' But nobody wanted to go and live in a council house. We wanted to stay in Dock Street. So this went on, they're coming down more regular and this went on now for a couple of months, telling us, 'Well, you're a silly lot.' And he'd always pick a bad day. 'Now, look what you've got to put up with, the walk you've got to have, and all that.' But we still kept telling them, 'No, we didn't want to go and live in a council house.'

161

Eventually they beat us down more or less and told us we had to move out. We told the councillors we were only prepared to go on condition they put us in the one row of houses, and which they promised faithfully to do. We didn't want to be separated from all our Dock Street neighbours. 'Oh, yes, yes, you'll be all in the one street.' So we thought, 'Oh, lovely, now we won't mind going.' And they said we'd be paying the same rent.

So anyway, we finally had the notice to leave. They didn't keep any of the promises. We were spread out all over the town. We went up the office, mind, and we played war about it, but nothing they could do. We'd been allocated this house and we could take it or leave it. So we had to take it. It killed the community, didn't it? It was a terrible thing, if they only realized what sort of a street we lived in before, what sort of neighbours we had. We weren't neighbours, we were one family and that is the truth. We were like one family. I think it was terrible and our first week's rent was one pound two and eleven [£1 2s. 11d.] not six and seven [6s. 7d.] like we was paying in Dock Street.

We moved in in October – my son was born in the December and I loved my kids. I had two daughters and I really loved my kids, but I just didn't want to be even bothered with my son. I wasn't with him all the time like I should have been. I was upstairs crying all the time. I broke my flippin' heart, and that's the truth, when I moved from there, and I think most of 'em did.

CHAPTER FIVE

Call me Mother

During the first half of the century as many as one in ten of all children were partly or wholly brought up by someone other than their natural parents – foster mothers, housemothers in institutions, relatives, siblings, step-parents, or nannies. The standard of care among substitute parents varied greatly from one family or institution to another, but generally it seems to have been low, often characterized by lack of love, regimentation and harsh punishments. Many of those brought up by substitute parents seem to have had an unhappy childhood.

One of the more successful forms of substitute parenting at this time was the nanny who was especially important in the upbringing of middle- and upper-class children. Nanny – or Nurse as she was sometimes called – was responsible for the care and control of the children in her charge from babyhood until they left home to go to boarding school at around the age of eight. In the first decades of the century more than a quarter of a million nannies were looking after the children of the well-to-do with little or no interference from the parents. In the hierarchical world 'below stairs' Nanny enjoyed higher status and pay than most other domestic servants. Most nannies came from a rural working-class background – country girls were considered by their employers to be more honest and reliable than city girls. A girl could join a household as a nursery-maid or an under-nurse; after several years spent working under the household's nanny she would become a fully fledged one herself, usually by moving to new employers. From the 1900s nursery training colleges began to emerge, the most prestigious of which was the Norland Nursery School, originally based in Notting Hill, West London, which often attracted girls from slightly better-off families. The vast majority of nannies, however, continued to be trained on the job and had no college training or qualifications whatsoever.

Nannies were expected to work long hours with only Sunday afternoons off. This meant that few opportunities arose to meet anyone outside the family they served and many nannies remained spinsters, devoting their lives to the children they brought up. Nanny spent most of the day with the children, and would eat, live and sleep with them in the nursery. Her influence and responsibility were so great that she was expected to adopt the manners and social graces of the class that she served. Many nannies were traditional and disciplinarian in their attitudes to the children. Every day would revolve around a rigid timetable of washing, mealtimes, walks in the fresh air, playtime in the nursery and ritual meetings with parents, usually after tea. But despite the elaborate rules that governed this nursery world children often formed a close relationship with their nanny, whose job was to give them endless time and attention. They saw little of their parents and the love they felt for Nanny was sometimes stronger than that for their parents. When Nanny left it could be traumatic for the children and for Nanny herself.

While many middle- and upper-class parents chose to subcontract the upbringing of their children to other adults, at the poorer end of the social scale large numbers of children were 'taken into care', due to circumstances beyond the control of their families, and placed in residential institutions. The first decades of the century were the heyday of the 'live in' institution in which staff assumed the role of parents. The prevalence of ill health and poverty meant that many parents could not cope with bringing up their children, and high mortality at childbirth meant that many others, left with just a father, were placed in orphanages. Illegitimacy, too, added to the numbers in institutions, for an unmarried mother was seldom able or allowed to keep her child. Children caught stealing or committing other offences were removed from their families and placed in reformatories for a long period, while many disabled children went to institutions for the blind, the deaf and the 'crippled'. More than 100,000 children were brought up in a wide range of live-in institutions at this time.

Many of the prejudiced assumptions made about the undeserving poor were often used against children in institutions by the staff, who considered them part of the 'great unwashed', ignorant, immoral and feeble-minded. In short, they needed to be saved from themselves and their families – if they had any family. One of the main aims was to instil in them a discipline to prevent them becoming a public nuisance or living on Poor Law hand-outs in the future. To achieve this, a strict, regimented daily routine was established in most institutions which revolved around early rising, cold baths, drill, simple manual labour and, above all, corporal punishment. Also, the authorities often tried to keep any contact with parents to a minimum, viewing them as a potentially corrupting or disruptive influence. In many institutions parents were only allowed to visit once a year.

Although a few of the staff had genuine affection and concern for the children in their charge, many of the matrons, sisters, teachers, officers and masters who acted in *loco parentis*, abused the extensive powers they enjoyed over the young inmates. They were often poorly paid, untrained, and the institutions in which they worked were overcrowded and chronically short of funds and facilities. All this encouraged autocratic methods and some acted with extraordinary cruelty and brutality. Since many institutions were run by voluntary societies and charities, with little monitoring by government inspectors, there were few checks on what went on and nobody to whom the children inside could complain.

From the 1900s onwards, however, a new trend in residential care for children stressed the key role of the substitute parent in helping inmates to develop into useful citizens. This could only work properly, it was thought, if institutions were dramatically reduced in size and attempted to reproduce a 'family atmosphere'. 'Scattered homes', providing care for twenty or thirty children, each one run by a 'housemother', gradually came to replace the big orphanages, especially during the inter-war years. Although these homes were often an improvement on the old impersonal institutions of the past, their regimes invariably remained harsh and disciplinarian. According to many brought up in them, they were characterized by a lack of real love on the part of the house-mother. who was often seen as no substitute for the parent or parents the children had lost.

Another trend in substitute parenting which became very important in the first half of the century was fostering. or 'boarding out'. and adoption. an option increasingly favoured by institutions caring for children. Foster parents would usually be paid a weekly sum to take in an 'orphan' and. in the 1900s. the Poor Law authorities boarded out around 8000 children every year. The advantages of this system for the authorities were that it was cheap and. if the new parents were genuinely loving. it seemed to be beneficial to the child. However. many women fostered children for purely mercenary reasons and recurrent scandals exposed the plight of children who were abused and half starved. The boarding-out system had a bad reputation in the early party of the century.

Fostering and *de facto* adoption by relatives was often more successful and had been practised for centuries among poor famil-ies. It became widespread within the extended family networks that grew up in working-class communities in the big towns and cities. Children whose parents could not provide for them or whose mother was unmarried or dead were often fostered by other. slightly better-off family members. They would 'take in' their own rather than see the children grow up in the workhouse or an orphanage. Sometimes a child would be fostered for several months or years to help a struggling relative; in other cases. the arrange-ment might become more or less permanent with an aunt or grandmother taking the role of substitute parent. Adoption within the family most often involved illegitimate children who from birth would be given to a relative to bring up as their own. to avoid the stigma of bastardy falling upon the family. Many of these children were never told who their real parents were and the substitute parent sometimes lived in fear of them finding out the truth.

If there were no relatives to take a child who the parents could not or did not want to support. some advertised them in local newspapers. In a few cases a child would be 'sold' perhaps for a few pounds. More commonly, advertising was seen as a way of finding a 'good' substitute parent without involving any institution of the Poor Law in the transaction.

Middle-class mothers who were unmarried or who had fallen on hard times — often due to the death of their husband — would advertise in the columns of the *Exchange and Mart*. They usually made the point that their child was of 'gentle birth' and that they were looking for a 'suitable' parent. The transaction would be made through a solicitor and the family background of the adopting parents would be scrutinized to ensure that the child was going to a 'good class' of home. Formal documents, handing over custody of the child, would then be signed by all the parties involved. With poor working-class mothers there were usually no such formalities.

A few examples of the extraordinary correspondence that sometimes accompanied the adoption of a middle-class child around the turn of the century have been preserved by the Children's Society. One letter dated 27 June 1898, sent by the London solicitors acting for a woman who had advertised her three-year-old daughter Olive for adoption, began:

Your reply to the advertisement in the *Exchange and Mart* relating to the adoption of a little girl has been handed to us to reply to. The child referred to is of gentle birth, not deformed and has no physical defect of any kind. She is pretty and remarkably intelligent. She had been well brought up and cared for and the only reason for seeking the adoption mentioned in the advertisement is that the mother, who is the surviving parent, is unable, due to a reverse of fortune, to bring up the child in a way befitting her station.

After providing two references as to his social standing and guaranteeing he would bring up Olive as a 'private lady', the adopter was sent a letter from the solicitors finalizing the arrangements for his adoption of the child — just two weeks after his initial reply to the advertisement.

We have decided to send the child to you but we feel that we cannot entrust it in the care of the guard of the train as you suggest and therefore propose that the lady under whose care it has hitherto been should take it to your house provided that as the distance is a longer one [the adopter lived in Hull] you could put up the lady for the night. The expenses of the journey will of course be borne by the mother and the clothing of the child handed to you . . . All we want is the child to be properly taken care of and brought up and that we shall have the right either ourselves or by any other person nominated by us, who is not of course to be the mother, to see the child from time to time. This is however a right which would be exercised in a very reasonable degree.

In the first decades of the century there was no adoption law and the natural parents had the legal right to claim their child back, even if an apparently legally binding contract had been signed. This occasionally led to custody battles and blackmail by the natural parents who would demand money of the adopters in exchange for the right to keep the child a little longer.

However, more and more genuine middle-class couples desperately wanted to adopt a child. The role of the married middle-class woman was increasingly revolving around the home and the care of children; those who were childless often felt a strong desire to adopt. There were, also, many widows from the First World War who did not want to remarry but who wanted a child. With this growing demand for 'adoptable' children went an increasing dissatisfaction with the lack of any law protecting adoptive parents. Pressure for reform helped to bring about the Adoption Act of 1926, which gave adopting parents full legal rights over their child and safeguarded them against interference from the natural parents.

This legislation led to a further surge of demand from would-be substitute parents. Legal adoption was dealt with exclusively by church-based organizations; local authorities did not become involved until the late 1950s. Children's homes began to set up adoption agencies and departments to deal with the many requests for 'orphans'. In the 1930s around two or three thousand children

170

were adopted each year in Britain and demand was massively outweighing supply in the Church of England Children's Society homes; Only one in ten got the child they wanted: girls were generally more popular than boys, and few wanted to take on babies or infants in nappies. The age of five was the most favoured for adoption.

The low opinion of institutions for their child inmates was reflected in their reluctance to let parents adopt straight away: they normally insisted on a probationary period of a few years' fostering, fearing that the institutional child, because of hereditary and personality defects, might not come up to the expectations of the new parents. The children were given intelligence and personality tests, and information of this, together with details on their natural parents, would be passed on to the new parents for consideration. Adoptive parents were vetted to a rather lesser degree by the adoption agencies, although they were particularly concerned with their religious beliefs and practices. Anyone wishing to adopt before the Second World War had to prove that they were regular church-goers.

A minority of children returned to their institution after a 'trial period', either having rejected or having been rejected by their new parents. In most cases, however, according to the records of the adoption agencies, they liked their new homes, and their new parents liked them. Certainly, for most of the children involved, to be living in a family home must have been preferable to institutional life. Adoption was an important factor in reducing the huge numbers of children in homes and orphanages during the early decades of the century.

One final form of substitute parenting was step-parents. Traditionally the presence of a step-mother or step-father in a family had been due to the death of one of the natural parents. The numbers of parents who died young from ill health, poverty and lack of proper medical care meant that step-parents were not uncommon during the first half of the century. In the 1900s either the mother or father died in around one in every six families with dependent children. The gradual decline in Victorian mourning

171

rituals and taboos on remarriage after the death of a partner, together with the mass slaughter of a generation of husbands and fathers during the First World War, gave an important impetus to second marriages. By the 1920s around one in three of all bereaved parents with children would remarry. However, with improvements in the standard of health of parents, remarriage because of a partner's death gradually declined.

Second marriage through divorce would − much later in the century − become much more widespread and important than second marriage through death. Although divorce was on the increase in the early part of the century, it remained quite rare. In the 1900s there were only about 500 divorces a year in a married population of around 11 million. But when legislation during the inter-war years made divorce slightly easier, the rate went up to around two to three thousand cases each year. In the first two decades of the century the divorce laws were heavily biased in favour of the husband and father, and many who wanted custody of their children obtained it.

Little is known about how step-parents treated children during the first half of the century. It is an area dominated by folk myths of wicked step-mothers, step-fathers and step-sisters. Fairy tales like *Cinderella* and *Snow White* express a deep-rooted anxiety and fear of step-families (this represents the other side of the idealization of 'normal' family life) and memories of step-parents have probably been influenced by them and by loyalty to natural parents. The notion of the cruel and wicked step-mother − which recurs in much of the reminiscence we have collected − was also probably fuelled by the loyalty of the child to its mother − if only to her memory: the step-mother could not replace or displace her. The step-mother's role was difficult and potentially stressful: she was usually expected to step into the mother's shoes, to look after her newly acquired step-children as if they were her own, and develop a close and loving relationship with them. The evidence we have collected, even allowing for the child's emotional reaction against its step-mother, suggests that this rarely happened, and that relationships between step-mothers and step-children were often characterized by conflict and rejection on both sides. The folk myth of the step-mother seems to have been grounded, at least to some extent, in experience.

Discrimination against step-children and favouritism towards natural children by parents in second marriages seems to have been very common. Step-children were often excluded from 'treats', made to do much of the domestic work around the home and were punished especially harshly. In the worst cases, girls might be sexually abused by their step-father; this was recognized in the early reports of child-saving agencies like the NSPCC. In the memories we have collected, the treatment of children was often most brutal when the step-parent had no natural children of their own. They frequently had no interest in the children they had 'inherited' and perceived them as a hindrance to the ideal relationship they wanted, as well as being new, costly, time-consuming and rivals for the love of the new partner.

Step-parents were set to become an increasingly common phenomenon in the second half of the century as divorce became substantially easier: the divorce rate increased 1000 times between the 1900s and the 1990s.

Charlotte Huggett

Charlotte was born in 1903 in Wateringbury in Kent. Her father was a farm labourer and she had two brothers and two sisters. Charlotte left school at fourteen and got a job as a daily girl. walking four miles to work every day until she started as a nursery-maid when she was fifteen. She became a nanny at the age of nineteen in 1922. and worked as one until recently: she has cared for over forty children. Charlotte has never married.

I always thought what a lovely job it would be to be a nanny and so I started off by looking after two little boys. I was put into a big house when I was fifteen. I was to help in the nursery and I grew up from there to be nanny. I was made nanny when I was nineteen. So I was really nursery trained not college trained.

You were always called Nanny. Nanny meant a great thing to you when you suddenly became nanny and you didn't have to wear a cap, that was one of the greatest privileges, not to wear a cap. Because you'd read books about nannies and you were very thrilled to be a nanny. I still am called Nanny – I still enjoy being Nanny.

I've always loved children. And as a nanny you're responsible for the child from the time it wakes up until it goes to bed at night. You're responsible for its manners at the table, you're responsible for the way it talks, you're responsible for it to be polite, which is a great thing, I think, politeness.

You went round to your children and gave them biscuits to start the day while you were getting washed and dressed, and then you got them all up for breakfast and then mostly you took them out because the parents always liked their children to be out, and you tried to make the walk as interesting as possible. And then you brought them in and gave them lunch, then after lunch they always had an hour's rest. They had a good tea, and, well, six o'clock was bedtime but before six they used to go down and see their parents.

The children were quite strangers to their mothers because the mother would come up into the nursery in the morning and just see them and then the children, quite often, didn't see them until the end of the day, when they went down to see their parents in the drawing room.

I think it was quite a torture for the children sometimes because they didn't know what to do with Mother when they were down there. They were rather in awe of their mothers because their mother was always very beautifully dressed and that was different from the nannies and the nursery. To see this lady coming in all beautifully dressed and their father. Well, the father seemed to lead an isolated life and he liked to see the children now and again, but if we met him in the garden he didn't understand. One day the children were in the garden and he said, 'It's all right I'll look after them.' But he didn't. One child fell in the pond because he wasn't looking after them and so after then he had them down to his study after tea and one day the children came up with handfuls of gold sovereigns which he'd given the children to play with because he didn't know what to do with the children there. They were, sort of, quite strangers to him.

Usually they were only with their parents for about a quarter of an hour a day, then I had to go down and fetch them to come up to the nursery where one played with them or amused them until it was bedtime.

The mother would come in and give them a quick kiss and say, 'Well, darling, what are you going to do today?' And the children would chatter on what they were going to do but they always looked up at Nanny to see if she approved of what they were going to do or say.

She would sometimes come over and say, 'You're a little bit pale, my darling, aren't you, this morning?' And when her mother had gone one little girl used to look at herself in the brass knob and say, 'Do I look a little bit pale this morning?' taking off what the mother always said.

The mother would tell you her plans for the day if it involved the children or the nannies. You always took advice from the mother what they should wear – she would always tell you what they were to wear but the children looked at you, it was you who sat them on your knee and nursed them. If they wanted the children dressed in a peculiar way I dressed them in a peculiar way because I knew in the end it would get round to my way. I've always respected the parents and respected what they wanted of me. But if they wanted us out wet or fine sometimes the children would like to be in so I insisted that we had an afternoon in where the children were able to play their games and able to chat. If they were in Hyde Park I used to take clothes out and re-dress them so that they could climb trees and then dress in their Hyde Park clothes to come home, in case the mother came past in the car. They had to look a certain way. Or it might be that the mother was going calling, they would go out calling and leave a card. It was rather torture for the nanny to go out with them then because the mother would sit and criticize how their hair was done, so they had to have their nails cleaned and every-thing in order. 'I'd like the children to be ready by three', and you would have to be in the hall waiting at three o'clock, not a minute after. It was rather a painful thing to be driving with the mother, although you felt very privileged. I was never nervous of the mother; I was very frightened of her criticism that I hadn't done my work as a nanny.

The children were much happier to be up in the nursery with Nanny. They regarded Nanny rather as a friend instead of their mother and father. They were quite happy for the parents to go out. I've seen the children wave happily to the parents going off abroad and I've seen the tears coming down their cheeks when Nanny was going out and quite often the children said, 'Why do you have to go out? Mummy doesn't know how to look after us, why do you have to go out? You know how to look after us.'

When the children were punished they had their sweets stopped and that seemed to be a great punishment or go up to their room – you sent them up to their room – and one little girl was sent up to her room and I found all the contents of her money box, everything, put on my pillow because she was so sorry that she'd been naughty. Sometimes the mother would come into the nursery and say that she would like the children to come down into the drawing room after tea and the child had been told that it was to go to its bedroom after tea so I would say to the child, 'Your mother wants you after tea. Mummy mustn't be punished for what you've done so you go down today but you'll go up to your room tomorrow night.' When tomorrow night came I would say, 'Well, you've been specially good so we'll forget about it.' And that's how you worked it out.

Being out such a lot with the children you got terribly tired and I can remember waking up finding myself asleep in the bath because I was so tired. But you had to be up and ready the next morning and not show your tiredness, but we were allowed to go out to a dance once a month. You had one half-day from two o'clock until ten – you had to be in by ten or you were locked out – and then you had half-day every other Sunday and sometimes you had a Sunday morning to go to church but not always.

When we were on holiday the mother and father came but they always stayed in a separate hotel and not the same hotel. Some days we didn't even see the parents, the children depended on Nanny. On the beach we would make sandcastles and show them the boats. It was very, very exciting because we lived in a very isolated place in the country. I think the children enjoyed the freedom of the sea and also they didn't have to wear such fine clothes. They were wet or dirty – it really didn't matter.

You never thought of it as being a job that you were being paid for, but the love of the children, I think, was a great reward. You couldn't possibly look after somebody else's children without the love. And I think the children must have looked upon me as a substitute for their mother because if they were ill it was always Nanny they called for to sit beside their bed.

The very first time I had to leave my children for another position, having been with them for six years and seeing them from baby stage to children running about and having a governess, I was so ill that I had to go back again to see them, to make quite sure they were happy. I could see that they still loved me but I could see that I'd got to go on and I'd try not to get too fond of the children but, of course, you do. A few days before I was going to leave the children I talked to them, telling them that somebody else was coming and then somebody else did come in and was with them for a few days, and gradually they took them out for walks, and gradually they did things for them, so that the shock wasn't too much for the children. The day that one left one didn't say goodbye, you just told them that you were going off and that the next person would be looking after them, but there were lots of tears all through those few days. Because you yourself was feeling very poorly about it and so the children themselves felt the atmosphere that you were going to leave. I was always a person that never cried – you controlled your emotions in the nursery, you never showed in front of the children that you were angry or cross or something had upset you or they'd upset you, you always controlled yourself.

I think that what keeps a nanny going is all the remembrances of all their children and being very interested in the children writing to you after you'd left. You keep in touch even with those young people so you feel you've got a big family. I had lots of letters from them – sometimes a little bunch of feathers and sometimes a few leaves that they'd found in the woods. All these children, they all meant as though they were my own children and I still think of some of them as being my own children although they're grown up and one of them is a grandma. I still think of her as being one of my children.

Left: 'Nanny' Charlotte Huggett escorting one family's children on a holiday abroad in 1936.

Below: Charlotte having a picnic with some of her charges on a day out in 1930.

Bottom: Nannies taking their charges for a walk in a London Park during the 1930s. At that time there were more than a quarter of a million nannies looking after the children of the well-to-do. (*Mary Evans Picture Library*)

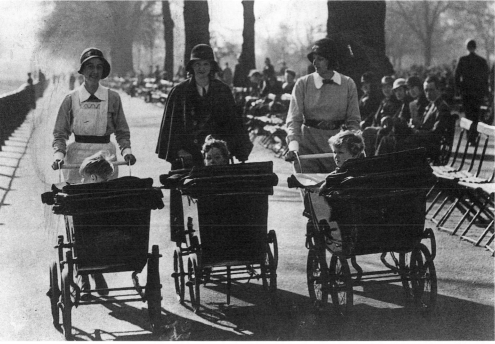

Above: Kate Organ's three youngest sisters in the dresses that Kate made for them to attend their mother's funeral in 1931.

Top Left: Kate Organ's mother. She died of tuberculosis in 1931 when Kate was just nineteen.

Top Right: Kate Organ, pictured in 1934. After the death of her mother Kate became a substitute parent and brought up her brothers and sisters.

Below Left: Marjorie Jacques, *right*, and her elder sister in the 1930s. Marjorie had polio when she was a baby and was sent to the Chailey Heritage Institution for Disabled Children in 1923.

Below Right: Vera Butterworth, *right*, with her step-father and step-sister in the 1930s. Vera's family was destitute, often having to sleep in workhouses. She was taken in by her step-parents when she was six and lived with them over the cake shop that they owned.

Top Left: Lavinia O'Donoghue's three children in the 1930s, with Reg in the centre. When the war started the children were evacuated to Newton Abbot in Devon.

Top Right: Mary Cole and her daughter, Valerie, on Clapham Common in 1943.

Above: A father saying goodbye to his son. As children were evacuated their fathers were being called up to serve in the armed forces. (*The Hulton-Deutsch Collection*)

Top Left: Mary Cole's husband with Valerie after he returned from the Navy in 1944. He did not see her for three years after she was born.

Top Right: Air-raid wardens search through the wreckage of houses and shelters after London's first bombing raid on 23 August 1940. Although a few thousand people died in the first weeks of bombing in London the death toll was not as high as had originally been feared. (*The Hulton-Deutsch Collection*)

Above: Mothers sheltering with their children in fields in Kent. Many families quickly lost faith in the official shelters in the cities and trekked out into the countryside, desperately seeking safety. (*Popperfoto*)

Top: A mother and her daughter outside their air-raid shelter in Downham, south-east London. Many suburban families spent their nights in Anderson shelters in the back garden, taking their bedding and food down with them. (*Topham*)

Above Left: Kathleen Teale-Jones and her first son, who was born in 1942.

Above Right: Elsie Huntley with her family. Derek, who died after a direct hit on their air-raid shelter, is on the left.

Top Left: Edith Throp, dancing with her first husband in 1936. Edith was one of many women whose marriages ended as a result of the long separations from their partners and the wartime strain.

Top Right: Jessie Shuttleworth's husband in Burma, 1943. At the end of the war Jessie had a nervous breakdown and he was sent back to England.

Above Left: The photograph that Florrie Dukes sent to her husband in 1945. When he received it he realized that she was ill and was sent back to England on compassionate leave.

Above Right: Jessie Shuttleworth and her first daughter in 1944. At this time Jessie was working for twelve hours every night at a factory making Churchill tanks.

Right: A mother reckoning up her family's weekly ration allowance. Women had to spend long hours queuing for a few basic ingredients out of which they then had to produce a meal. (*The Hulton-Deutsch Collection*)

Below: A welcome-home scene for a father returning at the end of the war. After the initial euphoria of the reunions many families found it difficult to pick up the threads of everyday life. (*Topham*)

Mary Siddall

Mary was born in 1899 in Rhosllanerchrugog, North Wales. Her father was a coal miner. Her mother died in childbirth in 1902 and when Mary was fourteen her father remarried. By this time the family had moved to Oldham. Mary's step-mother has three children of her own but Mary was the only one of the children who was sent out to work half-time in the cotton mill as a doffer. She met her husband, who also worked in the mill, in 1919 and they were married in 1921. They had ten children and Mary now has twenty-two grandchildren, twenty-three great-grandchildren and one great-great grandchild.

Well, my own mother died when she were twenty-six, with a second baby, when I was two years old, but twelve years later my father got married to this second mother. She'd three children of her own.

I thought she was so nice and then she changed, when she got married. She had no love for me, I never had no love off her, I were nobody's child, really. Me father thought, seemed to think, more about his step-children with his second wife. Always jealous of me, she used to pawn me things to save me going out. I'm looking for me shoes: 'Well, I've pawned them,' she says, because we've had no money, so I couldn't go out. It were the tricks she did. I hated her, I did really.

When my step-sisters were ready for bed, and my step-mother used to kiss them goodnight, and God bless, when it come to my turn she didn't kiss me. I used to say to her, 'You love me too, don't you, Mam?' She never answered me. I used to cry. Never made a fuss of me at all. I might have been an outcast. I knew very well I wasn't wanted.

I was the little slave at home. I used to come from work, blacklead the grate, clean the fire, then all the pans, with pan shine, see your face in them. She were very particular, you know, I used to help her to scrub clothes, she was taking in washing and I used to help.

179

My step-mother asked us to light the fire and I couldn't light it, so she got hold of the lamp oil bottle and hit me on the head with it. Because there was a gash I said, 'Let's go to the doctor's', and I told the doctor a lie – I'd climbed in a field underneath some railings – to save her from getting in trouble. My father didn't know, I told him the same story, and another time she hit me with a shovel. My father would have murdered her for things he knew she'd done to me. I were frightened of her, she used to leather me for next to nothing nearly. I daren't tell me father, even me sisters didn't know half what I went through.

Eleven o'clock at night, they were in bed. She was having me scrubbing, helping to do, and I had to go to work at four in morning, half-time. I were twelve when I started, half-time I worked at this mill, be there at six, to twelve o'clock, and then go to school in the afternoon. And we was that tired, we used to fall asleep, doing our writing, we used to work hard for that half a crown. And I got, must have had a twopence out of it. I was frightened of all the machinery, everything was so big to me, but I worked there a good few years while I were eighteen. I used to stand hours. I were the only one that went half-time. The others didn't go, I were the oldest at home, you see, I were happier there than when I were at home, had more company. I used to take some coppers out. She used to take it, but I had to wait on pocket money, give her my wage, very seldom I had pocket money out of it. My step-sisters, they got what they wanted, what they could afford, anyway. They'd often have an apple, orange or a piece of cake.

When I were about seventeen I come home eleven o'clock one night, I'd been roller skating – I used to love it, you know. She met me at the door. She says, 'Where have you been up to now?' and she went on and on and on and on, I couldn't stand no more. If I'd have had a knife I'm sure I'd have stabbed her, I could have murdered her. I give her one across the face. Shook her up a bit, you know, I thought she'd have come after me again – the door was open to run out – but she didn't. It frightened her. And I left home for three days, and went to live with me aunties. I felt like committing suicide. I felt like throwing meself in the canal, I were only little, you know, and I couldn't stand much more. I were really depressed and I got so far down and I saw this water, I looked at it and I thought, 'No, I can't, I can't go in, I've all the world to live in.'

I were glad to get married out of the road although I were twenty-one, but I went through it all them years, stuck it.

Mary Morton Hardie

Mary was born in Wishaw, near Motherwell, in 1912. She had two sisters. Her father worked as a civil servant but in 1914 joined the army to fight in the First World War and was posted abroad. In 1916 he was declared missing, presumed killed. After several months Mary's mother met another man who came to live with the family. At the end of the war, Mary's father returned home from the prisoner-of-war camp where he had spent the past two years. He was horrified to find that his wife, thinking he was dead, was pregnant by the man she was now living with. Mary's father filed for divorce and was given custody of his daughters. After placing them in a home for six months he remarried and took them to live with their step-mother on the Isle of Rothesay. The girls were forbidden even to talk about their mother and had no contact with her until they were in their late teens. Mary met her husband, James, in 1929. They had eight children and now have eleven grandchildren and six great-grandchildren.

M y mother received a telegram to say that he was missing, believed killed, in 1916. Of course, everyone was very upset but after two years had gone by my mother took up with another man who was a tailor and the two of them tailored in our house. We were all very happy. We never thought about Father being away. Then right at the end of the war another telegram came to say that Father had been released from a prisoner-of-war camp, was on his way home and would be arriving the next Saturday. Well, my mother fainted. My uncle Hugh, as we called him, he was really upset, Mother was eight months' pregnant to him at the time. So, on the Saturday morning Mother disappeared with Hugh.

We all went, my sisters and I, with my father's family to meet him coming off the boat train. And we brought him home. The first thing he did was to look at us and then he said, 'Where's Mary?' That was my mother's name. My granny told him what had happened. He was very angry, his face was scarlet. And he said, 'I've heard about this happening to others, but I never thought it would happen to me.'

Next morning when we wakened up, we were told we were going into a home and that he was going to sell the little house. Grandmother couldn't possibly look after three of us, she was too old. Dad was furious and applied for a divorce.

Our mama was a very sweet and happy lady, always singing, cuddling us and giving us little treats and titbits which were difficult to come by during the war. She always managed to give us little parties for our birthdays. She asked for custody of us children in court. But Father said, 'The slut'll have none of my children.' He was so angry about her being pregnant. I think that was the worst bit for him to swallow.

We were put into this home where we stayed for six months. Then it was suddenly announced that he was coming to take us away. He had bought a house in Rothesay and he was married to someone.

Father took us to the boat which would take us to Rothesay. It was crowded and we dashed up on board to the top deck. That was quite exciting – we came down on to Rothesay pier and it was beautiful. It was all set out in the sunshine, sparkling. Lots of people around, big families with children. I was looking forward very much to having a home with Father and, I suppose, his new wife too.

So at last we came to the house, White House Crescent was the place, and it was there that I had my first glimpse of my stepmother and she was a very pretty woman. But from the very start she said she'd have nothing to do with us. Father had to take us in hand. He said I was to be called Minnie. And I said, 'Why? I don't like that name.' 'Because your mother's name is Mary and I don't want to hear that name ever again.' I felt very hurt that he should so want to get rid of any connection with my mother. And he said, 'This is your new mother, call her Mother.' I said, 'I will not call her Mother, that's not my mother.' And he gave me a resounding slap. Beatrice looked at me, his new wife, and I always remember the awful look she gave me as though she hated me from that moment.

We were put in the kitchen immediately. We were not to go near the sitting room or our new mother's bedroom, and not to use her bathroom. There was a toilet in the kitchen and we were to sleep in the kitchen which we didn't think very much of.

A timetable was laid out for us and we had to do all the housework. My father had us all lined up like a regiment of soldiers. My sister had the fireplace to do, the great range to clean, blacklead every morning. I had the sitting-room fire to clean out, then I had the porridge to make, breakfast to set, and little Gina, she had to clean the spoons, put them down and brush the shoes every morning and Father's too, for the office. We were up about six o'clock to get all this done. Then Beatrice came down for breakfast just about half past eight and looked all about her to see that we had done all our jobs. If it wasn't done we were told what our punishment would be when we got home. Then we took a tram car to Rothesay Academy. As we got out of the door we had to call out and say, 'Goodbye, Mother,' to let all the neighbours see that we called her Mother. I would say, 'Goodbye,' and mumble, which made her very angry.

She didn't want us to go to school. It took money away from her, paying these expensive fees, and she was determined that we would not do our lessons properly and she used to burn our books if she got the opportunity or tear them up. We did our homework on the tram car coming home and put our books hidden away in the kitchen.

Every day we were in a tram car and we watched all the people and all the families with their children playing on the sands, the donkeys, the organ-grinders, jugglers. But we were to come straight home every night, come home, have the vegetables all done and ready for the dinner at night, for Father coming home.

We weren't allowed out on the beach at all. On Sunday Father, step-mother and us three walked along the prom, which was about two miles, and we could see everything that was going on, but we had to walk sedately behind them, all the way there and all the way back. Father thought this was wonderful, my step-mother made us not to come within six steps of her.

One day we were just a little late coming home from school and she put me in the coal cellar. I was terrified of the dark, I was terrified of rats and I was in there for a long time crying and screaming and banging on the door. When it was time to fill the coal pails, I was let out. I had to fill about six coal pails and carry them in. And every time I went in she gave me another slap, 'Just to help you on your way,' she said.

My step-mother was very free with her hand. She was always slapping us for the least thing. But I had very long hair and she just loved to pull me. The worst bit was when she took either Father's belt or the stair rod to us. That was very painful. She never left a mark where it was visible – always across the shoulders, the buttocks or the legs. She made out to Father that she was a wonderful mother to us. 'They're only blathering,' she used to say, if we told him or he'd seen us crying. She said, 'There's not a mark on them.' We felt like saying, 'Look, look at our legs, look.' It was on the tip of our tongues to say, 'Mother hit us,' but we couldn't, we just couldn't get it out.

She really hated us. In fact, I think she wanted to make us so miserable that Father would send us away back to Granny. She wouldn't even allow us to wash in the bathroom so we had to wash in the kitchen sink. We had an old sack thing for a bit of towelling and once the teacher sent us home to get properly washed and this, of course, was a great insult. And she scrubbed us with a scrubbing brush till we just about lost our flesh. We were scarlet, scarlet and screaming when it was bath-time.

During the school holidays we had to work, spring-clean the house, never allowed out. If visitors came we were all shut up in the spare bedroom and told not to make a sound on pain of a good thrashing afterwards. She didn't want us to be recognized as her children which would have made her out to be too old. She thought of herself as a sweet young thing.

Right from the start I wanted to find my mother. It took me

185

seven years, but eventually I did. I traced her to Ireland when I was sixteen years of age and I sailed over to Belfast. I'd looked forward all those years, expecting her to treat me as she treated me as a child. I was sick with longing to meet my mother, somehow I never pictured her with a family. I remembered when I last saw her. I got off at the pier, and I stood and nobody was left on the pier, and there was only one lady sitting there, a very stout lady dressed all in black with two great baskets, and I went up to her and it was something about her eyes that I remembered. She says, 'Hello, Mary, how are you or do we call you Minnie now? Do you not recognize me? I've something to ask you. Call me your aunt. I have a young family and they don't know that I have a family, so don't call me mother.'

I was so disappointed I really cried all night and I couldn't understand. It was Uncle Hugh who I remembered and he comforted me. It was him who said, 'Look how the cinders in the fire glow.' I was so far down in spirit that I felt life wasn't worth living, and he said, 'Now, if you blow on a cinder it'll fan into flame. You'll find something that'll make your life worth living, and the cinder will glow for you.'

And it wasn't long after that that I met James. We just fell in love right away. He was genuine, no nonsense. Very sensible and he made me feel life was worth living. He made life just stable. Before that I didn't know anything, where I was going to be or if I had any future. So we realized that our future was together. I was alone in the world, so we had a little money between us and we bought a little house and I thought I was in heaven and I have been ever since.

186

Violet Hudspith

Violet was born in 1923 in Kenilworth, Warwickshire. She had two brothers and three sisters. Her father was a master cobbler but was not married to her mother who was left to look after the children alone. They lived in a basement flat in Leamington Spa and Violet's mother worked as a cleaner to try to support her children. When Violet was seven, her mother was caught taking a tin of meat from a shop. She was prosecuted and the six children were placed in different homes. Their mother was denied access to them and Violet did not see her again until she traced her many years later. Violet grew up under the harsh regime of a 'scattered home' in Charlotte Street in Leamington Spa. She left school at thirteen and became a domestic servant. She met her future husband in 1941. They had two sons in 1942 and 1948. She now has one grandchild.

We lived in this basement flat and we were poor. My mother got a cleaning job across the road. My brother and I used to go up to the hills and pick these primroses. We used to pick quite a few wild flowers and bring them back and I remember sitting tying them into little bundles, you know, and then we used to go top of the Parade and sell them, a penny a bunch. We used to go back and give the money to my mother and then she could go and buy food, we were more or less on the breadline. You have to admire her when you think she'd got five of us by then and I can't remember being hungry but I must have been.

She was a very loving mother. I can remember her cuddling me. I can remember going out with my mother, going shopping. I remember we went into the shop and my mother did some shopping, we came out, crossed over the road and all of a sudden a man appeared and he put his hand on my mother's shoulder and he said, 'I'm arresting you for shop-lifting.' I looked up in amazement. We were taken down to the local police station, my mother had to appear in court the next morning. All I can remember seeing was this tin of meat, that's all it was, on the dock. And I remember seeing my mother standing there. I suppose her idea was to take it home and make a pie so she could feed us all. She looked absolutely ill.

The judge said, 'You will go to prison and your children will be taken off you.' The next thing we were whipped off in this car to the workhouse, then they graded us and just separated us.

I was sent to this home in Charlotte Street, my brother went to a home in Warwick, my other brother went to another home and my sister went to what you call a nursery school, and my eldest sister, she would be fourteen, I don't know what became of her.

When I got there I remember this woman, she wore glasses, she was tall and she said, 'You're going to live here and you're never going to see your mother.' I must have looked at her and I started to cry. And I did cry for two or three days. I was just heartbroken and I ended up going to hospital. I can remember this terrible crying. I remember standing at the stairs bottom and crying. I wouldn't let anybody touch me, you know. I couldn't believe that me mother wasn't there with me. I was calling for her. The housemother said to me, 'You will call me Mother.' It really took a lot of saying to call her Mother. I was resentful, very bitter. She was a very cruel person. You'd think she'd hear a little girl of seven crying, you'd have thought she'd have had a bit of feeling but she didn't. I was the lowest of the low, kind of thing, as far as she was concerned.

It was instilled in you that you just did not talk to anybody, you mustn't have an opinion about anything, you mustn't answer back, you mustn't speak until you were spoken to, no messing about there. The housemother had a way with that.

She was no cook, we all had to help with the cooking, and when we came home from school, like, she couldn't cook liver, it used to be raw and I couldn't eat it this day and she said, 'You're going to eat that dinner.' And I said, 'I can't, there's blood coming out of the liver.' Next morning at breakfast it was still there, I ate it by that time because I was hungry. If you sat down for meals, if you so much as scraped your chair or didn't sit down very quietly, or if you coughed or spoke that was a penalty in itself, you know, and I remember this one day, I don't know whether I smiled but I must have done something. That was the first experience I had of being beaten.

There used to be a little cubby-hole and she'd take you in there and she'd pull your dress or whatever you'd got on at the top, pinafore, and she would beat you across your back. And I remember going to school and we used to have to get undressed for gym and one of the girls saw it first and said to the teacher, 'Oh, she's got all marks on her back.' I remember her fetching the headmistress in, and she said, 'Oh, well, she's out the children's home, there's nothing we can do about it, just leave it.'

She knew I was afraid of the dark and at night time when we'd finished all our chores we used to have to put these traps out for the cockroaches. I was terrified of them you know and then we'd all go upstairs into what they called the sitting room and you had to sit and do your sewing and all your bits and bobs. And then she suddenly said to me, 'I want you to go downstairs and fetch me something,' and I swear to this day it was done on purpose and I used to be absolutely terrified going down these dark stairs – there was no light. And I had to find this thing which she had left down there, probably on purpose. I think she must have had a certain amount of pleasure doing it.

At Christmas time they used to march us in crocodile style up the Parade and they used to take us into Woolworth's, which was the cheapest shop you could get in them days, and they'd let you pick two little things, then you got those Christmas morning, with two sweets, I think, and an apple and an orange. There was a pantomime, it wasn't a thing of choice, it was a thing we had to do, we had to dress up and make the costumes and learn a few lines and then these people from the local authority would come and watch us, you know. But I never enjoyed doing it, for some reason. You had to pretend you were happy.

I couldn't smile, well, they knocked it out, they knocked

everything out, you had to become a zombie, really, it was unreal, there was no laughter, they knocked all the laughter out of you if you had any in you.

Course, Mother was never allowed to come and see us. That was one of the stipulations that the court made. She just became a memory but I never forgot her. She didn't do anything wrong in my eyes, she just tried to survive. She could have done hundreds of things, she could have lost us, she could have abandoned us, but she didn't. In their eyes she was just a thief. But they didn't look at her side of the story. She did it just for her children, really, she probably went hungry herself 'cos she was a very thin woman, that was her only crime.

I think they've got a lot to answer, 'cos they didn't only do it to her, they did it to us as well. My brother was very bitter, he came to see me, I would be eleven then, he'd be fifteen, he met me out of school, he shouldn't have done it but he did, and he said to me, 'I'm going away. I've got to get away from this lot, I can't take any more. I'm going to join the navy.' Which he did. They never found him.

Catherine Keating

Catherine was born in 1908 in Devon. the daughter of a forester. She had ten brothers and sisters. After leaving school when she was sixteen she started work as an assistant in a grocer's shop. She met her husband in 1929 when he was working as a stud-groom. They moved to Sussex together and he got a job as an operating theatre technician at Chailey Heritage Craft Institution for Crippled Children. In 1943 Catherine started work at Chailey as a care assistant. Then. like many institutions for children with disabilities. Chailey was run in a harsh. regimented manner. Catherine. however. managed to form close bonds with the children and soon became known as Mum by them all. She worked there until she retired. Catherine has two children. born in 1939 and 1943. and seven grandchildren.

At Chailey I was a care person and then I sort of graduated to Mum, and I thought that was marvellous because they all looked on me as sort of a mother figure, and I tried to treat them as my children. I was Mum to the staff and Mum to the children, Mum to everybody, so I used to take that as a great compliment. I'm sure a lot of them looked on me as a mother, you know, because I used to go back into my room very often and find them sitting there waiting for me. Perhaps they had a tummy pain or something had upset them.

When they came back after being on holiday at home we used to cope with it as well as we could, give them a little comfort and a cuddle and try and get them over it, there wasn't very much homesickness. It was always lovely to welcome them back, they seemed to get in a routine quite quickly, to listen to their little stories of incidents that happened at home, they all settled down very well. They used to say that they were coming back to 'this old dump', but they didn't really mean that, I don't think.

You used to let them sit for a while and perhaps give them a drink or something, and sit and talk to them, and then they'd go back quite happy and sometimes there was nothing wrong with them at all, but they just wanted to come and talk, you just used to accept that.

And the children used to talk to me quite frequently about their homes. 'Oh, dear, my mum and dad have some awful tiffs, you know, and my mum'll throw something at my dad.' A lot of the children had very difficult lives at home. Personally, I think sometimes that when the child went home it used to very often cause problems between the father and the mother. They were quite glad to get back to school again, you know, to get back to the atmosphere that we had there. You used to wonder sometimes because some of the children used to come back and say that, oh, well, I just stood at the gate all day and watched the people go past, and, you know, not much of a holiday for them.

I did advise them sometimes if they were sort of trying to be a bit silly or something like that, you used to try and talk to them as you would your own child, and they used to listen and they would act accordingly.

Very often I used to think that the discipline was very strict, but, then, with so many children you had to have discipline, otherwise it would be impossible to organize a place, you know, that size and you had to have discipline.

They used to sit at three long rows of tables in the dining hall and it was silence during the meal. If any of them were caught talking, they were in trouble, and they used to all pass the plates up at the end, a great clatter of plates coming up to the end, and it was all done in a very methodical manner.

You had to be very careful because each child had a number and you were never allowed to call them by their Christian name. They did have punishments, nothing very severe, I think a bit of cuffing used to go on, but the most that I can remember was standing in a corner, never any really harsh punishment. If there was punishment to be meted out, it had to be done through the house-master or the teaching staff.

There was no visiting. There was only one day a year that the parents were allowed to visit and that was really very strict, and it used to affect me quite a lot, you know, to think that they didn't see their parents until they went back again for their holiday. The children used to look forward very much to the visiting day to see their parents and everything used to be over so quickly, that we were – you know, they were back to the routine again, it didn't seem to have a lot of effect on them. Some of the smaller children missed their parents very much after they'd gone, but if you had to talk to them, and that, they used to come round quite quickly and there was never any long-term sadness.

It was against the rules at the Heritage to show too much affection towards the children and if they fell over or anything they had to get themselves up, you weren't allowed to help them up in any way, and I used to find that very hard sometimes, and used to feel as if you wanted to go and help them up. But there was lots of other ways that you could show affection to them. You used to have a talk to them and show affection in lots of other ways and they all used to appreciate that: it didn't feel as if they were badly treated, where a lot of the love sort of grew up between the children and oneself.

I used to do the best I could for them and I think they all appreciated the affection and the love – it's frightfully difficult when you have a large number of children.

I used to be very, very fond of the children and when they left we missed them very much, and it was nice to think they were just going away for the holidays, but when some of them left for good there were tears very often on both sides – used to feel the tears pricking your eyes when they used to come to say goodbye to you if they were leaving, and that was, you know, how I used to feel towards the children, I used to have that affection for them and I think they had that affection for me as well. There was too many of them to keep in touch. I very often think about the children. It's nice to look back and think of all these years, you know, and I really enjoyed my years at the Heritage. It was a marvellous experience.

Marjorie Jacques

Marjorie was born in 1920 in Guildford. Her father was in the army and fought in the First World War. The family moved around the country a great deal and they spent several years on the Isle of Sheppey. When Marjorie was eleven months old she contracted polio which left her legs, back and right arm paralysed. At the age of three she was sent to Chailey Heritage Craft Institution in Lewes, Sussex, a home for children with disabilities where she stayed until she was ten. In March 1949 Marjorie met her husband-to-be at a British Polio Fellowship dance. They married in September the same year. They have one son, Peter, who was born in 1951.

I had polio when I was eleven months and three weeks old. We were about three miles away from a hospital, and Mum had to put me in a pram, I was unconscious, and she had to put me and my sister in a pram and walk three miles to the nearest hospital. I was unconscious for three weeks. Then they found that I was paralysed and so they put sandbags all round me. Because my father was working in the army, Mum was finding it very hard going to look after me and my sister who was a year and five months older. She was having to take me to hospitals for treatment, massage and electrical treatment. Money was very short and when they promised that I would have treatment, medical treatment, and care and attention if I went away she thought it would be best. It took a lot of responsibility off her shoulders, made it easier for her life at home, obviously, because when I was at home she was massaging my legs every night of the week with olive oil. And they had to sign for me to stay in the institution until I was sixteen, thinking that I was going there for my own well-being and going to be looked after. So I was three and a half when I was sent to Chailey.

I had some treatment, I can remember having electrical treatment and being measured up for boots occasionally. But mainly the thing at Chailey was the routine and the terrible, terrible strictness.

I was always being punished for being naughty, or even just for doing nothing. If you wanted to go to the toilet in the night you had to crawl on your hands and knees and go down the dormitory through the hallway to the toilet, and then you had to lift yourself up off the floor onto the toilet, and it was an impossibility. And I was too scared to go. So consequently you'd go back to sleep and when you woke up in the morning, you found you'd wet the bed. When I was at home, I never wet the bed, ever. My mother used to come in about eleven o'clock at night and put me on the potty and I'd go, and I'd be all right for the rest of the night. No trouble at all. Well, you'd get punished for wetting at Chailey. I had to sit by my bed when I came home from school at night, go into the dormitory instead of going to play with the others, and I had to knit these black stockings. Those days you used to wear black stockings with a sort of a seam stitch up the back of the stocking. And if you knitted that wrongly you had to unpick it and do it all again. I knitted lots and lots of black stockings but I never ever remember finishing a pair! Well, then they brought my mug of tea in and bread and treacle and a lump of margarine on the plate. And that was my tea. And then I had to take the cup and the plate down to the inner bowl room, as it was called then, and wash it up, and once I slipped over on the floor and I broke the mug. So I got punished for that as well.

Or you were shut in an alcove overnight with just a bed and a chair and you had to sleep on your own there, and in the morning if the floor was dirty you had to scrub it with just an ordinary piece of soap and a scrubbing brush and a bucket of water. I can remember doing that several times. And this was the sort of thing that went on.

We had a sister there, I always remember she used to wear little pince-nez glasses and she looked over them, like, she was a very big lady, you know, she was a horror, nobody liked her, she was really horrible to us. Friday nights she used to make us drink this liquorice, for your bowels, and it was horrible stuff, mug full of liquorice and it was yellow, and if you didn't they'd pinch your nose and hold your head back. I don't think she liked me because I had plenty of go in me, I wouldn't kow-tow to her, and, she said something to me one day and I rebelled against it and I said, 'I'm gonna tell my mum of you when I go home. She won't let me come back.' I used to say things like that. And she got some sticking plaster, sent me to bed in the dormitory. I went to bed and she came round to put sticking plaster over my mouth. And it was on, oh, it must have been on there for an hour or two, until Matron came round in the evening for prayers and hymn, and before she arrived – before Matron arrived – one of the nurses would be sent round to take the sticking plaster off. And they'd come along and just rip it off. They were mentally cruel, more than anything.

On my birthday Mum would send me a lovely birthday cake. Now on one occasion I was naughty and they wouldn't let me have my birthday cake on my birthday. So, they locked it in a cupboard over by the dining hall and it was there the next day or the day after. 'Bout two days later they allowed it to come out. And when they took it out it was full of ants and had to be thrown away. And I couldn't have it at all. I was in tears.

I just didn't like being kept down under. And this is what they did and it was so regimented, it was really like being in the army. I think that I was just starved of love at the time, you didn't get any love and affection from anybody, not after you'd grown out of the baby stage. Nobody gave you a cuddle. And you certainly didn't have any teddy bears or things like that. You weren't allowed anything like that. I mean my teddy bear was at home. I can't remember having any toys at Chailey of my own.

We had visiting day on Easter Monday once a year. Now both of my parents couldn't afford to come so one year my father would come and another year my mother would come. And we looked forward to visiting day, we used to put on plays and we used to have to sing songs – do something on the stage. We used to have a walk around the grounds and around the gardens. I used to

196

show them my garden you see. then we would have to assemble in the schoolroom for the concert. Visiting day was a great occasion.

Finally the holidays would come round. That was what I used to look forward to most. going home. When we used to get in the train. going towards London we used to sing. 'Bye bye. Chailey.' And we used to sing that at the tops of our voices. And when we got to Victoria. there was Mum. or Dad. waiting. When I got home. of course. I was always hungry and I'd go through the cupboards. When I was home on holiday in the summer. Mum and Dad used to take my sister and I to the paddling pond. in Sheerness. these little paddle-boats. and the four of us would get in those and have a ride round in these paddle-boats. It was great. somebody would take photographs of us all together. My sister and I would go down on the beach. And we'd take tea in a Camp coffee bottle and some sandwiches. And we'd have our swimming costumes on and I used to crawl down to the water and get into the water. and providing I could put my hands on the bottom. I was OK. and I loved it. And I'd say. 'Oh. look. Mum. I'm swimming!'

When it got nearer to the date when we had to go back to Chailey I used to cry myself to sleep of a night. next morning it was all get ready to go back to Chailey and off we'd go on the coach and I was all right until I got to the railway station. and then I'd start crying. And it was a really upsetting time then. Everybody was waving. all the mums were wiping their eyes. Oh. we were crying our eyes out. all the kids. in the carriage – it was a special train sent down – everybody was crying because they didn't want to go back to Chailey. And when you got back. the worst part was taking your own clothes off and they used to tie them up in a parcel and give you a uniform to wear. and that. that was really heartbreaking. And you wouldn't see your clothes then until you went home. either summer or Christmas. We did cry ourselves to sleep.

Tuesdays was letter-writing day at Chailey. In the schoolroom we used to have to sit and write out letters to our parents. every week. and you couldn't put anything in there that was against the school. because they were read before they were put into the envelope and the teacher used to stick them down. After a few years. I began to get crafty and I'd try to be good so that. you know. the teacher would like me enough to let me put my own letter in the envelope myself. And. by her doing this I used to write little notes on the bottom of the letters saying what they'd been doing to me. like plaster over the mouth. et cetera. That's how they got to know. really. what was wrong. and I was able to put it in the envelope. you see. she used to give me permission to put it in the envelope and while she wasn't looking. while she was reading somebody else's letter I would scribble a note. I wanted them to know what was going on. I'm knitting another pair of black stockings for punishment. things like that. Just little things. You didn't have time to write very much. you had to do it very. very quickly because the teacher would look round and you'd be caught and then you'd be in trouble.

One year. when I went home in the Christmas holidays my boots were two sizes too small for me which caused my large toe on my left foot to go right under. My mother had to take me down to Freeman. Hardy and Willis and buy me a pair of boots and had to take them to the local 'snob'. to have these sockets put in the boot so that my irons could go in. And I had chilblains. well. they were shocking. My mother had to sit me on the kitchen table night after night and massage my legs with olive oil. I had awful rough hands through all the scrubbing they made you do. and all the housework. They were all chapped and they were raw and bleeding and I had all warts over the backs of my hands. and my mother had to buy a stick of caustic soda from the chemist. and dab it on these warts.

That was when I was ten and a half. My parents thought. well. they'd had enough of me being in such a bad condition. they were so disgusted at the way I was sent home. boots too small and everything. that they decided there and then I should leave. they spoke about it when I was in bed. they had to get permission from the local Kent Education Committee for me to stay at home. and they granted the permission. providing I went to an orthopaedic clinic once a month.

198

So then I went to a school with children who were able-bodied. and I was the only disabled one there. When there was a fire drill. my teacher used to sling me over her shoulder and run down the stairs with me. But every time I was naughty my mother used to threaten me. 'I'll send you back to Chailey!' So. course. 'Oh. no. Mum. I'll be good.' It was so wonderful to be at home all the time. lovely. and to go to the school. It was the start of a new life for me.

Kate Organ

Kate was born in Bristol in 1912, one of ten children. Her father was a painter and decorator but, due to poor health, he was often unable to work. As the eldest daughter of the family Kate seldom went to school and spent much of her childhood helping her mother with the housework and looking after her brothers and sisters. When her mother died of tuberculosis in 1931 Kate took over the care of the family completely, as well as working full-time in a laundry. She married a bricklayer in 1935 and they had two children of their own, in 1935 and 1938. Kate now has six grand-children and three great-grandchildren.

As far back as I can remember, being the eldest girl I was there to do everything. My mother was so busy having babies that I used to sort of do the running around for her, do the shopping, what I could just to help. I used to do the washing up, breakfast things, dinner things, I thought it was my duty to do it because I was helping me mum. She was never ever very well. Each child she got weaker, it was every fifteen months, eighteen months, that's all I can remember of my mum, having babies.

I used to be a bit nasty about it. I used to think, 'Oh, Mum, why, why?' Of course, in them days there was nothing to stop it – she was a staunch Catholic person and that was it.

I never had a child's life of me own, nor a teenage life. I don't think I ever did a full term at school but then again I think the teachers understood the situation because I was never, sort of, shouted out over it. I mean, the priests and that used to come to the house to find out about it and obviously they must have gone back and said about the situation. I used to get annoyed some-times, especially when friends of mine used to go out and come for me and I always had to say, 'No, I can't come out, I gotta mind this, or I got to do that.' I just did it because I thought I had to do it. Apart from that there was no one else to do it, it was either that or live not very clean, and I'm afraid I was a stickler for cleanliness.

Mum got weaker and then she was so ill for quite a while at home that in the end they took her to Southmead hospital. I used to have to go down every dinner-time, miss me dinner hour and see her, she wouldn't have no one, even my dad, visit her. One time I'd go in, she'd shout at me for not bringing this in, another time it was for not bringing that in. This was all from work on a dinner-time. And then I'd say, 'D'you want anything brought in tomorrow, Mum?' 'Yes, bring me in a rosary.' I'd take the rosary in and she wanted a prayer book. I'd take the prayer book in then she wanted a handbag. When she was dying the doctors from Southmead hospital sent to the laundry for me and I went straight down and then I phoned my dad and he did manage to get on a tram – I can remember us both coming along dreadfully upset.

All the children had to come with me to the funeral, I said I didn't want them in black but in black and white and so I gets so many yards of stuff and a neighbour cut them out and I just stayed in a few nights sewing them up. We had an old Singer sewing machine and I made sure they went to the funeral. Even though I don't think they understood a lot of it.

When Mum died we didn't do anything about having them adopted or anything, took it for granted that we'd all cope. The nuns decided to give it a month's trial to see how I was going to cope, in the meantime they still kept an eye on us, mind, they did come and visit us to see that we were all right.

The priest used to come now and again, but I'm afraid my dad used to shut the door and tell him we were out. Didn't want no truck with them.

After that I took full control, I mean, it was much harder because I had to do everything then. I felt confident that we could manage. Eileen was three, Amy was about five or six, Doris was nine, Frank was about eighteen months older than Amy when our mum died, then it was Pat, our Albert was next to me after Ellen. I love 'em all dearly, but Eileen was my baby. Being the baby she needed more looking after.

I used to get up between half six and seven, I got the children ready. I washed them and dressed them, clean clothes every morning which I had to wash every night because we didn't have lots of different clothes for them in those days. Then they mostly went to school. I had to work in the day and cook for them in me lunch hour. Then after work I had all the shopping to do and the housework. It was hard in those days, nothing to help you do it, just hard elbow grease. And all the children would be around my feet especially if it was raining and they couldn't play out. Then tea and bed for them. But I just had to wash all their things and get them ready for the morning. I couldn't ever go out.

Then as they got older they learnt to look after theirselves. It was a bit easier but I still had all the responsibility for them. My life started really when I met the man I married, although it was difficult for us even then because I looked after the children right up until they left home. But Vic accepted me as it was. We never went out very often. He accepted my position and that was it. I mean, he either had to put up with them or clear off. They were all there at night, the only time we had together was when they all went to bed. We never had no downstairs toilet, so they used to take a bucket upstairs to spend a penny in the night, and when Vic was there I used to say, 'Don't you dare bring that bucket through that room when Vic's here.' So what they used to do was go out the back door, go right round the front into the front door and go up the stairs, but the clatter of them and the bucket we knew what was going on anyway. Vic and I very often used to laugh at it.

Neighbours used to think I was their mother but if I never done it they would have been put in a home, it's as simple as that, and they was a pretty strong lot. I'm sure my mother would have wanted me to have done it. Well, I just hated the thoughts of them being put in a convent or an orphanage and I just thought it was my duty to look after them, and we did.

I wanted the family to stay together and I did anything I

could to keep them together and that's what I done, thank God. I felt meself as an older sister to them trying to do the right thing.

Vera Butterworth

Vera was born Rachel Robinson in 1923 in Bury. Her mother and father were destitute. They brought up their five children in workhouses and whatever lodging they could find. Her father made a little money as a rag-and-bone man. When she was six. Vera was taken in by a shopkeeper and his wife. Although later she went back to spend a brief time with her parents. she remained with the Hodgkinsons and although she wasn't legally adopted by them. looked upon herself as their daughter. She changed her name and tried to forget her early life. Vera left school at the age of fourteen and started work in the local slipperworks. She met her first husband. a miner. in 1941. They had two children in 1942 and 1945. Her husband died in 1966 and Vera remarried in 1974. She has one grandchild. six step-grandchildren and one great-step-grandchild.

I were born at Jericho, this workhouse. My mum and dad had no home, they lived in these doss-houses so if they were having a baby they went to workhouse. They had to work for their keep afterwards so, of course, the baby and the mother would be in until they'd paid off their debt. You were poor and that's how they treated you. This is how it used to happen; we was in and out, in and out, and in between that we lived in these lodging houses. There were no beds, we used to lie on the floor.

We used to do Ratcliffe, Bury, Haslingdon and walk as the crow flies, over the fields, climb the hedges over, backwards and forwards. I guess when Dad did have a bit of work it were the handcart going out for rags you know, rags and bones.

I don't remember sitting down to a proper meal. We would knock at doors and ask for food, walking from one place to another. Well, if we come across any cottages, the doors always used to be open then and you could smell the cooking. You would go and knock at the door and more often than not they would give you something, you'd sit down and maybe have a glass of milk and a crust, they'd be baking. And you'd pick things up off the floor, any food you'd pick that up. When you're hungry you'll eat anything, when you're thirsty you'll drink anything.

This went on and on for quite some time and I don't think we ever thought anything about it because it were just our way of life. That's how I met the Hodgkinsons, through travelling about and travelling down to their cake shop and looking in, I fancy it looked like Aladdin's cave, all these cakes. I guess to us it looked lovely and, you see, they started taking notice of us and sort of giving us stuff, you know, helping us along till we got very, very familiar. They used to buy us shoes.

I was the oldest of them that were looking through the window, maybe the cheekiest of them, and we looked in this window and see these cakes and then this lovely face of Mrs Hodgkinson as we peered through, and maybe she felt sorry for us but she were like an angel looking out and then she called you in the shop and give you something, and, well, I – I was getting to love them. I think they could see that I were, out in all sorts of weather, and they felt sorry and that's how I came to be taken in with them and it didn't matter to me mum and dad, they could probably see that I were being looked after better than any of 'em and I were off their hands, so I went to live with the Hodgkinsons.

A bed's a bed to everybody but to me it were heaven. I had a lovely soft bed, flock bed. It were like heaven having a lovely bed to go to, having nice clothes to put on, sitting down round a table and having a proper meal.

Well, I were called Rachel Robinson but when I did finally start going to school, I didn't want the schoolchildren that I were with to know what sort of life I'd been living, I didn't want them to know that I hadn't had a home up to recently, so, you know, I changed me name to Vera Hodgkinson, it wasn't Hodgkinsons that changed it, it were me, I were that adamant that I didn't want to carry this Rachel Robinson name. I wanted to change me whole life.

But the Hodgkinsons were just looking after me, they hadn't been able to adopt me or anything. So my real mum and dad could take me back with them any time they wanted. There were letters going backwards and forwards and apparently, I didn't know at the time, but there was some money being passed.

I've got some of the letters still now. You can see that my parents were asking for money for me to stay. 'Dear Mr and Mrs Hodgkinson, I write these few lines hoping this letter finds you in the best of health as it leaves me and my wife at present. Excuse me for not writing before now as we have not been in the best circumstances and we have had our baby in hospital with his face, but he is recovering. How is our Rachel going on? Is she not bothering about us? Or is she content? If she's all right we want to know if you will settle up with us. As you know, Mr Hodgkinson, we have nothing and we would not like to fetch our Rachel into a lodging house again, which you know, and I am doing nothing at all here for things are so bad. If you will settle up with us, Mr Hodgkinson, I am going to get a little business of my own, I mean to say, if she's not bothering and I know she's got a good home, one of the best, and I know she does not want for nothing. Yours truly . . .'

Then there's another they sent when they found out I'd been on a holiday. 'Just a few lines but I think you have a cheek to send our Rachel to Southport without our permission. You all have a good cheek. You'll have your own road with that child but we warn you for it. I'll be coming to Haslingdon and we'll let her stop a few more weeks, it won't do her any harm and then it will be our turn . . .'

They did take me back with them. I remember they took me away and we went to stay in a lodging house. There was a man on the scene at one of these lodgings, who he was I've no idea at all, but his face is so familiar after all these years to me and I know he did things that he shouldn't have done to me. Now, whether they were making money out of that I'll never know, whether me mum were having money paid to her, I don't know why it was, but I know I was a victim, it's something that I've always tried to push at back of my mind.

Then my mother and father were probably wanting more money again so I was back at the Hodgkinsons again. They were trying to adopt me and I think my parents must have been really worked up about this. They wrote a letter . . . 'Mr and Mrs Hodgkinson, I was very mad about the way you have our child but it is not yours and we will never sign. We have been to a solicitor and if she is not here before Saturday there will be further trouble. He has told us to write and tell you and I will take further proceedings. You have her very cheeky and that's not what she was when we had her . . . Mrs Hodgkinson whispering to it and telling it not to come home, the very idea, but we won't bother no more. In the first I did not ask you to take the child, you asked us while such time we got settled down. You don't think for one minute we've forgot her because you're mistaken. You had a cheek to have her name changed when you know what terms we were on. Well, no more at the present . . . Mother and Father.'

Mr and Mrs Hodgkinson didn't let on about all this but I think they were worried about it because they did really love me and they didn't want me back with my mum and dad.

I can remember this particular time, I'm growing up then, ten or eleven maybe, and I were playing out in this street, and I thought, they'll all have mums and dads, these children, and I've only Auntie Maggie and Uncle Edward, this is what I were calling Hodgkinsons, so I went in and I said, 'Auntie Maggie, can I call you Mum?' Well, she didn't answer me, she went upstairs. I thought, 'Oh, what have I done?' I were always frightened of having to go back with my parents, you see. So I told Uncle Edward what had happened and that I'd asked Aunt Maggie to call her Mum and that she hadn't answered me. Well, he never answered and he went upstairs and I thought, 'I'm going to have to go back.' And I went upstairs myself and went in bedroom and they were both sat on bed holding one another's hands crying. And they both said, 'Oh, it were lovely.' They'd never asked me to call them Mum and Dad, they'd let me choose it, so they knew how much I loved them, you see, I wanted to be their little girl. I didn't want to belong to anybody else, just them two. I'd forgotten the other life, I didn't want to go back to that.

I was always frightened of me mum and dad coming to take

207

me back again because I knew really that I hadn't been properly adopted and I thought they would have every right to take me back. I used to dress up. I don't think my step-mother meant to hurt me but when you dressed up she used to say that I favoured me own mum. That used to really upset me, I used to think I'll not dress up if I favour her.

I can remember coming home from school and I could see Mum and Dad walking up what were Peel Street in Haslingdon and I ran out back into backyard and locked the back door and I ran upstairs to me step-mum and I said, 'Emily Robinson and Tommy's out there.' And she says, 'You're not going back.'

I were playing with a ball another time and I were throwing it on to a board that had letters on and I missed it and it went down Wilkinson Street and I run for it and this woman picked it up and handed me it and when I looked I knew that it were me mother. I could tell meself from her. and I run like mad up into shop. locked the door. locked the kitchen door and then run upstairs. I'm shouting to my step-mother. 'Emily Robinson's coming.' Now then I wouldn't come down. and talk to 'em at all. I stopped up there. I were frightened of going back. As I got older they stopped coming any more. they must have got tired. and I think the Hodgkinsons said they couldn't have any more money for me so they signed a form so that after I lived with the Hodgkinsons legally. all the time. never saw my family again.

But even now I sit back sometimes and I've got this urge to find out what happened to me real mum and dad and I do wonder have I missed out on anything? How many sisters and brothers have I and what did I miss? I probably did miss out. but I had such a lovely life with my step-mum and -dad.

CHAPTER SIX

Bombs at Bedtime

In September 1939, at the outbreak of the Second World War families all over Britain found themselves in the front line of a new kind of 'total war': civilians had to face what only the military had encountered in previous wars. In the modern age of the aeroplane and weapons of mass destruction, every major town and city represented a military target for bombing raids from enemy aircraft. Mothers, fathers and their children were suddenly plunged into a terrifying world of air-raid sirens and gas masks. Civilian morale, the backbone of which was the family, was regarded by government experts as a crucial factor, which would help determine whether Britain won or lost the war. It was predicted that hundreds of thousands of civilians might die in the conflict. Not only were families expected to resist enemy bombardment, they also had to play a key role in increasing productivity and reducing waste on the 'Home Front'. The endless government propaganda which told civilians what to do and celebrated their achievements at home has helped to mythologize the family and parenting during the war. The image created by newsreels and newspapers was one of unflinching determination, defiance and strident patriotism: 'We can take it.' The reality, reflected in the memories that we document, is very different.

Evacuation is the first major event which highlights this distinction between official myth and reality of personal experience. During the summer and autumn of 1939 around 3,500,000 people moved from areas of Britain thought vulnerable to air attack or invasion to those considered safe. This mass migration of population away from the major cities like London, Birmingham, Manchester, Leeds and Glasgow had an immediate and disruptive impact on family life. Those who had the money and the means

often evacuated themselves – with some success – but most working-class families in the big cities were left in the hands of hastily
organized government schemes. under which in September alone.
almost a million schoolchildren were evacuated. Newsreels showed
mothers happily waving goodbye to their children but the partings
were – not surprisingly – traumatic as mothers and children
wondered if they would ever see each other again. When the
children arrived at their country destinations the billeting system
sometimes broke down and a kind of 'slave market' developed in
village halls with children being inspected like cattle. In many
instances nobody wanted to take the poorest and most ragged
children. or the innumerable bands of inseparable brothers and
sisters. Things often didn't improve much once the children had
settled in with 'receiving families'. who were frequently horrified
by the behaviour of city children. The conflicts were usually worst
in upper-class households where evacuees might find themselves
treated as servants or second-class citizens.

Many of the half million mothers and pre-school-age children
who were also evacuated experienced similar problems. The rural
homes where they were billeted often lacked space and facilities for
babies and small children. which quickly led to domestic conflicts
between the villagers and the newcomers. Also. many young
mothers felt lonely and isolated. missing the tightly knit communities where they had come from.

From the beginning a trickle of evacuees returned home
preferring to face the possibility of attack by the Luftwaffe rather
than a life of deprivation in the countryside. By December 1939.
when the mass bombings predicted by the government had not
materialized. the trickle turned into a flood: more than half of
the 750.000 mothers and children evacuated from London. for
example. had returned home before Christmas. Some families.
however. were not fully reunited until after the war was over: all
men in their mid-twenties and under – a total of one and a half
million – unless they were in a reserved occupation had been called
up for military service. followed. by the middle of 1940 by all men
under forty. Many mothers. though relieved to be home again.
now had to face the war without their husbands.

The nightmare of mass aerial bombardment. the Blitz. began in September 1940. London was the first and primary target. though there were sustained bombing raids in later months on most of Britain's major cities. During the first raids on the capital the emergency services almost broke down. Families discovered that the air-raid shelters erected by the government gave far less protection than they had been promised: some street shelters collapsed like a pack of cards. burying the occupants inside. when bombs fell near by. Bombed-out families. desperate for food. clothing and shelter. were bewildered to discover that practically no provision had been made for them. There were similar scenes in other cities like Coventry. Bristol and Hull after intense bombing raids. Although the horror of these raids was covered up by the press. the dominant memory of parents is of shock. panic and confusion. Many families abandoned the official shelters. rushing around desperately searching for cover wherever they could: under railway arches and in railway tunnels. in warehouses. crypts or churches. which were widely believed to have some holy immunity from the bombings. Sheltering in London's tube stations. later celebrated in propaganda films. was banned at first. but hundreds of terrified families bought tickets and evaded station staff in a bid to stay on the platforms all night where they felt safe.

Many thousands trekked out of the cities. struggling through cratered streets. pushing handcarts and babies in prams. to seek the safety of the countryside. Most slept rough in fields. under hedges or in barns. Disused coal pit workings were popular as they seemed to offer protection from the elements and from stray bombs. Some families even began living in caves: fleeing Londoners discovered a series of caverns at Chislehurst in Kent and. as with the London Underground. simply broke into them. After a week of the Blitz more than 8000 Londoners were living there. Each family colonized a small section. which was marked out as their territory. To begin with they slept on the stone floor but. after several weeks. beds. armchairs and tables were transported down in carts and lorries. Similar patterns of cave dwelling developed close to several other badly bombed cities: hundreds of Bristol families moved into the Portway caves beside the river

213

Avon while a few journeyed to those in the Cheddar gorge. Most of those who camped in fields and caves would set off from their homes in the early evening armed with sandwiches. Thermos flasks and blankets. They would spend the night out – most raids took place. of course. at night – then return home. wash. have breakfast. and send the children to school. All this placed an enormous strain on the families involved. especially the mothers. but they preferred to endure the discomfort. cold and insanitary conditions rather than facing the terror of night raids in the cities.

After the panic of the early days and as the bombings continued many families began to learn to live with the Blitz. The death toll was not as high as had originally been feared: only a few thousand died during the first few weeks of bombings in London. Most survived a scare or near miss. which encouraged them to believe that they and their family could see the bombings through. After the initial chaos and disruption. everyday life resumed its normal pattern with many shops. schools. hospitals. pubs and offices open-ing normally. and public transport continuing to operate. Although all this took place in a surreal city landscape of cratered streets and bombed-out buildings. the 'business as usual' approach had immense practical and psychological importance in helping parents to cope. The emergency services now began to deal with the aftermath of raids more effectively. with improved back-up facilities. such as soup kitchens. rest centres. and more workable evacuation schemes for bombed-out families. Even the caves where families sheltered were made safer and more comfortable: by the spring of 1941 the Chislehurst caves boasted bunk beds. canteens. a children's chapel and a cave hospital.

The Blitz was never as traumatic for most families living in the suburbs as it was for those in the city centres. Many suburban families. whether on a private development or a council estate. spent the nights in an Anderson shelter. a corrugated iron shell supplied by the government and buried in their back garden. The family's routine often carried on much as it had before the war. though parents and children might find themselves playing board games and reading books by candlelight in a cramped shelter rather than in a modern living room. Most of these parents seem to have been remarkably successful in protecting their children from any sense that the family was in danger, and made special efforts to ensure that nights spent in the Anderson shelter when raids occurred, were seen by young sons and daughters as an adventure and not as a threat to their lives. By virtue of their low-density layout, suburban homes were far less prone to direct hits and mass destruction than the packed streets and tenements in the central areas of cities, which enhanced this comforting sense of normality.

The Blitz on most British cities ended in the summer of 1941 after Germany invaded Russia. From then onwards the main thrust of the Nazi blitzkrieg was directed against the Soviet Union. Although many parents had learnt to live with the Blitz the respite in the bombing was greeted with a deep sense of relief – although this was tempered by the possibility that the Luftwaffe might soon be back.

Britain now faced a crisis of war production and manpower. Its economy urgently needed to be geared up for war and a counter-attack on Nazi Germany. The changes that this brought about in family life were almost as dramatic as those occasioned by the Blitz: with most men away fighting the government turned to its main alternative source of labour – women. In December 1941 conscription for unmarried women into war work was introduced, but as this still did not solve the labour shortage the government turned to mothers with children. This involved an extraordinary shift in attitudes: in the pre-war years a woman's duty was seen to be, first and foremost, to care for her children. The Ministry of Labour began running campaigns to recruit mothers into the factories, and in tandem with this the government rapidly expanded nursery provision all over Britain. The experiment worked. Officials were surprised at how many mothers were keen to go out to work once the care of their babies and pre-school children was assured. During 1942, residential nurseries were opened in industrial areas and some day nurseries began taking children overnight, becoming twenty-four-hour nurseries, to cater

215

for mothers doing shift work. Eventually 80 per cent of married women in London. for example. were employed.

However. the heroic propaganda picture of mothers joyfully leaving their children in the nursery before going off to do the night shift was misleading. Many became worn out with the double burden of running a home and doing a full-time job. It was common practice for mothers with young children to be expected to work a ten- to twelve-hour day. six days a week. The work was frequently arduous and exhausting. and on top of this it took sometimes considerable time to get to work. especially if a mother was employed at a remote 'green field' munitions factory. As a result. absenteeism was high: mothers were constantly forced to take time off to do housework. shopping and look after their children when they were sick.

Rationing made life at home difficult for mothers too. On average the spartan adult weekly ration was two ounces of tea. four ounces of butter or margarine. two ounces of sugar. two ounces of cheese. four ounces of bacon or ham. two and a half pints of milk and 1s. 5d. worth of meat. In addition. each month a person was entitled to twenty 'points' worth of tinned goods. which would buy. for example. a tin of Spam. or five tins of baked beans. plus one packet of dried eggs. The consequent diet seemed to all but the poorest families both meagre and boring. To make matters worse. the women often had to spend long hours queuing for their rations. then more time trying to transform the sparse ingredients into a family meal. Ministry of Food campaigns. featuring characters like Potato Pete and Doctor Carrot. offered good advice on how to make nutritious meals out of. for example. a few potatoes and a cabbage. but in practice many mothers found it difficult and time-consuming to produce something that their children would eat. Similarly. although the 'Dig for Victory' and 'Keep a Pig' campaigns meant that families might enjoy some extra vegetables or meat. it often meant more work for the already over-stretched mother. The same was true of 'Make Do and Mend'. which aimed to encourage people to recycle old clothes. and the constant recycling of all kitchen waste on the so-called 'Kitchen

Front'. It seemed to many tired mothers that almost every hour of the day was occupied in supporting the war effort.

All this stress and strain was often made more difficult for mothers to bear because they had no husband at home to share their problems or to take some of the load. It was especially difficult for those whose husbands had been reported missing or dead and who were now single-parent families. Many whose husbands were posted overseas – and whom they never saw from one year to the next – felt as if they were in much the same position. Some women began to take advantage of the new freedom that the war had given them to go out 'unescorted'. Paid work outside the home gave them money to spend and a new circle of friends with whom they could enjoy the occasional 'girls' night out' at the local cinema or dance hall. This could open up new horizons, and it was here that many met servicemen not just from all over Britain, but also from many of the Allied countries.

The American GIs – 'oversexed, overpaid and over here' – were expecially glamorous. As an ordinary GI earned four times the wages of his British counterpart, and as he also had easy access to tinned foods, cigarettes, nylons and 'candles', strictly rationed among civilians, he could be an attractive friend for a mother whose husband was away. In the wartime atmosphere of 'living for the present' friendships often led to affairs which in turn led to the break-up of marriages.

Fathers posted away from home also enjoyed a new freedom and independence: some of them, too, had affairs that led to the end of their marriages. As the war continued, even those with successful marriages wondered how long a husband posted away would remain faithful.

It was in this atmosphere of war weariness that families in London and the South-east had to face one final terror – attacks by secret weapons developed by the German High Command to undermine civilian morale. It began early in the summer of 1944 when the Luftwaffe launched the V-1, a pilotless plane designed to explode on impact. These flying bombs, shortly to become known as 'doodlebugs', were hurled from camouflaged catapult bases in northern France. By the middle of June they were falling on London at the rate of around seventy a day. The missiles brought a new kind of devastation to the capital: they were of such force that they damaged houses and shattered windows within a quarter-mile radius. Those who were within fifty yards of the explosion were usually killed or buried alive. Even more disturbing. the warheads were so small that they could not be picked up by radar defence systems so there was no warning of their arrival. Mothers. tired after five long years of war. were ill-equipped to face renewed suffering and the doodlebugs. as the Nazis intended. had an immensely damaging effect on morale. Most of these robotic bombs were aimed at central London but as they could not be targeted accurately many fell on the suburbs around the capital. The new geography of the bombing brought into the front line suburban mothers who had escaped much of the devastation during the Blitz. After two weeks of flying-bomb attacks about 1600 had been killed. 10.000 injured. half seriously. and over 200.000 houses damaged. Many mothers who lived along the main doodlebug flight paths were on the verge of nervous breakdown.

Government censors allowed no information to be disclosed about the appalling effect the bombings were having on family morale. and to begin with they refused to allow the press to report that these attacks had happened at all. Urgent government action was taken. however. to avert a crisis: a new and more successful evacuation scheme enabled half a million mothers and children to escape from the capital to billets in the countryside: new purpose-built underground shelters were opened in London: and. perhaps most important. the defence system was improved so that very few doodlebugs got through from August 1944 onwards.

The cycle of censorship. devastation and despair was to be repeated between November 1944 and April 1945 when the V-2 rockets were launched against the capital. most of which. again. fell in the suburbs. When the war in Europe was finally over in May 1945 there were no greater feelings of relief than among suburban families in London. They had borne the brunt of the final terror of the war and civilian morale – especially among mothers – had plummeted to a dangerously low level.

In the victory celebrations that followed the end of the war
many parents looked forward to a new world for themselves and
their children. The experience of the war had changed them and
their ideas about what they wanted in the future. To begin with,
the war had led to the mixing of people from different social classes
on an unprecedented scale. Evacuation, for example, for all its
drawbacks, had opened the eyes of better-off families to the abject
poverty in which many parents were forced to bring up their
children in the city slums. Middle-class volunteers, who had
worked for the emergency services in blitzed cities, were also
horrified by the conditions poor families had to endure. There was
a new vision of family life in a fairer and more equal society. Many
working-class people shared the dream of a classless Britain –
especially the younger generation of parents who had struggled
through the war. Their aspirations had been reflected and
reinforced by wartime government propaganda – and by the
Beveridge Report – which had promised them a better standard
of family life backed by health and welfare services that were
worth fighting for. It was because the Labour Party expressed
some of these ideals that it won the landslide victory in the
post-war election of 1945 which turned Winston Churchill out of
office.

But after the euphoria that accompanied the end of the war
had died down and after the emotional reunions between husbands
and wives, many found it difficult to pick up the threads of family
life and 'return to normal' as they were expected to do. State
nurseries were closed and women were told to leave their jobs to
make way for the returning men, much as they had after the First
World War. Some were thankful to be at home full-time, relieved
of the burden of doing two exhausting jobs, but many resented
that most of the opportunities for paid work for married women
which had opened up during the war were now being taken away
again. Many experienced deeper marital problems which had a
profound effect on family life in the future. Some had married
hastily under the pressure of the war and were far from sure that
they wanted to settle down again with a husband they hardly
knew, while others preferred a new partner they had met during

219

the war: divorce and the break-up of parents and their children, which in pre-war years had been rare, was about to become much more common.

Betty Dennison

See also Chapter One, page 35. When war broke out Betty's husband joined the Merchant Navy and she was left alone to look after the three children. He was killed at sea in April 1940 and Betty struggled to bring up her children with the help of her mother. When the war was over Betty remarried, a family friend who had also been in the Navy. She had three more daughters with him born in 1946, 1949 and 1955. Betty now has fourteen grandchildren and two great-grandchildren.

I was a mother with three under school age. We went in the first lot of evacuations. My husband was at sea and me mother said, 'You'll have to go with them bairns because it's too dangerous to stay here.'

We all got to the station, I had these three children and we got iron rations. Hundreds of kids and mothers on these trains. We just went out into the country. And I was the last one to find a place, 'cause nobody wanted anybody with three kids.

Anyway, I got with this real old couple. No lights. You had a candle in this big old farmhouse right up in the attic and then I was wanting to make a bottle for John. 'You can't do this, oh, you can't do that.' There was no water. I was in this attic with the three kids and we were all in one room. Don't know how we got to bed that night, really. Took 'em out to see if I could find a shop and there was loads of women with their kids, they was all walking about looking for shops, looking for summat to eat. 'Cause we didn't get no meals or anything there. We had to find places to buy some food.

I don't know how we managed that first day. Then I found this garage and this taxi driver, and I said, 'Oh, can you take me back home?' But he said that with the petrol being rationed he would get into trouble. So I said that I'd have to get home with the three bairns because they wanted something to eat. And really begged him and I told him he'd get paid so in the end he took us back to Hull.

There's loads came back after. They couldn't stick it. You might as well be at home where you're happy and the kids are happy. If you go in the shelters then you'll all go together. You're not happy when you're away with strangers. I was happier to be at home, though after we got back we were very badly blitzed, we had bombs and raids every night.

Well, the shelter was only down the terrace. We'd set off with three children, you know, two would be hanging on to me skirts, and I'd be carrying John. You had to carry him on your hip because he was so big. We'd be walking slowly and look up at the sky and you'd see all these flashing things. And you always thought it was nearly on top of you. You'd only feel safe once you got there, down that shelter. You're so worried about the children that really they take over. If we couldn't get to the shelter, if we didn't have time, we'd have to go under the stairs. We'd have a blanket on the floor so we could lay the bairns down but it was worse because you could feel the vibrations which you didn't feel in the shelters because they were all concrete. They had bunks at each side, wooden bunks up and down. Put your bairns on the bunks, and your stuff. There were no lights so we all had a torch, like, some had candles. When the bombs were dropping you thought, 'Oh, that's near.' If it was quiet then somebody'd be praying and somebody'd be singing. If the kids were awake, some of the older kids, they'd be singing or they'd be playing with something and the men'd be singing.

And if the bairns didn't go to sleep and then if they was crying they'd maybe want a bottle, or they'd maybe want a wee and you can't satisfy 'em, you can't give 'em everything they want at the time, can you? It was very, very hard, and then you'd nothing to look forward to, only the same thing tomorrow. It was tiring because all you wanted was to just have a rest, like, or go to sleep. You couldn't because you daren't go to sleep and leave them awake. And there was too much noise with all the planes. It was all over when the sirens went, maybe three or four o'clock in the morning. Then you'd really want to go to bed and have had a good sleep and you couldn't because the children wouldn't want to go to bed.

It wore you out, you know, so that you'd no energy for anything, like. We was desperate for it to end. I didn't think it would. Then you see when you went out next morning it was shocking, people walking about through all these great big hose-pipes and old buildings aflame, and homes still burning. And then my husband was killed. When they're in the Merchant Navy there's no bodies or anything, is there? They just say that the convoy's gone down. There were about two hundred ships with all those men on and there wasn't a body found. That was '41. You only got a letter. 'The ship's been sunk, he's presumed drowned.' And you don't know really how to cope with it. What do you do about it?

I was out for so many days I didn't know what I was doing. If I hadn't been at me mother's the bairns wouldn't have got looked after or anything. I didn't really seem to care, I didn't seem to know whether they was getting fed. I think I started to lose my mind.

And it was then when I was feeling so low, like, we was bombed out. We were in the shelter but then in the morning you go out into what's left. I saw the house and I was absolutely shattered. All the windows were in, I don't think there was even a door on, everything all in flames. We rescued what we could get out. Got the bed, cots and different things. Luckily we had a lot of stuff in the shelters with us. I had to go to me mother's and take the bairns.

Everyone was so frightened, especially then when we didn't even have a home left. The raids were so regular that we started going out with the coal carts into the country. We'd go out to the outskirts of the town and sleep rough in the fields. We felt safer there so we did it almost every night. The coalmen would take load after load of mothers and children. They dropped us off and we would sleep anywhere. You just put the baby down on a blanket and so long as I fed him he went to sleep, good as gold. But the older two, they would never sleep much. They would be prancing about and going round to see the different families that were sleeping around. But at least we were away from the bombs and it felt safer.

I don't know how I coped really, though, not with the house gone. I'd lost my husband and then I'd lost everything. It's the bairns that keep you going. The bairns bring you back to normal 'cause you know they have to be looked after. They did bring me back.

Lavinia O'Donoghue

Lavinia was born in 1905 in Walworth, south-east London. Her father was a builder and she had four brothers and five sisters. She left school at fourteen to work as a machinist in a print shop. Later she took a job in the kitchens of a restaurant in Oxford Street and it was there, in 1926, that she met her future husband who was then a chef. They married in 1927 and settled in Walworth. Their children were born in 1928, 1930, and 1933. At the start of the war Lavinia's husband joined the Home Guard as his occupation was reserved. The three children were evacuated with the rest of their school, to Newton Abbot in Devon but after visiting them in their billets Lavinia discovered that they were not being properly cared for and she brought her two sons home. After that during bombing raid the boys went with their mother to underground shelters near the dockside. Lavinia now has five grandchildren and three great-grandchildren.

W e had a letter around to say would we assemble at the school and they got all the children together and then they all marched out. We had to go to the railway station and see 'em off. They all 'ad their gas masks on. They'd got in the middle of the carriage so they couldn't get to the window to see or to wave to me. It was really chaotic because they were all crying.

I suppose, really, you gave a sigh of relief to think they'd be out of danger and at the same time you were so upset. You'd think, 'Oh, I've lost my family.' We came home and it was so desolate here, there wasn't a sound. And I was really worried about them. Reg used to walk in his sleep and I used to get up and sort of trail him back to bed. So when he went away I said to my husband, 'There's only one thing, I wonder if he'll sleep down there.' So we decided to send tins of Ovaltine for him to help him sleep better.

I went down to them after a couple of weeks and Reg said this woman who he was staying with wasn't looking after him a bit. He said he hardly had any food. When the woman was out of the room, I looked and as I opened the top cupboard there was all the Ovaltine tins – she hadn't given it to him.

All her mind was on was these soldiers and sailors she had lodging with her. Just the money, that's all she wanted. I said to Reg, 'Well, what's she giving you to eat?' He told me he hardly got any food and that he was really starving, like. I confronted her, I said, 'You're not looking after 'em at all.' 'I'm doing it to the best of my ability,' she said. I said, 'Well, it's a very poor ability that you've got.' I couldn't cause too much trouble, I knew my boys had to stay there till I got the money to get them back with me to London.

I was very upset. I was angry as well. I thought the teachers were lax, they could have told me, couldn't they? Kept an eye on them. He didn't even go to school. I was furious, really, more than upset, anyhow I said to my husband, 'There's a blooming fine turn-out, they're supposed to look after 'em.'

Then when I got back to London I went to the council offices in Peckham, 'cos they used to supply me with the money to go down there, and I told them and they said they would blacklist her.

Directly I got the money I was down there again like a shot. I was worried, worried sick about them. I went down there on the train and I went to see our Reg. By that time he was in the hospital. When I got there he came out and he looked dreadful, so thin. We went up to the park and I said to him, 'You don't look very well, do you?' So he said, 'Well, it's this head.' He had like a white cap on him and when I moved the white thing there was all these sores all running. Oh, it was hopeless. I cut all the hair off. I brought him and his brother home and they stayed with me till the end of the war. Their sister stayed in her billet, she had a good one, but I couldn't leave the boys. I got them home and I got our Reg back right. I was over the moon to have them back.

Reg O'Donoghue

Reg was born in 1933. He was evacuated to Devon with his brother and sister during the war. He stayed there for several months until his mother, Lavinia, took him back to London, concerned about the bad treatment and lack of care that he had received. Reg spent the rest of the war in London. He left school at sixteen and became a telephone engineer. He married in 1958, and has a son and a daughter and one grandchild.

I thought the end of my world was coming. I was leaving and that was it. Mum was just a speck in the distance. I was squashed against the window, sort of thing, and just waving. Everybody was crying, I think. Crying into me gas mask with my ticket on the side. I just thought I was being sort of thrown away. It's the first time I'd ever been away from home, first time I'd been away from me mum.

The billeting officer took a party of us round, dropping one off as we was going down the street. 'You can stay here, you can stay there.' Me and me brother and sister had been told to stick together and not get split up, but nobody could take us all so I was on me own.

I remember he took me to this house and the woman first of all said, 'Oh, he'll be OK here, this is gonna be his bedroom and this is where he'll sit and where he'll sleep.' All very nice in front of him. But I don't think she took too kindly to me from the start. I was crying and when he'd gone it was, 'That's the first and last time you come through the front door. In future you always go round the back door.' That's always the tradesman's entrance. I don't think I slept even one night in that bed. I was on the floor or under the table.

I got no food, or very little food, from the woman that I was staying with. I can never remember having one meal in that house at all. I had to go out and fend for myself. I used to skulk around all day. I didn't go to school at all, I was too busy trying to find places, I suppose, to feed myself and keep out of trouble. No proper sleep of a night but not being in bed, never any meals in the house, so I spent my days sort of wandering around the back streets of Newton Abbot trying to find food. They never sent anybody from the school round to find out what the problem was.

This went on for some time because I was vastly underweight. I had to scrounge for food from the army centre which was just close by. I quickly got to learn to go there at the right times when the meals were finished and the army corporal came out in his white apron and threw what was being left into a big dustbin. I used to have to climb up over the top. And I can remember I used to try and reach into the middle of what he'd just put in so that it hadn't touched the sides of the dustbin and that's how I used to survive, we used to eat from there.

Until one day I decided I'd had enough, I wanted to get home. I found out where she kept money on the shelf. I took it and found me way back to the station and actually purchased a ticket to London. I didn't get that far. First stop was Exeter, and the police boarded the train, come into my compartment. They was absolutely appalled at my condition.

They took me back to the police station and I can remember being given a big doorstep sandwich and a steaming mug of tea which I just ate ravenously. Then they took me to hospital and I was admitted straight away.

They cut all my hair off because I had what they call impetigo. My head was full of lice. The hospital made me wear a little white cap with a rubber band around it. I'm not too sure how long I was in the hospital. I can remember my mother coming in screaming virtually, well, she couldn't believe it, the state I was in, and she said, 'I'll take him home. If you can't get him right, I will.'

Well, when I saw my mum all the pent-up feelings flooded out. I begged her to take me out of the hospital and take me home.

Grace Goodman

Grace was born in Calcutta in India in 1910 where her father was
a property dealer. She had two brothers and one sister. She first
came to England when she was sent to boarding school at the age
of eleven. After leaving school she settled in England and became
a secretary when she was nineteen. She married her husband, a
salesman, in 1934. Their only daughter, Rachel, was born in 1938.
At the beginning of the war Grace and her family were living in
Manchester. Her husband was not called up because of an injury
although he become a fire watcher. Grace and some of her friends
were alarmed by stories of Nazi atrocities on Jewish women and
children; fearing for their own families because they were Jewish.
Grace and her friends devised a method of committing suicide
rather than suffering in the event of an invasion. She now has
three grandchildren.

We decided, if there was an invasion, and we knew that the
Nazis were coming closer, we would kill ourselves and
kill the children. We knew a lot more than was commonly known
about what the Nazis did, we knew from Jewish people who had
managed to get letters through, some had escaped through various
routes and they came with stories. We knew some of the things
that they did to the children. They cut off their arms and legs to
see if they could live, could the body just exist. And in various
tortures they used to dismember children and kill them to get
their parents to say where their friends were hidden, where there
were other Jews hidden.

The whole horror of it was there, and rather than live under
those terms we'd rather die. We decided that it was better we'd
go, and go together. We thought of all sorts of dramatic ways of
doing it, cutting our wrists and this and that, and then we thought
of getting the pills. We got some sleeping pills from the doctor
and he very carefully told us, 'Don't take more than two, and if
you take the lot it will kill you.' We thanked him, nobody spoke

229

openly to him as to what we were going to do, but he knew and we knew.

We saved our rations so that we'd give the children a really good party, we'd really make ourselves sick with food, and then do ourselves in. We'd all ring up, let each other know that we were all going to do it. So that anyway if there was an after-life we'd all be together still.

I think I could have done it because I was so very close to Rachel. I had every intention of doing it – there was a chocolaty pudding that she liked, and I'd saved the chocolate, I'd put this aside, so that I would make it very sweet and use all the sugar, give her a really good taste, and the pill would have been in the chocolate so she wouldn't have tasted it. It had nuts in it so that if she got the pill I'd say that's part of the pudding.

It seemed sad to think that eventually one had to do this, end her life, but it seemed inevitable, you just have to accept what is, that's life. Possibly if I'd had enough faith in God I'd have let her live, but from what was happening to the Jews certainly, it didn't seem that that faith was justified. It's because I loved her so very much. It wouldn't have taken long, you see, I mean, I'd have made sure she'd gone and then I would have taken it. I knew I was going to make quite sure that I wasn't going to live. It was a choice for my husband whether he wanted to take it or not. That was up to him, but I felt my daughter was my responsibility, I wasn't going to allow her to be hurt in any way.

Rose Townsend

(See also Chapter Four, page 153.) During the war Rose and her family were living on the Southmead Estate in north-west Bristol. Her husband was posted abroad to Italy. Rose worked at the Rolls-Royce factory making aeroplane parts while her children were at school. During the Blitz on Bristol, in 1940 and 1941, she took them to shelter in the Rocks Railway Tunnel, in the Avon gorge.

I didn't think we'd be safe in the air-raid shelters because they were coming over the fields at the back of us dropping the flares and they might mistake the estate for the aeroplane works. We were going on from shelter to shelter, taking the children and trying to do different things for 'em, they'd be coming over with the planes and then you'd be up shaking like a leaf in different shelters. I was so frightened, we went to the caves to have a bit of peace so that the children wouldn't hear the bombs coming down.

I took the children to the Rocks Railway. They were really tired, you know. 'Mum, will we be safe in there?' I said, 'Yes, of course, you will. You've got Mummy with you, haven't you? They won't touch us.' I said, 'Now where we're going, it'll be cold and damp, but I'll wrap you up in blankets and you'll be safe. That's all I want,' I said, 'you being safe.' They weren't aware of the real danger that was going on around them. So they believed me and they were all right then.

We went inside and there was all this water running down the walls of the rocks and so I thought, 'I'll put up the deck-chairs for the children.' And I 'ad the blankets and I wrapped it all round them – they wore their coats, they didn't take their clothes off, I seen them settled down for the night and I put a pillow behind their heads. I done as best I could for 'em. Well, I couldn't sleep anyway. It was too cold and I was so worried about them. I didn't know whether these rocks could stand it, if they bombed it or anything, I thought a stray bomb might come down near the entrance, and block the entrance, we wouldn't be able to get out and we should have to fight our way out. All sorts of things was going through my mind, but I wouldn't let the children see that I was worried. I just set their minds at rest, told them they were safe and that. It was awful, and the bbzzz, all the planes coming over. Oh, it frightened me to death. I thought, 'Oh, gosh I shall be glad when they're over, gone over. And there's loads of them there together and all this noise.' I were tossing and turning all night and then on me back, on me side. At two o'clock in the morning, the little girl said to me, 'Mum, I want to go on the toilet.' The boy said, 'And me, Mum, I wants to go.' So I took 'em up round the rocks. 'We gotta go to school, Mum, after we've been sleeping up 'ere all night?' Used to have a laugh in there and that, mind, tried to cheer one another up. They used to play with the other children, they used to bring a lot of games with 'em. Then it was cards.

But when we came home there was so many houses down, so many houses, people killed. Oh, it was terrible. I seen the town and it really did upset me 'cos everything I knew was down, I couldn't find nothing.

I stayed sheltering in the caves every night for a month and I couldn't stand no longer. I did really, you know, come to the end of me tether. I thought, 'Oh, this is it, Rose. If you goes on much longer you're going to end up in hospital with a nervous breakdown or something.'

Marie Daniels

Marie was born in 1910 in Victoria. south-west London. She had two brothers and one sister. Their father was a private chauffeur. Marie left school when she was fourteen and became a Court florist. She met her husband. a waiter. when she was sixteen in Kennington Park. They had four sons born in 1930. 1931. 1935 and 1940. During the war the family were living in Sidcup. in Kent. Marie's husband worked as a fireman and much of the care of the four boys was left to her. She sheltered with them in an Anderson shelter in their garden until they were bombed out of their home in 1941. It was then that they began to go to the nearby Chislehurst caves. After a year of travelling there almost every night Marie and her children were evacuated to South Wales where they remained until the end of the war. Marie now has seven grandchildren and six great-grandchildren.

I felt complete and utter panic for my family and for myself, for everybody, the siren went and we all rushed for gas masks. Nothing happened. The terrible part about the gas mask was, my three eldest sons could put the gas mask on themselves but the baby was very small. He had to go in a great big contraption. You tried to get him in this thing but it was very, very hard. He was tiny and wriggly, and it was very awkward to get him inside. He just squirmed, he cried, you more or less gave up.

You had rigged the Anderson shelter up to the best of your ability, with all the bedclothes and the warmth down there. When the air-raid siren used to go I used to roll the baby up quickly in a big towel, had everything ready for him, take him down the shelter. I tried to keep as normal as I possibly could under the circumstances. The four children and myself, we all sort of ran like mad to get down there. You were even afraid of tripping. Once you were down there you felt a certain amount of safety, but not an awful lot. Course, you knew jolly well that you were safer down there than you were in a house. You were thankful that you had somewhere to run to, but at the same time it was pretty horrible when you'd been in a decent bedroom and you suddenly felt something crawling over you. And it was so damp, so smelly, awful really. We took torches down, a little bit of food for the children, my baby then was three months, he was being breast-fed. But at the same time I had to take nappies and gripe water and all in case he was naughty. And we had spiders, beetles. I hated it because sometimes you would be laying there, you had all these sorts of things crawl about, walking over you.

Then you would hear the bombs outside above you. And having heard these terrible explosions, I thought, 'My God, it can't keep you safe.' I never felt safe. I don't think I hardly slept I was so worried. I was so afraid for the children. I just used to hang over them like a sheet covering them, with my arms round as many as I could get. I felt that that would save them, it was a stupid thought, really. But they didn't appear to be really frightened. I think they were at the age where it was a sort of an adventure. A baby really doesn't know what's going on.

One night we had a terrific raid, worse than the others it seemed. It shook our air-raid shelter just like a jelly. There was water and bricks and mortar and stuff all over the top of our Anderson shelter. So after that it really did shake us up quite badly and my husband said that we couldn't stay there, that we'd have to go away. He insisted, so we packed up very quickly.

We went to the Chislehurst caves. My husband had heard that people were going sheltering down there and he thought that would be the best thing for the five of us.

So every night round about five-ish, I used to get all the children dressed and packed up in warm clothes and get together the bedclothes we had to take down. And off we went. So many people were making their way into the caves, you were one of hundreds of families. I felt surely to goodness it couldn't take all these people.

When we first went to the caves, none of us had bunks or anything like that. To sleep in the early days in the caves it was, for me, almost impossible but for the children, thank God, they slept pretty well and that I was grateful for. I just took as many eiderdowns as I'd got in my house and made a sort of mattress of them.

But I was so worried all the time. I was so worried, too, because the baby wasn't being looked after as a new baby should. We had a sort of niche in the caves and we put a curtain up and we were rather private. The baby often had bad nights, and you'd hear somebody shout out, 'For goodness sake, keep that child quiet.' You couldn't really, it was a normal thing for a child to wake up in the night, he was so young. And the other people around you quarrelled if they saw that you had a niche in the caves. 'How did she manage to get that?' People did get a little bit edgy towards one another.

As time went on and more and more people were going down there, they improved the caves, they brought in bunks. We had bunks and I had a little sort of wicker carrycot that I took down with me for the baby. But it was so claustrophobic, I couldn't get used to that closed-in feeling. And very damp, there was water running down the side of the rocks, and that made it very smelly. We were just like cave dwellers.

They used to have little dances and sort of concerts down there for the children. You were pleased to just let them have their run round the caves because you knew that they couldn't do that when you were at home, because you kept them round you all the time. There was a canteen down there so if the children got hungry, they could have a little snack. I suppose there was a sort of community feeling but as far as I was concerned I had my little community round me and I didn't have the time to sort of mix. It was just the children and myself, when my husband had his leave he came too.

Then the morning would eventually come and the All Clear would go. All I wanted was to get home to bath the children and bath the baby. Fortunately there was a bus stop very, very close. There used to be all the office workers on this bus and they were rather snooty and they used to sort of sniff, weren't very pleasant about us coming on the bus after we'd been in the caves all night.

My children was my life. The children sort of kept you sane in a way because you knew that you had to pull yourself together, you daren't let them know how worried you were and what you were thinking of all the time. I cried, at different times I cried, I cried a lot when they weren't there. It was just the feeling that they weren't having what they should have. They didn't have their schooling, they didn't have proper food really, and they were so good. It was a big problem, the children not getting any schooling. Very upsetting, really, because they were all bright children. Fortunately the school wasn't far from where we lived so that we were able to get a couple of hours in the afternoon at school. It was sad because the teachers sometimes they could turn up, sometimes they couldn't, the teachers did their best.

The doodlebugs were absolutely terrifying because you just didn't hear a thing, and suddenly this terrific bang. People were exhausted because prior to the doodlebugs they were beginning to feel as if, 'Oh, well, thank God we're getting to the end of it all.' But when they came people were absolutely distraught with fear, including myself, of course. It was really a panic in the caves when we knew what was happening, that you couldn't actually hear them until they were nearly on top of you, you know, it's a horrid feeling. People were ill, mentally and physically. I lost an awful lot of weight. I'm a very tall lady and I went down to seven stone. I think it was the mental anxiety really. The thought that this other thing, this new thing had arrived.

It was them that made me and my husband decide to evacuate ourselves to South Wales. I mean, the house had been blasted, the roof was off and the windows were out, water was pouring through. We went to South Wales, to a mining village. We all stood in this big hall waiting for people to take us in. I think we were about the last family to be taken, could you blame them? In the end we were put with a couple and they were absolutely marvellous. They actually got out of their own bedroom to give it to us because it was the biggest room in the house so the four children and myself slept in the same room.

When the peace was declared I just couldn't put into words

how I felt. how millions of other people felt. It was one of the happiest days of my life. I knew my children. thank God. had been spared. and my husband. bless him. It was a wonderful feeling. I felt so relaxed that at last I could let my children out of my sight. let them do the things that normal children do like running in the fields. They were able to go to school and have their lessons.

Phoebe Lee

Phoebe was born in 1904 in Walworth, south-east London, one of eleven children. Her father worked on the production side of the *Daily Mail* in Fleet Street, and her mother was a bookfolder. Phoebe left school at fourteen and started work in a Lyons tea shop. She married in 1924 and had four children, sons in 1936 and 1930, a daughter in 1932 and another son in 1945. When war was declared Phoebe and her family were living in Catford, also in south-east London. Her husband worked as a bridge inspector and spent most of the war travelling around the country. After experiencing some narrow escapes during air raids spent in an Anderson shelter, Phoebe's husband arranged for his wife and children to shelter in the Chislehurst caves in Kent. The family set up a makeshift home and lived there until Phoebe was evacuated to Wales to have her fourth child, Peter. Phoebe now has ten grandchildren and three great-grandchildren.

I couldn't help crying, I used to cry on my own, I never let Joe know, my husband. I didn't used to let him think I was worried. It was so awful to have to lift up my children and take them out of bed and roll them up, and take them down into the Anderson shelter, and I had to run with the little one, Jean. Her little feet used to go pitter-patter down and I used to think to meself, 'This is dreadful.' And then, of course, the guns were sometimes going, you could hear people being bombed. I was frightened for the children. I loved them and I was afraid they might get crippled or something like that. I was scared for all of us.

We had a bomb dropped three houses from me, it shook our house, it took our windows out. We were down the Anderson shelter then, and it was full of water. So the next night we had to pack up our things and go straight down to the caves at Chislehurst. We lived quite near but I met many people that had come miles and miles to get there, that had lost their homes. We used to go on the train. It was packed, it looked like a fair. There was people everywhere, we were all friendly, there was not a bit of bitterness.

When I first got to those caves I dreaded going in, I felt they were falling in on me, I was really terrified every time I went down. It was just grey walls, it was like walking under the earth, and I was really terrified. I said that it could fall in, if a bomb dropped on top. But my hubby said, 'No, it wouldn't it's too thick, the walls are too thick.' But it was really uncanny, I think, to be walking under the earth. I used to look at the top before I went in and think to meself, 'Supposing a bomb dropped on top, that would be bound to shake something down on us.' And that used to worry me. I didn't like it and I used to go cold, I used to dread it, but I had to go because I knew it was safe. Then I used to feel, 'Supposing the Germans got here, supposing they landed.' I used to have nightmares. I used to cry some nights, but it was no good crying with the children to think of. My two boys weren't scared, they used to say, 'Come on, Mum.' And they used to help me with Jean, one was eight and one was twelve.

It was a nightmare, really. I used to go to sleep thinking about the caves collapsing around us. I used to dream about it. I used to dream that I was struggling, you know, to try and help the children out of the clay. And then if they weren't there I used to worry where they were, whether they'd gone somewhere, you know, where p'raps it wasn't safe. I imagined them screaming, it was a terrifying thing.

I used to pray to God, I used to wonder if God was there, I used to say, 'Where are you, God, to allow this?' I used to go to the cave chapel say a prayer and pray to God that it would all finish, and then I used to have a little snivel and I used to say to myself, 'Oh, it'll get better.'

We used to go round and have a little chat with the other people and there was sometimes a bit of a sing-song down there and then I'd go and make the beds up for the children, put them to bed, give them a drink, my husband used to sit on one bunk and I slumped on the other. We kept our clothes on and I put jumpers on the children. You did fall asleep because you were so tired, but it wasn't very nice, when you feel the fright of the banging of the bombs. And it was cold down there, like a cemetery feeling.

And down the caves, as time went on, there was so many people going down there that they started charging everyone a penny to get in. And they put proper toilets in. They had a piece of cloth in the front which you used to have to lift up to see if anybody was in there. Then the electric lights come on, of course. We had lamps when we first went down there. And my brother started a café up. My two boys had a ball down there. They went all over the caves, went round to where they threw money down an old well, they really enjoyed it. My children and I had a nice little place, called Rookery Nook, a little alcove which was very nice and we used to take the clothes down there and make the bed, and in the morning we woke up and had a cup of tea from the café.

Then I was bombed out of the house. One morning we got back there from the caves and it was just like a wreck. My husband said then that it was good to keep coming backwards and forwards from the caves and that he would get a shed to put up for us to live in just by the entrance of the caves. He put a little cooker in there for me, I had a little washing machine, a Hoover machine, and we stayed there. And so every night when the sirens went we had hardly any distance to go down into the caves. As soon as the warning went we were in the shed, we slid down and went into the caves. I used to say to the kids, 'If you're not near me when the siren goes, run down to the gate of the caves.' And they used to do that. I always found them if the warning went. Sometimes we'd be having our dinner and the warning went and we'd have to rush down there, and the boys used to many a time run down with their plate with their dinner on it, down to the caves.

It was scary when you could hear the bombs. I felt like screaming really but you didn't, you just held onto your kids and prayed to God that we'd be all right. What was the alternative? I mean, an Anderson shelter wasn't much good, was it? If you're in a home on your own you're lonely, aren't you? Just on your own, whereas down there we were all together.

Mary Cole

Mary was born in 1918 in Dobcross near Saddleworth in York-shire. The family moved to London when she was a year old and her father got a job as a clerk in an insurance company in Threadneedle Street. She married in 1940 and had two children. Valerie in 1941 and John in 1947. Her husband was working as an accountant when war was declared but he registered for service in the navy almost immediately and was called up in 1941. He was posted abroad three weeks after the birth of the couple's first child. Mary was left to bring up their daughter alone for the next three years. She now has three grandchildren.

It is amazing how we survived on what we had. I'd never eaten rabbit before, rabbit was sort of a poor man's or a country man's meal. When you went to the butcher's you had to queue up for everything, you had very little meat allowance so if they had a rabbit and you were friendly with the butcher, you would say, 'Will you save me a rabbit?' Then you asked the butcher how you'd cook it and what do you do with it and he chopped the legs off for you. He just said, 'You get hold of the skin and you pull.' So it was trial and error. The first one, I must admit, was rather pulled to pieces. Put it in with lots of vegetables and there you got a meal which lasted you literally all week for two of you. The legs, you could do those like you would do a chicken leg today; it was a very good meal.

Well, people used to think that it would be terrible to pull a rabbit to pieces because they are nice fluffy little things and you think, ah, aren't they pretty, but when you're short of food and when you've seen people blown to pieces, you lose all your softness towards rabbits. You forgot about it being a living animal and you thought of it just as a lunch or dinner or a piece of meat. They were nice and filling and it meant that you'd saved your meat ration so you could have a little bit more meat the next time; it was a very inexpensive and good meal to have.

We had an allotment; now, they were brilliant. They dug up the cricket pitches on the Clapham Common. First of all the hardest part was getting the turf off because it had got all the grass on and you had to dig the grass up, then you would bury the turf and you would work your way down, as soon as you got a clear space you would plant something. We used to get a terrific amount of food off that. Out of one year we got a hundred pound of tomatoes. About six hundred shallots, which of course then we had to peel and bottle, you cried all day, and broccoli, sprouts, cabbages, you mention it and we grew it. We grew a lot of potatoes because that really was a staple food, you could get forty-eight pounds of potatoes off seven rows of potatoes. If you could get vegetables you could have a meal so anybody who wanted to make life better for themselves would get a vegetable plot and grow their own. You were better off digging than queuing – it did you more good, though it was very tiring, you ached all over, and very often you'd get drenched.

I'd never gardened at all beforehand but there were loads of posters to dig for victory, it encouraged you to start digging. I was never interested in gardening before; it was a case of you just read the instructions on the packet and you planted the things and hoped they would grow. You just expected them to grow. You didn't take it into account that they might die off, you just put them in and they said they would be up at a certain date and, funnily enough, they nearly always were.

Up until the war it had been mostly been seen as a man's thing, digging and growing vegetables – women didn't tend to do that sort of thing. This was something a bit new and different. Everything was different, sort of topsy turvy. Your husbands weren't there – there were no men about so you did what the men did.

I don't think people really thought they were digging for victory, they were really digging for themselves, weren't they? They were digging to increase their supply of food. Everybody felt that they were helping in this war effort by not sitting back and expecting everything to be done for you; so whatever you did to help you felt it was a good thing, you weren't being a burden on anybody, you were sort of being much more self-supporting than you would have been without a war. I don't think you really thought about the patriotic side of it. You really did it for yourself and your family and for the boys who were fighting.

Oh, Valerie used to love going up there on the allotment because she could play, you know, and she used to love digging for worms and she liked, she quite enjoyed helping you; I mean, very often her help was more of a hindrance but at least she thought she was helping. When she was little it was all right 'cos she was in the pram; but once she got to toddling you had to keep your eye on her, you couldn't work so well 'cos you'd find her on the next allotment sort of picking apples, picking tomatoes or something like that, you turned round and she was walking over one row of shallots. She was very good at picking tomatoes except that she would find a small green one and pull that off and say, 'This is green,' and throw it away. She used to like digging worms. We also had a little dog, well, a puppy dog, and so it was quite entertaining, shall I say, to watch the two of them and get on with digging and planting. There was a hard tennis court adjoining the allotments and, if the door were open, you could put them in there and leave them to play and it was like a huge playpen, and then you could get on without any trouble.

It was difficult, though, 'cos we were about half a mile walk from our allotment and, of course, you had to carry all your tools. You used to put your spade and your fork and all your bits and pieces in the pram on top of the child in it and coming back Valerie very often had to walk back because you'd got produce as well in there. You also had to carry water. Now that was a bind because you had the pram full of bottles of water as well as the children and the tools.

We used to have quite a lot of horses, obviously, because cars were off the road so if you saw a horse going along and it left any manure it was a case of first one out got the manure. And that meant humping the manure up there as well.

You never threw anything away. They provided pig bins which weren't terribly popular with a lot of people but you put all your peelings in them and they used to be collected regularly. Dogs would occasionally knock the top off or even cats, the bin overturned and all the rubbish, which was rotting by this time, would be in the road.

When we had the raids we had guns on the common and the shells used to come over the house if they were firing our way. They used to have two naval guns that sounded entirely different; they were very, very noisy, so the letterbox used to rattle with the repercussions of the guns. They were a bit nervous, children, when something different happened, so I christened them Popping Penelope and Keyhole Kate. I used to say, 'That's one of Daddy's guns.' And she used to say, 'Is Daddy there?' I'd say, 'No, but they're guns off his ship.' She'd say, 'Are Popping Penelope and Keyhole Kate coming tonight?' And she really felt that when they were there she was safer.

Well, my husband had gone away when Valerie was not quite three weeks old. He went into the navy and he didn't come back for three and a half years. Of course, Valerie grew up and she got to the stage where she realized that other children had daddies because most of them seemed to come home on leave.

So she had photos of him and when she started talking she would jabber away to him and she said to me one day, 'Daddy doesn't talk, does he?' And I said, 'Well, Daddy does but the photo doesn't.' This photo really was her daddy in her mind. She used to talk to him quite regularly and when we had a letter she would go and pick up the picture and kiss it and say, 'Thank you, Daddy, for the letter.' And of course she used to try and write little letters to him with a lot of help but she felt that was keeping her in touch.

I always bought her a present on her birthday and Christmas from Daddy. I bought her a dolls' house on one occasion and I left it on the doorstep and got a neighbour to ring the bell and she went down and there was a note from Daddy, from his ship. So he was a real person to her.

We were on the common one day and I turned around and she had her arms round the leg of a young sailor and she said, 'Here's Daddy.' The poor boy – there were about six of them – and he was the youngest of the lot and he was covered in confusion and, of course, it was a huge joke to the others. She obviously had a picture in her mind of him.

Although he was away three and half years, she wasn't at all shy with him and when he got back home they got on very well, really. She followed him round everywhere when he first came home and wondered why she couldn't go into the toilet with him and the bathroom with him.

There was a certain amount of jealousy and it was mostly the fathers who resented, not outwardly but you could feel that they resented, the amount of attention that the child was taking because you've got to watch a three-year-old all the time.

Kathleen Teale Jones

Kathleen was born in County Tipperary in Ireland in 1921. the daughter of a soldier. She had one sister. In 1934 the family moved to Solihull. near Birmingham. Kathleen left school aged seventeen and became a shorthand-typist at the aero division at Wilmot Breeden. She had met her future husband at school in 1934 and they eventually married in 1941. He was an engineer and they had two sons. in 1942 and 1943. Kathleen's husband was sent to work as an engineer at the American airfield at Upper Heyford. After her second child was born Kathleen decided she wanted to go back to work. She found a job at the SU Carburettor Company near Solihull. placing her children in a nearby nursery from 1944 until the nursery was closed down in 1946. She was then forced to give up her job. Kathleen now has seven grandchildren.

I was approached to work for the manager of the SU Carburettor Company in Shirley and they informed me that there had been a nursery set up near to their factory and would I like to go along and check it out. So I went along and found it was a very, very large Victorian house and it had been set up specifically.

I talked to my friends before I actually sent the boys to the nursery and they all said, 'Oh, my goodness, you're not going to do that, they're going to have all sorts of scars, they're psychologically going to be warped and you're actually going to be storing up an awful lot of trouble for yourself, you should be at home looking after your children, that's your position and that's your job, that's what you've taken on.' I went home and thought about all this and I thought, 'That's not for me.' I wanted to go to work. I couldn't see any future in pushing food into children one end and clearing up the mess at the other, it definitely didn't really turn me on.

I didn't go back to work for patriotic reasons; I went back to work because everybody else seemed to be putting their shoulder to the wheel more than I was, to help everyone to get out of the

mess. I have all my life regarded women's contribution to anything as being undervalued and not appreciated and the war gave
us the chance to prove we could work as well as the men.

But it was really an expedition to get the children to the
nursery and to get them back in the evenings. I used to have to
push them in the pushchair up to the main Stratford road and
then catch the Midland Red bus, a quarter of an hour on the bus
then a walk to the nursery, put them in the nursery and then get
on my bicycle and go to work and, of course, it all had to be
repeated in the evening. But in spite of all that I loved my work
and I really wanted to work.

The nursery was very well run, very clean, the children had
good food, so we had their coupons and I was able to get a bit
of extra food with them. They were put to sleep every afternoon
and they had medical checks even to the point that they decided
that my eldest son needed his shoes built up on the inside because
there was some problem he had and they arranged that.

As far as the children being in the nursery all day and you're
supposed to have this terribly maternal instinct about what they
are doing and whether they are all right . . . well, I didn't have
it. My children always were aware that I would always come
back to them wherever they were and they had great security
from me. They never looked back at me after the first two or
three days, and I felt very secure and very happy that they were
being well looked after. They were very happy and contented
children. When I picked them up in the evening they were always
happily engaged playing with water or playing with sand and
being talked to and stories read to them.

They closed the nurseries more or less straight away when
the war ended. I was absolutely shattered, devastated because
there was nobody that would be able to look after my children.
I had an interesting challenging position and then it meant that I
had to return to the boring mundane work of being at home
with nothing challenging, nothing to make life interesting. Just
housework and children. It was absolutely dreadful, it completely
devastated me.

Edith Throp

Edith was born in 1908 in Manchester, one of six children. Her father was a joiner's labourer. She left school at the age of fourteen and went to work in the textile mills in Bradford where her family lived. Edith was married in 1936 and had a daughter in 1938. During the war her husband was posted with the RAF to Halton. Edith placed her daughter with a baby-minder and worked in a munitions factory before getting work as a bus conductress. After they had been parted for some months Edith discovered that her husband was having an affair and despite making efforts to get back together the couple divorced shortly after the war. Edith went on to remarry and lived with her second husband in Australia for many years. She now has two grandsons.

It was always heartache, having to leave her. I mean she were a very, very quiet sort of placid little girl, she just wanted her mummy. She just wanted her mum and to stop at home with me. Whenever I went to work, all the time she were just pulling at me dress. She wanted me all the time. So it was bad when I went and left her with the baby-minder. I left her crying all the time. The woman used to say to me, 'She's all right, love, just go because it's only as soon as you've gone she's all right.' And I'd go and shut the door and I could 'ear 'er all the way down the street, 'Mummy, Mummy, Mummy.' And that's how I went to work, working all day heartbroken and then when I went at teatime I knew she'd been crying.

It was hard work. You had to be up early, six o'clock in the morning even for ordinary textile work and you were coming home at half past five and six o'clock at night and then you'd cook and clean and wash and iron and everything before you went to bed. Sometimes I didn't know whether I were getting into bed or getting out of bed for work, I were that tired. But I had it to do so I had to do it.

I were that tired that I decided to go and visit me husband

where he was posted in the army in Bedford. I took my little girl
and I was really looking forward to surprising him. But anyway
it was me who got the surprise. I turned up where he was living
and some of his mates tried to stop me from going to see him.
Then I found out he was living with some woman. Him and his
friends had been billeted to live with this woman and one by one
they all left and that left him on his own with her. By the time
I got there they were living together like man and wife! I couldn't
believe it.

I was shocked, absolutely, absolutely devastated. I never
thought it would happen. I never thought he would do it to me,
and I really was upset, I were sickened, you know, crying and I
couldn't believe it, to think that he'd always said what a lovely
wife he had and a lovely baby and he was the only one. It had
never entered me 'ead that we'd split up . . .

Well, he came home on compassionate leave hoping that it
might be all right but because of what he'd done, because I knew
what he'd done, sleeping with somebody else, I couldn't make it
all right. Well, we were having our dinner, sausage, liver and
onions and Yorkshire pudding I'd made. He was up on one side
and I was up the other and Pauline in the middle on the chair and
the dinner was all laid out but I couldn't eat mine, I couldn't eat
a thing. I couldn't swallow and it suddenly come over me that I
knew then I could never forget what he'd done. So I didn't touch
my dinner and he said, 'Is it always going to be like this?' And I
said, 'Yes, I'll forgive but I can't forget. I never will, I'll never
forget.' So he left and that was the end of us.

Well, naturally it did affect my little daughter but more so
because she had to rely on me all the time – she wanted me all
the time. She realized that all the other little ones had their daddies
home and she was always wondering why her daddy wun't
coming home. I was sickened over her not having a daddy, I was
sickened over being left with her and having to cope.

I blame the war entirely for everything, we would never have
been parted I don't think for one minute if the war hadn't started.
We were perfectly happy, had a lovely little baby growing into

a nice little girl. It was moving away to a strange town, temptation and women prepared to make 'em suppers to take all their
thoughts away from their wives for a while. We were perfectly
happy and he loved me, I know he did, and I loved him and we
never went anywhere without each other. My life would have
been different altogether if the war hadn'ta come on.

Robert Williamson

(See also Chapter Three, page 99.) Robert was called up to the army in 1941 and became a driver in the Royal Signals. He spent much of the war in the Middle East and India. He had one daughter, born in 1932. He did not return to his family until 1946 when his daughter was fourteen. Robert now has four grandchildren and five great-grandchildren.

I joined up on 6 November 1941. I felt rotten about it. If I'd have had the guts not to go, I wouldn't have gone, but I didn't have the guts.

When I came home on embarkation leave I thought I'd never see me wife again or family. They don't tell you where they're going to take you even. I went to Bristol, to Avonmouth, and set sail there and I wakened up in Palestine. I felt I'd probably never see home again, and I didn't see home anyhow for about two and a half years.

I sometimes didn't think I'd get back home. They were constantly in me thoughts. I never had women out there, it was too risky – some of the fellows did do, but I weren't that type of a person and I missed 'em terribly.

The main lifeline that we had was receiving mail from home, these were red-letter days – they really lifted everybody in the unit. They brought memories back and you thought, 'I wonder if I will see them again?' But there were never a week went without I didn't write to either our Norma or me wife, and in return I used to get plenty of mail. Sometimes it was a long while coming because you were always moving about, you'd send one address and by the time they got that letter you were at another address, you'd moved on somewhere else. Some fellows never bothered if they didn't have a letter, you know, because they didn't want to write one back. But I spent most of my evenings writing letters, given the chance.

If I didn't get one when the mail came in, I felt very despondent, but given the next delivery and there was one there, it was better still, you'd get two, one from Norma, one from Hetty.

I missed my daughter because I were missing her growing up. I had a locket with me daughter in one half and me wife in the other half – gold locket. There were times when you felt embittered. I mean, when I got home she were as big as me! And she could play the piano and things like that which she couldn't do before, you see. They'd never let me know this which was a lovely pleasant surprise when I arrived home on leave.

Going home, the flags were out, everything were trimmed up, big cake an' all, welcome home. It were very emotive, afraid I cried with joy, you know. They were stood at the gate waiting. And I remember picking our Norma up – big cardboard box in me hand with me demob suit in and a green trilby in me hand. I think we all cried, tears of joy. There was an air of expectancy on both sides – and joyful reunion lifting our Norma up, kissing her, hugging her and the wife, Hetty, never forget that time – very emotional.

Elsie Huntley

Elsie was born in 1913 in Camberwell. London. She had five sisters and one brother. Her father eked out a living doing odd jobs for people in the area. Elsie left school when she was fourteen and became a baker's assistant. She met her husband. a motor mechanic. when she was sixteen and they married in 1933. Their first son. Derek. was born in 1935. followed by three more in 1942. 1946 and 1952. During the war Elsie's husband was posted to Catterick Camp in Yorkshire. Elsie stayed in the family home in Mitcham. Surrey looking after their two sons. In 1944 she was sheltering in a brick shelter with them when it received a direct hit: Derek. who was then nine and half. was killed instantly. Elsie has nine grandchildren and two great-grandchildren.

Y ou used to be scared stiff if you had your wireless on and the sirens would go off. And you knew then that something was going to happen, the planes were going to come over dropping their bombs. But you knew you had to cope. I mean, if you'd got a man in the army, and you're on your own you've got to cope with those two children and you mustn't seem frightened because otherwise you make them frightened. It's no good letting them see that you're scared out of your life, is it? 'Cause if you do that what are you going to make them? A bag of nerves. So you had to put a sort of brave face on it and, you know, say, 'It's all right, darling, nothing's going to happen, you'll be all right.' If we were in the shelter we used to all play together, little games. So that took their minds off what was happening outside.

As the war got on a bit more the old doodles started coming which were terrible, these pilotless bombs. They were the worst because they used to just drop and go anywhere. Nobody knew where it would drop. We used to go into brick shelters outside the house. This particular night it was very bad, exceptionally. In the morning there was my four women neighbours, another man, myself, my Derek, he was nine, and my baby in the shelter.

I went into the house and I said I'd make a cup of tea. After a few minutes Derek came running in and said, 'Mummy, quick, there's one coming over.' I told him to run in and lay on the bunk. Worst thing I could have said for him to do, really. I rushed back into the shelter, course, you heard it stop and when it stopped you knew something was going to happen and course, crash, the shelter just collapsed on top of us all, screaming, naturally. And I had the baby in my arms and I just bent over. All the screaming was going on and I just thought, 'Oh, help me, please, God, help me. Get me out.' I was trying to ease myself away, so that baby could breathe 'cause he was squashed hard to me, you just thought you couldn't breathe, you were tightly squeezed. It had all collapsed in the middle. And then I could hear noises above, where people were trying to rescue us. And I'm shouting, 'Please get me out. I've got a baby in my arms here.' I could hear them digging away. Getting all the rubble away. I didn't know what was happening. And Derek was laying on the bunk where I was bent over. There was two bunks like, see, one bunk down and one bunk up. And he was laying on the top bunk, so I wouldn't have known whether he was on top of me and I managed to get my hand out and somebody held my hand, and said, 'Well, hang on, lady, hang on. We'll get you out quickly.' They pulled my baby out, then me and put me in an ambulance. And I said, 'My little boy's in there.' I didn't see anything when I came out, just hoping my son was OK.

They whisked me off to hospital, took the baby from me and I didn't see him till they come round in the casualty ward. They had to cut my clothes off me, because I still had all dirt and grit that I had been laying on and clean me up a bit. I had a chipped bone in my spine and a double fractured leg. Never thought I was going to be bombed. Never dawned on you that it could ever happen to you. And when it did, you couldn't believe it, such a shock. Then nurse came round with my baby saying, 'Who does this baby belong to?' I told her I had another little boy there somewhere. Well, I didn't know anything till the morning.

They told me next morning that Derek had been killed and

all my four neighbours were killed. I didn't know what to do, really. Nobody can explain the feeling of losing somebody like that, anyway. He had been actually killed outright, I just broke down and cried. I don't know how badly he was injured, they never ever told me. I didn't want to know, I just thought he would have been all right, safe in the bunk. I would never have told him to go in the bunk had I known. I think even now that if I hadn't done that, he might have been slightly injured, but I think, even now, I would have still had him. I felt the end of the world had come really, you think you'd all been laughing and talking in the evening all about things that had happened during the day, and then you'd lost your son, you can't really describe the feeling. I broke my heart.

But it was no good giving way to anything because you still had to carry on living and you had to live for your little boy and for your husband. If I didn't carry on, who was going to have my baby? I had to look after him, his daddy was in the army.

And at the end of the war, at the victory celebrations I felt just sad, wished Derek was there. My hubby wasn't with me, couldn't get off leave, so I just stayed indoors, nobody could bring Derek back. Or anybody back. I couldn't have rejoiced.

As time went on, naturally, you heal a little bit with your feelings, but even now all those years ago, I'll never ever forget that day or losing our boy like that. Terrible feeling. He'll never be out of my mind, it will live with me for the rest of my life.

Florrie Dukes

Florrie was born in Shepherds Bush in London in 1916. She had four sisters and one brother. Her father worked on the railways as a carriage cleaner. Florrie left school at thirteen and started work in the Royal Borough Laundry. She met her husband when she was sixteen and they married in 1937. He was unemployed for much of the 1930s, managing to get occasional work on the railways. They had one son who was born in 1940.

Florrie's husband was posted abroad in 1942 and did not return to England until 1945. When her son was two years old she put him into a day nursery and went to do war work in a factory, making heavy vehicles for the troops. Florrie had twin girls in 1950 who died shortly after their birth. She now has three grandchildren and eight great-grandchildren.

I waited till Jimmy was nearly two to see if I could get a job then I saw outside Roots they wanted helpers so I went in. They said it was fixing up lorries, and that I looked tough enough to do it, so I took the job.

It was quite easy to get Jimmy into the nursery. They had been putting leaflets through the door telling us about it, that we could put our kids there and go out to work. It cost five shillings a week and it was quite close by so that I could go from home, take Jimmy to the nursery and then go on to work. I'd got to put him in the pram, especially in the winter time, that hurt me most, taking him out round about half past seven in the morning. Although it was only just round the corner it was cold to bring 'em out of a warm bed and take them round to the nursery. I used to take his coat off and hang it up. I said, 'Look, there's your peg, Jimmy.' I was quite pleased because the first time I took Jimmy round I saw all the babies the same age as him and they all seemed to be enjoying one another's company but I don't think Jimmy was old enough then to realize that he was going to be left all day and I think, as the days went on, he gradually got to know – that upset him. It went on quite well for quite a while. My mother used to pick him up because they used to close at four o'clock and I used to have to work till five.

One day, I went to get Jimmy and Mum told me he'd gone missing. We were looking all over the place, he was only toddling. We went all round the neighbourhood and when I went home again there he was sitting on the doorstep. Then that happened again a few weeks later, he went missing again. I said to the women at the nursery, 'Your're supposed to look after our children while we're at work.' 'Well,' she said, 'he'll never go down to sleep of an afternoon.' It was worrying me so much that every chance I got, me tea break, I used to come from Roots, run across to see that he was all right and then run back again.

They didn't have enough girls to look after them. They're supposed to have been qualified child nurses. He used to cry when I used to leave him. I used to be crying going to work when he used to say, 'Don't be long, Mummy, don't be long.' He couldn't tell you much, he never used to mention much about the nursery because he was only two but it was what I saw myself that I realized that he wasn't happy.

And also the food they were giving 'em, it wasn't very good. All this dehydrated stuff. I used to come from work, pick Jimmy up from the nursery, go in and have a lunch, take him back to the nursery and go back to work. Otherwise he didn't get fed properly.

And then my job was very heavy, putting the wings on the lorries and then putting the engines in, it was on a pulley. It used to be two of us, between us, to get them dead central, then we had to tighten them all up. Then one of the men used to come along and try the engine and see that it was going all right, to see it didn't wobble. We all brought in the old bits of blankets so we could lie down a bit 'cos it was on the concrete floor.

I think the men thought that women couldn't do that sort of work but, my God, we worked harder than what the men did. I used to get cross, I did, because we were working hard and they were just standing around. It was hard for us going home looking after them and getting the children from the nurseries and things. I mean, well, you could see every one of us was getting exhausted. Your arms used to ache because you had to pull these things into line. More often than not when I came home all I wanted to do was to sleep for a little while but having Jimmy to look after you couldn't sleep.

We'd have to get up and take the baby over to the shelter. That tired you 'cos no sooner you'd get there than the All Clear went. Sometimes you just slept standing up. One night we had this bad night and we was in the shelter with all the neighbours, standing up all night long, like, with Jimmy in me arms, and in the end I slid down on to the floor and managed to sit down and fall asleep for a little while; that was during the heavy bombing raids.

When my Jim came home on one of his embarkation leaves, he said to my next-door neighbours, 'Mr Edwards, keep an eye on Flo, make sure she takes Jimmy and herself over to the shelters.' Well, Mr Edwards used to come in and wake me up and I used to say, in the finish, 'Mr Edwards, will you please stop coming in I am not going over the shelter. 'I'm fed up with it and if I'm to go I'm going to go in my own bed with my baby.' I'd had enough. I wanted to lay in my own bed and then when the sirens used to go I used to say to Jimmy, 'Come on.' And we used to get in bed together and just hope for the best and thank God that we came through it all right.

Then they advised us to let the children go away, be evacuated because it was getting exhausting taking them home and then going into the shelters of a night time. So we let him go and I was lost. I had nothing. He'd only been away a fortnight and I decided I'd go down to see him, to High Wycombe where he'd been sent. Well, I got there I saw him and he just had a vest on, no shoes on and a pair of shorts and he was sitting on his own. Course, he ran up to me and we hugged. I said I'd sooner die with a bomb on us than to know that my child was down there. I couldn't leave him there so I took him straight back with me.

We got home and I dumped him in the sink to bath him, but

as I was undressing him on the table he kept itching himself. He said, 'Me itch, me itch.' And when I looked I could see these lice in his head. I had to cut his curls off, we put newspapers on the table and I cut his curls off and these crawly things all dropped out. It made me feel sick. My mum had to look after him after that because I wasn't sending him away again without me and the nursery just wasn't good enough for me.

Towards the end of the war I was really fed up. We'd got sick and tired of waiting for the sirens to go. Shall we go shopping? Will the sirens go before we get back? We was waiting to have our men back home. All I wanted was Jim to come home and let us be a family together again.

Then the rockets started coming and they were frightening because you didn't hear 'em and you didn't know where they were going to fall and the damage they done was terrible. The thing I was frightened of most was that Jimmy wouldn't see his dad again or his dad wouldn't see Jimmy again. If one of those rockets came down it would kill everybody around it and I did used to worry then, especially when I was laying in bed. I used to think, 'Oh, don't let no rockets come over tonight, don't let no rockets come over tonight.' I kept saying that to meself over and over again because I had the fear of 'em coming and I'd never see Jim again. He was missing such a lot, all our boy's growing up and everything, he was missing all that and I was missing him so much that I think that was the beginning of me starting to be ill.

There was one occasion when I'd had a hard day at work and I went home, got a meal, got Jimmy undressed, and I said we'd go to bed for a little while. I didn't wake up until six o'clock the next morning. I wasn't undressed. I was just laying on the bed. I really was getting too tired to work, too tired to carry on. I used to wake up in the morning and get Jimmy ready and I was just too tired to go to work. I used to undress Jimmy again, put him back in his cot. They used to send one of the foremen over and I just used to say that I was ill. I couldn't care less if I lost the job because I was too tired to do it any more.

I used to write to Jim nearly every day, I had to because it kept me going, you know. It made me feel as though he was near me, you know. If I missed one day it used to be a double letter the next day. I started losing weight, but I had to look after myself and Jimmy. You had nobody else to look after you. I used to sob my heart out, I'd cry at anything and everywhere I went I used to say to Jimmy to come with me. I wouldn't walk from one room to the other without him. I was afraid of dying. I didn't wanna die on me own. He was six years of age and when I used to be taken bad, I used to faint over and he used to put a cushion under my head and go in next door and say, 'Oh, Aunty Kath, come in, Mummy's asleep on the floor again.' He was a good kid. I was in and out of hospital quite a lot, I lost the feeling in me hands. They told me at the hospital it was the exhaustion, the war, the nerves and everything, and also my husband being away, not being there when I needed him most.

Then I sent my husband this photo of me writing to him. He showed it to his CO and I looked so bad that he was told to pack his bags and get home. He was transferred to England, stationed at Woolwich for the ending of the war.

Course, I wasn't expecting him home. I was bathing Jimmy and I was kneeling down and in come my husband. He dropped his kitbag on the floor he says, 'Ah, caught you at it, have I?' It was a relief. We cried and we laughed. We was all together again and we hoped never to be parted again.

Jessie Shuttleworth

Jessie was born in Coventry in 1922. She married in 1940 and had two daughters in 1941 and 1946. During the war her husband was posted to Burma and Singapore. Jessie remained in Coventry looking after their daughter. In the last two years of the war Jessie worked a night-shift in a factory making parts for Churchill tanks. Her mother looked after her daughter Sylvia while Jessie was at work and Jessie took over during the day. At the end of the war, overcome by exhaustion and the stress of the past five years, Jessie had a nervous breakdown. She was sent into a mental hospital for two weeks until her husband was sent back to England on compassionate leave to look after her.

All I wanted to do was survive with my baby. She was the most precious thing to me. That's all I wanted to do, survive with her. You talk about terror. You're down there in the shelter, didn't take the pram, because there was nowhere to put it, I used to have to carry her to the shelter. And you used to take a bottle wrapped in a hot-water bottle. In a bag on me arm. Because that's all she needed, some Virol and a dummy. It was no good taking a napkin to change, or another nightgown, or anything. This was a waste of time. People were coming in, and saying the world was coming to an end, that we'd all be burnt alive, the city was a ring of fire. And they put the fear of God into you. And that's when you really, really, really got terrified. Because you believed it. During the lulls, people would talk to you. People would sort of grip you. Your arms. Anything just to get a human touch to somebody else.

By the next morning, when you got out you see what's happened. Many times that we've come back from the shelter they've been digging people out of houses. You had a job to get by. If you took your pram it took you ages to get back home, because you had to find ways of getting round. You'd have to climb over all the rubble to get home, and you wondered if your house was going to be there. Perhaps there ain't no windows in, the doors have been blowed out, no gas, no water.

I used to have to go and get buckets of water, carry it from a standpipe at the end of the road. Put the baby's napkins in to soak, wash 'em. Go back and fetch more water. Swill 'em, and then boil them on a black range. Then again when it got dark the sirens would go, I got her wrapped up in me arms and it was back down the shelter for the night.

Sometimes you didn't even get to the shelter before you could hear the bombs. And the fear, fear drives you on. I knew that I'd got to get to the shelter because I believed the shelter was the safest place to take her. Me putting her in a pram. She was such a good child she used to sleep. Trying to find the best way, it was quite a way to go to that shelter. Looking up and seeing things like the incendiary bombs coming, or hearing a thud. And all you wanted to do was get to the shelter. It drove you inside because you were so frightened. It was fear that done it. And you'd hear people screaming. But you didn't stop, you didn't. Your one aim was to get to the shelter. And as long as you could get to the shelter then you felt safe.

They were terrific raids, they were. You sit there with your baby and you wait. Then you hear these thuds, when a bomb dropped. You never hear the one that hits you. One night we had a near miss, blew the lid off. We did hear it screaming down. When it hit this canteen, the whole shelter rocked. We're in the earth, but it absolutely moved the earth. Then comes the blast. Like a big, big thing sweeping over you. The force of it. I must have got it in me face, and my baby got it on the side of her face. Because she had a mastoid afterwards. She's deaf to this day, it perforated her eardrum. Then people come screaming down the shelter. 'Oh, they've all been killed.' It makes me go cold. And you're petrified. For a minute everything stands still, just like slow motion. For a few seconds afterwards nobody spoke, nobody, nobody done anything. Then the reaction sets in, everybody starts screaming, 'cause there is no light. You're in the dark, all the lights went out. You just think you're going to be buried alive. But then somebody'll say, 'Oh, well, it hasn't hit us because we heard it coming. Wonder where it's hit, who's it got.' All the time your stomach is churning over and all you want to do is to survive. You've got to believe that you're going to survive.

I never dreamt that I'd get killed, nor our Sylvia, my baby. I just lived for her, and to survive with her. From day to day, and from night to night, that was the only thing that I lived for. You were alive. That's all you cared about, and your baby was alive.

Course you did feel sorry. You'd escaped but them poor devils had been killed. It's self-preservation. Get home. I'm all right.

I never even thought about going away from the city. Where could I go? I hadn't got nowhere to go. I weren't going out in the country and taking a new baby to lay under the hedges. Oh, no, no.

When it was dying off a bit the bombing I started to work nights at the Mechanization works, I earned good money, you see, and they were clamouring for women to work. And the women, they all mixed together, all friends together. Everybody was in the same boat. They'd either got their husbands at the war or they'd lost people or they'd been bombed. One big family communion. Nobody was snobby to each other, you shared what you'd got. Now cigarettes were very hard to get during the war. But if somebody had a packet of cigarettes, they would share everything.

Me mother used to have the baby for me. I used to work twelve hours from eight till eight on a big machine, making cogs for Churchill tanks. The work that I did was very hard. These big, big tanks. I'd stand there and it was like sleeping on a clothes line because I'd have ten minutes sleep, literally go to sleep standing up. Then at eight o'clock in the morning I'd go back to me mother's. And I'd sit there and have a cup of tea, and I'd perhaps have half an hour's sleep. Then I'd take Sylvia out, in the pram. We'd go to one of the big parks, just to try to get away from it all for a while. I'd have her at home at the weekends, I'd have her home in the daytime, then take her back to me mother's probably on me way back to work. Sunday nights as well, six nights a week. Only had Saturday night off. I did that for two years.

I stopped work when I had my second baby, Pauline. But then it started. First of all it started with very bad headaches, then I wouldn't go out. I wouldn't take the children out, under no circumstances. And I used to imagine that things were coming through the wall or people were talking through the wall about me. And I used to dread it, I wouldn't even put me foot outside. I just didn't want to do anything at all, and it gradually built up. I did go to the doctor's, he gave me some tablets. 'You'll be all right,' he said. They never done me any good. And me head used to get like hammers and I used to feel like it was going to burst. I could bang me head against the wall but I couldn't sleep.

This particular night, I hadn't got any energy, hadn't got any strength, I just couldn't do anything. I'd just about had enough, just wanted to go to sleep, I didn't care what happened. I'd put the children to bed. Behind the back door was the gas stove, a very old-fashioned gas stove. I got this cushion and I opened the oven door, and I put it in. I was going to turn the gas on, and this knock came on the back door. He said, 'Are you all right, Jess?' My neighbour came in and he saw what I was doing. Of course, him and his wife got the doctor straight away. He came within an hour. And within two hours they'd taken the children away, to an open-air school. They took me to the mental hospital.

That hospital was terrible. Iron bars up. They – they give you this – this stuff, this white stuff to drink in the morning. Then you had to get out of bed and make your own bed and then you had to clean underneath it. And then you got back into bed. They never allowed you to walk around. It was a terrible place. But I honestly didn't care where they put me, as long as I could get some rest. I didn't care what they done to me. Even me children, when they took them away, I didn't seem to care. When you don't sleep for weeks on end, your brain's ready to explode. They wanted to give me this electrical treatment, on my head. They sent for my husband, they brought him home from Singapore in three days because I was so ill. Then they said they wouldn't give me this electric treatment, but they'd let me come home, under his supervision.

When I first came out the hospital, I couldn't sleep. I used to go mad. Because me eyes burnt and me temples throbbed and me head throbbed, they didn't give me any medication from the hospital. I'd got nothing. And my husband used to hold me, and he used to say, 'Force yourself to go to sleep. Go to sleep. You've got to go to sleep.' Gradually it got that I'd sleep for ten minutes, then perhaps half an hour and then over a period, I got that I became normal.

I still had to go to see the psychiatrist down the hospital regular, once a week. He said everything that had happened over the years of the war was suppressed in me subconscious, built up and built up, that's why me head used to feel like it was going to explode. Five years it took for that to happen. He told me that once I'd got all this out of my system, and got back to normal it'd never happen again.

It always left me a bit nervous. But otherwise, I'm as strong as ever. Like in the war, you'd got to be strong. You'd got to stand up for yourself and your baby. That's all I cared for. To keep going for her. I'd put all the bombing and everything at the back of my mind. I just buried it, I buried it deep. I think my brain got so tired and so exhausted. The fear which was wrapped up inside, it had to have a release, it had got to come out some way or another.

FURTHER READING

Bailey. Doris M. *Children of the Green*. Stepney Books. 1981

Belsey. James and Reid. Helen. *West at War*. Redcliffe Press. 1990

Black. Clementina (ed.). *Married Women's Work*. Virago. 1983

Burchardt. Natasha. 'Structure and Relationships in Stepfamilies in Early Twentieth Century Britain'. *Community and Change*. vol. Four/Two Great Britain. 1989

Burnett. John. *Plenty and Want: a Social History of Food in England from 1815 to the Present Day*. Routledge. 1989

Chinn. Carl. *They Worked All Their Lives: Women of the Urban Poor in England. 1880–1939*. Manchester University Press. 1988

Fildes. Valerie. 'The History of Breastfeeding to c. 1920'. *Breastfeeding Review*. 13. November 1988

Fisher. C. *A Midwife's View of the History of Modern Breastfeeding Practices*. International Federation of Gynecology and Obstetrics. 1990

Gardiner. Juliet. *Over Here: GIs in Britain During the Second World War*. Collins and Brown. 1992

Gathorne-Hardy. Jonathan. *The Rise and Fall of the British Nanny*. Weidenfeld and Nicolson. 1985

Hardyment. Christina. *Dream Babies: Child Care From Locke to Spock*. Jonathan Cape. 1983

Hoggart. Richard. *The Uses of Literacy*. London. 1957

Holdsworth. Angela. *Out of the Doll's House: the Story of Women in the Twentieth Century*. BBC Books. 1989

Humphries. Steve and Gordon. Pamela. *Out of Sight: the Experience of Disability 1900–1950*. Northcote House. 1992

Humphries. Steve. Mack. Joanna and Perks. Robert. *A Century of Childhood*. Sidgwick and Jackson. 1988

Lewis. Jane. *The Politics of Motherhood*. Croom Helm. 1980
  Women in England 1870–1950 – Sexual Divisions and Social Change. Harvester Wheatsheaf. 1984

Llewelyn Davies, Margaret (ed.). *Life As We Have Known It*. Virago, 1984

Loudon, Irvine. *On Maternal and Infant Mortality 1900–1960*. Society for the Social History of Medicine, 1991

Mack, Joanna and Humphries, Steve. *The Making of Modern London 1939–1945: London at War*. Sidgwick and Jackson, 1985

Marks, Lara. *'Dear Old Mother Levy's': the Jewish Maternity Home and Sick Room Helps Society 1895–1939*. Society for the Social History of Medicine, 1990

Middleton, N. *When Family Failed*. Gollancz, 1971

Minns, Raynes. *Bombers and Mash, Lest We Forget: the Domestic Front 1939–1945*. Virago, 1985

Pember Reeves, Maud. *Round About A Pound A Week*. Virago, 1984

Roberts, Elizabeth. *A Woman's Place – An Oral History of Working Class Women 1890–1914*. Blackwell, 1984

Smith, Donna. *Stepmothering*. Harvester Wheatsheaf, 1990

Summerfield, Penny. *Women Workers in the Second World War*. Croom Helm, 1984

Thompson, Paul. *The Edwardians: The Remaking of British Society*. Paladin, 1979

Thompson, Paul with Wailey, Tony and Lummis, Trevor. *Living the Fishing*. Routledge, 1983

Thompson, Paul. *The Voice of the Past: Oral History*. Oxford University Press, 1988

Ward, Colin. *The Child in the Country*. Robert Hale, 1988

Weightman, Gavin and Humphries, Steve. *Christmas Past*. Sidgwick and Jackson, 1988

The Making of Modern London 1914–1939. Sidgwick and Jackson, 1984

White, Jerry. *The Worst Street in London: Campbell Bunk, Islington Between the Wars*. Routledge, 1986

Winfield, Pamela. *Bye Bye Baby: The Story of the Children the GIs Left Behind*. Bloomsbury, 1992

Wolfram, Sybil. *In-Laws and Out-laws: Kinship and Marriage in England*. Croom Helm, 1987